MW01254076

Inferentialism

Also by Jaroslav Peregrin

DOING WORLDS WITH WORDS
MEANING AND STRUCTURE

Inferentialism
Why Rules Matter

Jaroslav Peregrin
Academy of Sciences of the Czech Republic, Prague

palgrave
macmillan

First published 2014 by
PALGRAVE MACMILLAN

Palgrave Macmillan in the UK is an imprint of Macmillan Publishers Limited, registered in England, company number 785998, of Houndmills, Basingstoke, Hampshire RG21 6XS.

Palgrave Macmillan in the US is a division of St Martin's Press LLC, 175 Fifth Avenue, New York, NY 10010.

Palgrave Macmillan is the global academic Imprint of the above companies and has companies and representatives throughout the world.

Palgrave® and Macmillan® are registered trademarks in the United States, the United Kingdom, Europe and other countries.

ISBN: 978–1–137–45295–5

A catalogue record for this book is available from the British Library.

Library of Congress Cataloging-in-Publication Data

Peregrin, Jaroslav.
    Inferentialism : why rules matter / Jaroslav Peregrin, Academy of Sciences of the Czech Republic, Prague.
        pages cm
    Includes bibliographical references.
    ISBN 978–1–137–45295–5
        1. Meaning (Philosophy) 2. Semantics (Philosophy) 3. Language and languages – Philosophy. 4. Inference. I. Title.

B105.M4P465 2014
121'.68—dc23   2014021108

Contents

Part II Logic, Inference, and Reasoning

Acknowledgments

This book is a result of many years of my work on the topic, and there are many people to whom I am grateful for various kinds of critical comments and other impulses that I have projected into the final version of this book. My colleagues, who helped me directly with fine-tuning the text and to whom I am especially grateful, because without their critical comments the book would hardly have reached fruition, are Vladimír Svoboda, Vít Punčochář, Radek Ocelák, and Pavel Arazim. Others who have given me valuable comments or criticisms either directly regarding the manuscript, or more generally concerning my ideas concerning inferentialism, are Ondřej Beran, Bob Brandom, Christopher Gauker, Gary Kemp, Ladislav Koreň, Tomáš Marvan, Barbara Partee, Pirmin Stekeler-Weithofer, Ken Turner, and Michael Williams. I am also grateful to Clare Wille and Petra Ivaničová who helped me with the linguistic and formal side of the book. The work on this final version of the book was sponsored by Research Grant No. 13–20785S of the Czech Science Foundation.

1
Inferentialism: State of Play

1.1 What is meaning?

We may say, and we often do say, that what makes the difference between a word and a kind of sound that is not a word is that the former *has meaning*. Yet what does this mean? Thousands of books and articles have been written about the nature of meaning and I have no intention to survey them all here (needless to say, this would not be a humanly accomplishable task). For our present purposes it suffices to note that despite the immense efforts that have been put into these investigations no general agreement about the nature of meaning has yet been reached.[1]

The question regarding the nature of linguistic meaning is approached in multifarious ways. The first crossroad is opened up by the question of whether the phrasing 'has meaning' should be taken at face value, as expressing a relation between the word and some preexisting entity called *meaning*. Many philosophers have taken this for granted and have not seen it as disputable. A word, it is often claimed, stands for – or represents, or expresses – its meaning, and the reason it can do so is that we humans are simply symbol-mongerers: we have the peculiar ability to let one thing stand for another.[2] However, the trouble is that it is very difficult to explain, in a non-mysterious way, how we do it and what the relation so established consists in. Is there some unanalyzable power of our minds that is capable of establishing symbols, and is the symbol bound to what it symbolizes by some mental fiber? It seems to me that it remains utterly mysterious not only what the nature of such mental mechanism would be, but especially how the mind could establish such public links as are essential for public language, and what these would consist in.[3]

It also seems to me that attempts at explaining the links directly in a naturalistic, especially causal way have not been very successful.[4] Thus I am convinced that even if we disregard direct attacks on the coherence of such representational conceptions of meaning, due to Quine, Sellars, Davidson, and others,[5] there are reasons to be skeptical about the prospects of fleshing out such a theory in a non-mysterious way.

These quick glosses, of course, are not to be taken as serious criticism, their purpose being only to remind the reader that no such approach has gained general acceptance as an explication of the concept of meaning, and that an effort to look elsewhere for another, more plausible explanation of meaningfulness is understandable. (Inferentialism, as presented in this book, is often thought to be a counterintuitive doctrine, so it warrants keeping in mind the problems plaguing rival conceptions of meaning to see that they face obstacles the circumvention of which might outweigh some amount of prima facie counterintuitiveness.)

But, of course, we need not take the meaning talk at face value; we could take it instead as metaphoric talk about some properties of words. Maybe what is characteristic of words – as contrasted with sounds that are not words – is not, or is not literally, that they stand for something, or express it, or represent it, but rather that they have some peculiar property. (The fact that we tend to talk about having a property as about being related to some reification of the property is not in itself mysterious, for it is something we do as a matter of course: we do not hesitate to speak about things having height, color, etc.[6])

One of such explanations, the popularity of which has been on the increase over recent decades (especially thanks to the impact of the legacy of the later Wittgenstein), is that what characterizes a word is the way it is employed within our language games. According to this view, what we call meaning is, in fact, a reification of use. But the trouble is that all kinds of things around us have uses, and yet it seems that to be meaningful as a linguistic expression is something very different from being used, say, as a hammer. Could the difference consist merely in the complexity of the respective uses?

One alternative way of conceiving the difference is to distinguish between items like hammers, which merely have uses, and items like words, which have *roles*, where a role in the sense entertained here is something that is conferred on an item by *rules*. Here is where the underlying idea can be elucidated by comparing words with chess pieces (a comparison frequently used in this book): just as to make a piece of wood (or, for that matter, whatever substance) into a rook it is enough to subordinate it to the rules of chess, what makes a type of sound into an expression meaning thus and so are again certain rules – rules constitutive of our language games.

It seems to me that this opens up a non-mysterious way to explain meaning (chess does not seem to be a mystery!), and because such ways are in short supply, it is a view we might want to take seriously. Hence the idea is that what makes linguistic meaningfulness (aka having meaning) categorically different from other kinds of usefulnesses are the *rules* that govern the enterprise of language. According to this view, it is the fact that they are constituted by these rules that makes meanings into something special.[7] Moreover, the fact that meanings presuppose a very specific kind of rules (including, be it only in the background, a framework of most basic rules, rules related to what we call *logic*) makes them into a sui generis, into entities of a kind that has nothing comparable in our world.

Inferentialism, the topic of this book, is a specific version of this view, according to which the most important kind of rules that constitute meanings are *inferential* rules. The term was coined by Robert Brandom (1994; 2000) as a label for his theory of language, which draws extensively on the earlier views of Wilfrid Sellars (1949; 1953; 1954). (Brandom has engaged the term especially to contrapose it to the common *representationalism*, i.e., the doctrine that meaningfulness consists in representing, i.e. in 'standing for'.) However, the term is also naturally applicable (and is growing increasingly common) within the philosophy of logic,[8] and indeed it is in the context of logic that we can most clearly see how inferential rules are supposed to give rise to meanings. Let us, therefore, now turn our attention to logic.

1.2 Inferentialism and logic

Probably the first expression of what we can, retrospectively, see as inferentialism is a passage from the pioneering work of modern logic, Frege's *Begriffsschrift*:

> The contents of two judgments can differ in two ways: first, it may be the way that the consequences which can be derived from the first judgment combined with certain others can always be derived also from the second judgment combined with the same others; secondly, this may not be the case. The two propositions 'At Plataea, the Greeks defeated the Persians' and 'At Plataea, the Persians were defeated by the Greeks' differ in the first way. Even if one can perceive the slight difference in sense, the agreement still predominates. Now I call

the part of the contents which is the same in both, the conceptual content. (Frege, 1879, p. v)

The idea that the (logically relevant) content of a sentence is determined by what is inferable from it (together with various collateral premises) anticipates an important thread within modern logic, maintaining that the notion of content interesting from the viewpoint of logic derives from the concept of inference. This has led to the conclusion that the meaning or significance of logical constants is a matter of the inferential rules, or the rules of proof, that govern them.

It would seem that inferentialism as a doctrine about the content of logical particles is quite plausible. Take, for instance, the conjunction sign; it seems that to pinpoint its meaning, it is enough to stipulate:

$$\frac{A \wedge B}{A} \qquad \frac{A \wedge B}{B} \qquad \frac{A \quad B}{A \wedge B}$$

(The impression that these three rules do institute the usual meaning of $\wedge$ is reinforced by the fact that they may be read as describing the usual truth table: the first two saying that $A \wedge B$ is true only if A and B are, whereas the last one that it is true if A and B are.) This led Gentzen (1934; 1936) and his followers to study the inferential rules that are constitutive of the functioning (and hence the meaning) of logical constants. For each constant they introduced an *introduction* rule or rules (in our case of $\wedge$ above, the last one) and an *elimination* rule or rules (above, the first two). Gentzen's efforts were integrated into the stream of what is now called *proof theory*, which was initiated by David Hilbert – originally as a project to establish secure foundations for logic[9] – and which has subsequently developed, in effect, into the investigation of the inferential structures of logical systems.[10]

The most popular objection to inferentialism in logic was presented by Prior (1960/1961). Prior argues that if we let inferential patterns constitute (the meaning of) logical constants, then nothing prohibits the constitution of a constant *tonk* in terms of the following pattern:

$$\frac{A}{A \; tonk \; B} \qquad \frac{A \; tonk \; B}{B}$$

As the very presence of such a constant within a language obviously makes the language contradictory, Prior concluded that the idea that inferential patterns could furnish logical constants with real meanings must be an illusion.

Defenders of logical inferentialism (prominently Belnap, 1962) argue that Prior only showed that *not every* inferential pattern is able to confer meaning *worth its name*. This makes the inferentialist face the problem of distinguishing, in inferentialist terms, between those patterns that do, and those that do not, confer meaning (from Prior's text it may seem that to draw the boundary we need some essentially representationalist or model-theoretic equipment, such as truth tables), but this is not fatal for inferentialism. Belnap did propose an inferentialist construal of the boundary: according to him it can be construed as the boundary between those patterns that are conservative over the base language and those that are not (i.e., those that do not, and those that do, institute new links among the sentences of the base language). Prior's *tonk*, when added to a language that is not itself trivial, will obviously not be conservative in this sense for it institutes the inference $A \vdash B$ for every A and B.[11]

The Priorian challenge has led many logicians to seek a 'clean' way of introducing logical constants proof-theoretically. Apart from Belnap's response, this has opened the door to considerations concerning the *normalizability* of proofs (Prawitz, 1965) and the so-called requirement of *harmony* between their introduction and elimination rules (Dummett, 1991; Tennant, 1997). These notions amount to the requirement that an introduction rule and an elimination rule 'cancel out' in the sense that if you introduce a constant and then eliminate it, there is no gain.

Thus, if you use the introduction rule for conjunction and then use the elimination rule, you are no better off than in the beginning, for what you have proved is nothing more than what you already had:

$$\frac{\dfrac{A \quad B}{A \wedge B}}{A}$$

The reason *tonk* comes to be disqualified by these considerations is that its elimination rule does not 'fit' its introduction rule in the required way: there is not the needed 'harmony' between them; and proofs containing them would violate normalizability. If you introduce it and eliminate it, there may be a nontrivial gain:

$$\frac{\dfrac{A}{A \; tonk \; B}}{B}$$

Prawitz, who has elaborated on the Gentzenian theory of natural deduction, was led, by his consideration of how to make rules constitutive of logical constants as 'well-behaved' as possible, to consider the relationship between proof theory and semantics. He and his followers then developed their ideas, introducing the overarching heading of *proof-theoretic semantics*.[12]

It is clear that the inferentialist construal of the meanings of logical constants presents their semantics more as a matter of a certain know-how than of a knowledge of something represented by them. This may help not only explain how logical constants (and hence logic) may have emerged,[13] but also to align logic with the Wittgensteinian trend of seeing language more as a practical activity than as an abstract system of signs. This was stressed especially by Dummett (1993).[14]

1.3 Brandom's inferentialism

Unlike Dummett, Brandom (1994; 2000) does not concentrate on logical constants; his inferentialism extends to the whole of language. As a pragmatist, Brandom concentrates on our linguistic *practices,* on our *language games* and on their place within our human coping with the world and with each other, but, unlike many postmodern followers of Wittgenstein, he is convinced that one of the games is 'principal', namely, the *game of giving and asking for reasons*. It is this game, according to him, that is the hallmark of what we are – thinking, concept-possessing, rational beings abiding to the force of better reason.

To make inferentialism into a doctrine applicable to the whole of language we must make sense of the view that inferences are crucial for *all* kinds of words, including empirical ones. The weakest way to do this would be to claim that an expression cannot be meaningful without playing *some* part in *some* inferences, i.e., that each meaningful expression must be part of some sentences that are inferable from other sentences and/or from which some other sentences are inferable. This is a position that Brandom (2007) calls *weak inferentialism*. This position is clearly not necessarily incompatible with representationalism: believing that to mean something is to represent something is not incompatible with believing that sentences are inferable from other sentences. (Brandom himself conjectures that *everybody* would be a weak inferentialist, but I think that some representationalists would claim that an expression may be meaningful without being part of any sentence, or at least any sentence having inferential links to other sentences.[15])

A stronger version of inferentialism, which Brandom (ibid.) terms *strong inferentialism*, claims that this kind of 'inferential articulation' (i.e., being part of sentences that enter into inferential relationships) is not only a necessary, but also a sufficient, condition of meaningfulness – though construing the concept of inferential rule rather broadly, so that it encompasses 'inferences', as it were, from situations to claims and from claims to actions. (Hence it accepts such 'inferential rules' as *It is correct to claim 'This is a dog' when pointing at a dog*.) This is Brandom's own version, and it is a version to be discussed in this book – though not necessarily in Brandom's own terms, nor sharing his emphases. (Besides these two versions, Brandom also considers *hyperinferentialism*, the claim that inferential articulation is a necessary and sufficient condition of meaningfulness on the narrow construal of inferential rules, and he rejects it as clearly untenable for a language containing empirical vocabulary.)

Why language must be inferentially articulated is because of its crucial role of being the vehicle of the game of giving and asking for reasons. To be able to *give* reasons we must be able to make claims that can serve as reasons for other claims, hence our language must provide for sentences that *entail* other sentences. To be able to *ask for* reasons we must be able to indicate that a claim is in need of being justified, i.e., we must be able to make claims that count as a *challenge* to other claims. (We may, of course, ask for reasons for a claim without explicitly challenging it, but the most primitive way of asking for reasons seems to be a doubt expressed by a challenge.) Hence our language must provide for sentences that are *incompatible* with other sentences; our language must be structured by these entailment and incompatibility relations.

In fact, for Brandom the level of inference and incompatibility is merely a deconstructible superstructure, underlain by certain normative statuses that communicating people acquire and maintain via using language. These statuses comprise various kinds of *commitments* and *entitlements*. Thus, for example, when I make an assertion, I *commit* myself to giving reasons for it when it is challenged (that is what makes it an assertion rather than just babble), and I *entitle* everybody else to reassert my assertion deferring any possible challenges to me. I may commit myself to something without being entitled to it, i.e., without being able to give any reasons for it, and I can be committed to all kinds of things, but there are certain things the commitment to which blocks my entitlement to certain other things.

Brandom's idea is that living in a human society amounts to steering within a rich network of normative social relationships and enjoying many kinds of normative statuses that reach into many dimensions. Linguistic communication institutes an important stratum of such statuses (commitments and entitlements) and to understand language means being able to keep track of the statuses of one's fellow speakers – to keep score of them, as Brandom puts it. And the social distribution is essential because it provides for the multiplicity of perspectives the intersections of which make the objectivity of linguistic content possible.

This interplay of commitments and entitlements is also the underlying source of the relation of incompatibility: commitment to one claim excluding the entitlement to others. Additionally, there is the relation of inheriting commitments and entitlements (by committing myself to *This is a dog* I commit myself also to *This is an animal,* and being entitled to *It is raining* I am entitled also to *The streets are wet*), and also the relation of inheritance of incompatibilities (*A* is in this relation to *B* iff whatever is incompatible with *B* is incompatible with *A*). This provides for the inference relation (more precisely, it provides, according to Brandom, for its several layers).

Brandom's inferentialism is a species of pragmatism and of the use-theory of meaning: he sees our expressions as tools that we employ to do various useful things (though they should not be seen as *self-standing* tools like a hammer, but rather as tools, like, say, a toothwheel, that achieve useful results only in cooperation with other tools). Brandom gives pride of place to the practical over the theoretical, seeing language as a tool of social interaction rather than an abstract system. Thus any explication of concepts such as *language* or *meaning* must be rooted in an account of what one *does* when one communicates, hence semantics, as he puts it, 'must answer to pragmatics' (1994, p. 83).

What distinguishes Brandom from most other pragmatists and exponents of various use-theories is the essentially normative twist he gives to the pragmatist attitude to language. Thus we can say that what his inferentialism is about are not inferences (as mental actions or episodes of speakers or thinkers), but rather *inferential rules*. This is extremely important to keep in mind, for it is this that distinguishes Brandom's inferentialism from other prima facie similar approaches to meaning, from theories that try to derive meaning from the episodes of inferring rather than from rules.

1.4 'Normative' inferentialism vs. 'causal' inferentialism

This brings us to an issue that must be clarified right at the outset. There is a doctrine that, although superficially similar to the Brandomian inferentialism, should not be confused with it (as, unfortunately, often happens). This doctrine was discussed in the early nineties by Peacocke (1992), Boghossian (1993), and others and it has become popular under the term 'inferential role semantics'.

What this doctrine shares with the Brandomian inferentialism is the conviction that meaning is an inferential role, *viz.* the role conferred on an expression by our inferential practices. However, the crucial difference lies in the aspect of the practices taken to be relevant for the determination of the role. Whereas this theory concentrates on inferences individual human subjects really carry out, or have dispositions to carry out, Brandomian inferentialism concentrates, as we have seen, on inferential *rules*. Let us discuss this difference in greater detail.

Consider the exposition of the theory given by Boghossian (ibid., p. 73):

> Let's suppose that we think in a language of thought and that there are causal facts of the following form: the appearance in O's belief box of a sentence S_1 has a tendency to cause the appearance therein of a sentence S_2 but not S_3. Ignoring many complications, we may describe this sort of fact as consisting in O's disposition to *infer* from S_1 to S_2, but not to S_3. Let's call the totality of the inferences to which a sentence is capable of contributing, its *total inferential role*. A subsentential constituent's total inferential role can then be defined accordingly, as consisting in the contribution it makes to the total inferential role of the sentences in which it appears.

The role, then, is determined by what a subject does, or is disposed to do. In this sense, this theory appears to be a subspecies of 'conceptual role semantics',[16] and thereby a subspecies of the *functionalism* well known in the philosophy of mind.[17] As the functioning that plays the crucial role here is the causal functioning of the human brain (at least insofar as we see mind as supervening on the brain; otherwise it would be a pseudo-causal functioning of the mind), we can call this variety of inferentialism *causal* inferentialism. Hence there is a basic difference between this variety of inferentialism and the normative variety promoted in this book.[18]

The difference is more far-reaching than it might prima facie seem, and to appreciate it we must clarify the nature of the *rules* that play such a crucial role in the characterization of inferentialism. In Chomskian linguistics (and elsewhere too), rules are considered as something that can be directly implemented within the human brain; hence they are again certain causal mechanisms. But this – and this is the key point – is *not* the notion of rule essential for inferentialism. Rules as understood here are not causal determinants of human conduct, but rather something that it is *not* causally necessary, for any given subject, to follow; it is merely *proper* for the subject to follow them.

However, what does it mean that something is *proper* for a subject? Does this not lead us to some esoteric stratum of reality populated by *proprieties*?[19] Not really; for a propriety is nothing other than a resultant of certain attitudes of many people. It follows that to be able to accommodate proprieties, we need to consider the subject in the context of a society, with the interlocking stances of its members creating a filigree web of social relationships. A human as a social being not only reacts to her natural environment, but also reacts to her peers' reactions. In the course of time she develops what I tend to call *ought-to-be*-thinking (appropriating the terminology of Wilfrid Sellars), which means that she perceives some ways of behaving and acting as agreeable and others as reprehensible.[20] And what I call a propriety, or an (implicit) rule, grows out of such attitudes resonating throughout the surrounding society.

It follows that rules are far from etheric entities beyond the causal order; they are a social, and, especially, what we usually call *institutional*, matter. (As Wittgenstein and the post-Wittgensteinian discussion has taught us, rules in the relevant sense of the word cannot exist other than in the public, social space – for it is only this space that provides for *following the rule* not collapsing into *thinking one is following the rule*.[21]) Thus they are not a matter of merely resonating attitudes, but rather they tend to invoke a superstructure of customized and institutionalized reactions to *improper behavior* ('punishments') as also to *proper* ones ('rewards') that are often wielded in a cooperative manner. And such institutions, though they are a matter of the causal order, are *not* a matter of the causal structures of an individual brain. The existence of a rule is thus a matter of the interlocking patterns of attitudes, actions, and reactions of many people.

Saying that an inferential role of an expression that amounts to its meaning is instituted by such social rules, rather than individual dispositions, has profound consequences. First, there is straightforwardly room for *error*: the way somebody uses an expression may be *wrong*; her individual disposition may not chime with the social rule. And, second, social rules may govern only what is socially accessible; they may govern how we act, not directly what we think. As a result, what is governed by such rules will be the usage of words, expressions, and especially sentences, not our handling of any mental contents such as beliefs. (Though insofar as beliefs can be thought about as internalized assertions, the subjective mental reality may be thought about as influenced – if not formed – by the intersubjective normative one.)

1.5   Is inferentialism circular?

There is an objection often thought fatal to inferentialism, and so we will address it immediately. This is the objection that inferentialism is (viciously) circular: making an inference, so the model version of the objection goes, we must move from some propositions to a proposition, hence from sentence meanings to a sentence meaning; how, then, can inferences *constitute* meanings? To illustrate the crucial difference between the causal and the normative versions of inferentialism, let me consider the difference in the impact this objection on the two versions, in particular the fact that the normative version, unlike the causal one, is largely immune to it.

Consider this objection in greater detail: drawing inferences we typically move, so the story goes, from some beliefs to a new belief, i.e., from propositions to a proposition. These propositions should be definite: it should be clear exactly which propositions they are. I may, for example, move from the propositions that *if it rains, the streets are wet* and that *it rains* to the proposition that *the streets are wet*, and obviously I must be in their possession before I can make this inference. Hence the inference would seem to presuppose propositions, rather than help them into being.

The same holds for concepts insofar as they are seen as constituents of propositions. The proposition that *if it rains, the streets are wet* incorporates implication (rather than, say, conjunction). Hence I must be in possession of the concept of implication already *before* I put together this proposition, and hence before I carry out any such inference. Hence again, claiming that the concept of implication is *forged* by inferences of this kind seems to lead us to a vicious circle: we need implication to be able to substantiate the inferences.[22]

A way of circumventing this objection that might immediately come to mind is to insist that inferences are essentially linguistic, i.e., that they are carried out primarily with sentences, and only secondarily with propositions that the sentences express. But prima facie this does not help, for it would seem that for such a linguistic move to deserve the title *inference* (rather than being just a haphazard passage from one string of letters to another), the sentences must be *meaningful* – v̈iz.

express propositions. So the circumvention would seem to fail because we need propositions *before* we can do any inferences, and again it would seem that inferences thus cannot be constitutive of meanings, especially propositions.

In a recent paper, Boghossian (2014, p. 17) speaks of:

> something that should have been obvious, but that is often lost sight of, including by me...: and that is that reasoning is an operation on thought contents and not on symbols (that have content). That immediately implies that the usual ways of presenting programs of 'inferential role semantics' are confused – a logical constant's role in inference must be explained by its content; its content cannot be explained by its role in inference. Of course, it is always open to an 'inferential role' theorist to give up on the claim that concept possession arises out of the inferential manipulation of symbols, and to insist, rather, that both inference and concepts arise simultaneously out of some pre-cognitive operations on symbols. But it is not easy to see how to flesh out such a view in a plausible way.

I think that what inferentialism provides – or at least struggles to provide – is precisely the fleshing out of this view. Our version of inferentialism presupposes the existence of rules that in turn, as discussed in the previous section, presupposes the social nature of the enterprise of drawing inferences. Inferences are not subjective mental moves, but rather moves in a certain public, intersubjective game, and the rules of the game are constituted together with the constitution of the game itself.

Consider the following 'objection' aimed at chess: chess is played with chess pieces and not with mere bits of wood, hence the piece's role in chess must be explained by its value and its value cannot be explained by its role in chess. Or, put differently, chess moves are not made with bits of wood, but rather with chess pieces, hence we must have the pieces prior to the moves and independent to them. The obvious reply is that it is the rules of chess that confer the values on the bits of wood, i.e., make them into the chess pieces. Hence as soon as we have the distinctions between rules and moves, we may let the former constitute the pieces and the latter then 'operate' on the pieces. In other words, 'the piece's role in chess' is ambiguous, in between the role conferred by the *rules* of chess and the role we confer on it by the ways we use it in games. Once this ambiguity is sorted out, which, in the case of chess, is trivial, the 'objection' looks ridiculous.

And the point is that normative inferentialism can parry the objection of circularity in an analogous way. It can accept that 'a logical constant's role in inference must be explained by its content', whereas at the same time rejecting that 'its content cannot be explained by its role in inference'. We must only sort out the ambiguity of *inference*: the role of a logical constant (or, for that matter, another linguistic item) in inference$_1$ is explained by its content, where inference$_1$ amounts to the inferential moves we actually do with the constant, whereas the content is explained by the role of the constant in inference$_2$, where inference$_2$ amounts to what is *correct* to infer, *viz.* to inferential *rules*.

Of course there is a difference between language and chess consisting in the fact that the rules of chess can be stipulated (in language), whereas those of language cannot have come into being in this way. But this objection does not entail that such rules are nonexistent, and it will be one of the tasks of this book (especially in Chapter 5) to indicate how they could have come into being and established themselves in the form such that this parallel between language and chess turns out to be viable.

Thus, normative inferentialism maintains that for rules, as certain social institutions, there is a story to be told about how they emerged as means of fixations of certain social mechanisms (a story we will tell in detail in Chapter 6), and how they bestowed certain meanings on items the use of which they regulate. No such story appears to be available for a causal inferentialist; the only way a mind can acquire the required dispositions to operate with symbols so that it generates a language (or a 'logic') appears to be some kind of trial-and-error, and due to the holistic nature of linguistic and logical rules, there is no direct feedback that would make this path passable, i.e., that would make it possible to acquire the rules one by one. In contrast to this, the 'social version of the trial-and-error' that leads to the establishment of the rules of language is viable because the 'cultural promulgation' of the social rules makes them survive the demise of any individual mind and hence can wait for the slow feedback given by the external world to the whole system of rules.

Consider another variation on the circularity objection, presented by Fodor and Lepore (2007, p. 682):

[I]f, as we suppose, Brandom understands his Gentzen-style analysis of content as providing a *possession condition* for 'and' (more generally, for the concept of conjunction), then the treatment would seem to be circular on the face of it. So, for example, we're told that 'to define the inferential role of an expression "&" ... one specifies that anyone who is committed to P and committed to Q, is thereby to count also as committed as to P&Q, and that anyone who is committed to P&Q is thereby committed both to P and to Q' (Brandom, 2000, p. 62). But since expressions for conjunction (*viz.* '&' and 'and') appear on both sides of each equation, it couldn't be that Brandom's definition of 'and' is what is known by someone who has the word (/concept) and in virtue of which he understands the word (/grasps the concept). Nor, for the same reason, could it be what is *learned* when someone learns the word (/concept).

Of course, to *articulate* the inferential rules governing a logical constant we need a language with its logical vocabulary. But this only says that inferential rules cannot always be explicit, and that there is a sense in which rules have to be implicit to human behavior before they can come to be expressed. This is, of course, a nontrivial assumption and Fodor and Lepore question it; again, it is one of the principal tasks of this book to defend it.

I conclude that the allegation of circularity that is sometimes taken as a knock-down refutation of inferentialism rests on a conflation of the causal and normative versions of inferentialism. If we stick to the normative version, it loses its bite. (Clearly this loads a great deal of the burden of explanation onto the concept of rule, which is itself not transparent, but to unpack it is one of the main tasks of the first part of this book.)

1.6   Plan of the rest of the book

In what follows we will be talking about *normative* inferentialism, the kind of inferentialism introduced by Brandom. However, what I will be discussing may not be exactly Brandom's version of inferentialism, nor will it be presented within Brandom's preferred framework. I will explore the foundations of inferentialism in my own way (which I believe is in essence compatible with Brandom's).

Let me return to the trivial example of an inferential role: the role of $\wedge$ that is established by the inferential pattern:

$$\frac{A \wedge B}{A} \qquad \frac{A \wedge B}{B} \qquad \frac{A \quad B}{A \wedge B}$$

There does not seem to be much controversy possible over this simple case: as this pattern can be read as straightforwardly equivalent to the standard truth table for the connective, nothing seems to stand in the way of seeing it as delimiting the meaning of '∧'.

However, serious difficulties emerge as soon as we move on from this case. We can distinguish two directions along which we can move. One obvious direction is to try to extend inferentialism to expressions other than logical constants, to expressions that can be found in natural languages, especially *empirical* expressions. The most general problem then is to establish how this can be done at all: how empirical expressions that seem to be first and foremost means of *representing* the world can be treated inferentially. Another direction along which to move would keep us within the realm of logic, but would strive to scrutinize how the various kinds of logical constants can be accounted for inferentially. (Already standard disjunction, as we will see, presents a problem for the inferentialist.) Here the basic problems are much more technical. These two directions are dealt with by the first and second parts of this book, respectively.

Thus, in the first part we address the general problems of inferentialism with respect to the whole of natural language, including a discussion of the very sources of normativity that underlie the inferential rules governing it. I try to generalize the inferential construal of logical constants to the rest of the vocabulary, thereby reaching an inferential explication of the concepts of meaning and language. Discussing how the concept of inferential rule can be generalized so as to encompass the empirical dimension of language leads to the conclusion that the whole of language (in contrast to its purely logical part) must be understood as a system of *embodied* rules, i.e., of rules that constitutively incorporate the world. I broach the problem that at least some of the rules of our language are bound to remain merely implicit in our linguistic practices. I point out that such rules are carried by the *normative attitudes* of people, leading to the conclusion that normative attitudes result from the fact that we do not only state that something is the case, but also endorse that something *should be* the case. There follows an analysis of how the rules of our languages interlock to provide for propositions and concepts, and finally I discuss this fact from the evolutionary perspective.

The second part of the book concentrates on the inferentialist approach to the meaning of logical constants and to logic in general. We start from the disambiguation of the term *inference* and from the discussion of the relationship between inference and consequence. (It is often claimed that the necessary discrepancy between inference and consequence, as documented by the results of Tarski and Gödel, shows the irreducibility of the truly semantic notions to the 'syntactic' ones, but we argue that the relationship inference vs. consequence can be construed as the relationship between two layers of inference, namely one based on the usual strict concept of rule and the other based on a looser concept.) In view of the Priorian argument that not every inferential pattern is capable of constituting a reasonable logical constant, I consider the problem of characterization of 'benign' (or 'semantogenic') patterns, as contrasted to the *tonk*ish, 'malign' ones. I conclude, in accordance with Belnap's reaction to Prior's problem, that the inferential patterns constitutive of logical constants should be conservative. I also discuss the kinds of logical constants that can be introduced in terms of inferential patterns straightforwardly, and introduce a hierarchy of inferential (and consequently semantic) systems yielded by relaxation of the concept of inferential rule.

I also offer a story (based on the idea of Brandom) explaining *why* it is that the patterns constitutive of logical constants should be conservative. My claim is that it is because the role of logical vocabulary is basically *expressive* – that its *raison d'être* is to make explicit the inferential relationships between sentences implicit to our non-logical concepts. Exploiting this idea, I then discuss the notion of 'native' logical operators (generic operators needed for making the inferential relationship explicit) and I use it to shed new light on the differences among logical systems. I draw some consequences of this construal of logic for the very nature of logic: I claim that human 'possession of logic' should not be understood as a matter of knowledge of logical laws, but rather as a matter of possessing a certain kind of language, governed by a certain intricate set of interlocking rules. Finally I turn my attention to the interconnection between logic and reasoning, and concluding that the laws of logic are not rules of reasoning in the sense of tactical rules, I claim that they are rather rules that constitute the 'material' that is a necessary vehicle for reasoning.

Individual chapters of the book have absorbed some of the materials (mostly substantially reworked) that I have earlier published in articles. Aside from material from articles that had the character of prepublications and were printed in volumes that were not widely accessible, this also concerns some genuinely published papers. Thus, in the first part of the book Chapter 3 contains bits of the paper 'Inferentialism and Compositionality of Meaning' (*International Review of Pragmatics* 1, 2009, pp. 154–181), while Chapters 4 and 5 include some scattered fragments from 'The use-theory of meaning and the rules of our language games' (K. Turner, ed.: *Making Semantics Pragmatic*, Emerald, Bingley, 2011, pp. 183–204); Chapter 4 incorporates some material from 'Inferentialism and the Normativity of Meaning' (*Philosophia* 40, 2012, pp. 75–97);

Chapter 5 includes parts of 'Semantics without Meaning?' (R. Schantz, ed.: *Prospects of Meaning*, de Gruyter, Berlin, 2012, pp. 479–502); while Chapter 6 overlaps with 'The Enigma of Rules' (*International Journal of Philosophical Studies* 18, 2010, pp. 377–394). In the second part of the book, Chapter 8 draws on the material published (in greater detail) in 'Inferentializing Semantics' (*Journal of Philosophical Logic* 39, 2010, pp. 255–274); Chapter 9 partly overlaps with 'What is *the* logic of inference?' (*Studia Logica* 88, 2008, pp. 263–294), while Chapter 11 contains a small fragment of the paper 'Logic and Natural Selection' (*Logica Universalis* 4, 2010, pp. 207–223).

1.7 Summary of Chapter 1

In this chapter we have introduced the general concept of inferentialism as it has come into circulation both in logic and in philosophy of language. We have also attempted to clear away the most widespread misunderstandings, particularly stressing that inferentialism is not what has occasionally been called *inferential role semantics*. What was termed *inferentialism* by Brandom, and what we address in this book, is the doctrine that identifies meanings with roles vis-à-vis inferential *rules*, whereas the kind of inferentialism envisaged by Boghossian, Peacocke, and others is interested in roles with respect to inferences actually or potentially carried out by speakers. We have stressed that a proper understanding of this preempts the most frequent kind of objections to inferentialism, namely the allegations of circularity – objections that have no obvious force against the normative version of inferentialism we present.

Part I
Language, Meaning, and Norms

2
Words as Governed by Rules

2.1 Ross's 'Noît-cif tribe'

Alf Ross (1957), a leading exponent of the so-called Scandinavian Legal Realism school, invites us to imagine a community that he calls the Noît-cif tribe that maintains that

(1) if a person has eaten of the chief's food he is *tû-tû*; and
(2) if a person is *tû-tû* he shall be subjected to a ceremony of purification.

Ross argues that in this case the term *tû-tû* is redundant for its only role is in forging the link between the fact of eating of the chief's food and the obligation of undergoing the purification, where this link can be established directly, without the mediation of this term.

In this way Ross wants to make plain that words like *tû-tû* are anomalous – they are very different from prototypical words of our language that are truly meaningful in that they *refer to extralinguistic reality* (and subsequently he aims to show that some legal terms – like *ownership* – are anomalous in the same sense and hence are not 'really' meaningful). Here we want to use his illustrious example to show the contrary (in the spirit of the notorious 'one philosopher's *modus ponens* is another's *modus tollens*'). We want to indicate that *tû-tû* is not anomalous and that prototypical words of our language do not work in a substantially different way.

Let us call (1) the *condition of application* of *tû-tû* and (2) its *consequence of application*. As Ross notes, there may (and in reality probably will) be more than one *condition of application* (a person may be *tû-tû* not only when he has eaten of the chief's food, but also, say, when his totem animal is killed, etc.) and, likewise, more than one *consequence* (a person who is *tû-tû* is not only to be subjected to a ceremony of purification, but also, perhaps, not to eat until the purification, etc.) It is for the sake of simplicity and perspicuity that we concentrate on the case with one single condition and one single consequence of application.

Consider some word more mundane than *tû-tû*, say the word *spider* (or, for that matter, its equivalent in the Noît-cifian language). It also has conditions of application; perhaps

(1*) if an animal has eight legs and builds webs, it is a spider.

Also it will have consequences of application, e.g.

(2*) if an animal is a spider, killing it is not a crime.

In view of this, what is the difference between this word and *tû-tû*?

The first difference that comes to mind is that the conditions (1*) and (2*) were rather randomly selected among many other candidates. (1*) is probably imprecise (not every spider necessarily builds webs as far as I know); and (2*) is one among many other consequence of an animal being a spider. But this does not seem to be a deep difference. Impreciseness can be done away by consulting experts, and the fact that there is more than one consequence of application also does not constitute a decisive difference. Also *tû-tû* may have more than one condition and more consequences. As Ross draws the picture, the general situation would be

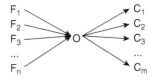

where the Fs stand for the conditions and the Cs for the consequences. Eliminating O then simply amounts to forging links between every F and every C:

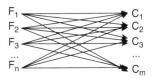

This indicates that O leads to a great economy of reasoning: whereas without its help we need $n \times m$ links, with it we can make do with merely $n + m$.

Another difference between *tû-tû* and *spider* may be seen as consisting in the fact that the conditions and consequences for the former were explicitly defined and are hence precise, while those for the latter do not have any such definition and are hence vague. Again, this does not seem to be a decisive difference. I do not think that anything in Ross's example hinges on the fact that (1) and (2) are explicitly formulated by the Noît-cifians. And, moreover, the boundary between terms that are explicitly defined and those that are not is not the boundary between the precise and the vague. A definition such as that of *tû-tû* above must – eventually – be couched in terms that are themselves not explicitly defined (*eat, food*...), which means that they too possess some amount of vagueness. On the other hand, even terms without an explicit definition can play useful roles in language only if there is *some* contrast between those things to which they are, and those to which they are not, applicable.

The last difference can be seen in that terms of ordinary language, like *spider*, may be thought of as having a function that eludes adequate capture by any definition of the kind of (1) and (2). This is to say that although a term may have some conditions and consequences of application, its functioning in language is something over and above them. But what is this functioning then?

2.2   *Tû-tû* vs. *ownership* vs. *fun*

Inferentialism, in its most general form, claims that there is nothing over and above this altogether. In short, Ross's *tû-tû* illustrates how ordinary words of our language function – illustrates this, to be sure, in an oversimplified way, but illustrates it fairly in that it does not conceal any essential sources of meaningfulness (like *reference*).

Ross himself, as we already have mentioned, performed his thought experiment in order to indicate that some legal terms, such as the term *ownership*, have the same status as *tû-tû*. He claims that both these terms merely forge links between some factual conditions and some normative consequences. His point is that the usage of the term *ownership*, at least in the legal context, is governed by conditions of the very same kind:

(1**)   If A has lawfully purchased an object, ownership of the object is thereby created by him.

(2**)   If *A* is the owner of an object, he has (among other things) the rights of recovery.

Hence Ross claims:

> [T]he 'ownership' inserted between the conditioning facts and the conditioned consequences is in reality a meaningless word without any semantic reference whatever, serving solely as a means of presentation.

The moral Ross draws from this exercise is that legal terms like *ownership* are not words meaningful in the sense in which 'standard' English words are. The background assumption seems to be that a term, to be truly meaningful, must obtain a reference; it is insufficient merely to have the conditions and consequence of application.

However, this is precisely what the inferentialist denies: her claim is that language is *not* a set of signs animated by their reference; she maintains that words become meaningful by being entangled within the network of inferential relationships. To be sure, these relationships do somehow involve a worldly dimension, but to see this dimension as a matter of reference is ill-conceived. (This is not to say that the concept of reference is itself ill-conceived, but it is to say that reference should not be seen as something independent and prior to inference.)

How could a reference be established and what kind of difference would it instigate between the allegedly merely pseudo-meaningful *ownership* and truly meaningful words like, say, *spider* or *fun*? Well, it is clear that the word *spider* must be somehow connected to spiders. And, indeed, an important part of learning the word is learning to use sentences such as *This is a spider* (or just *Spider!*) in appropriate situations, prototypically as an accompaniment to pointing at a spider. But this does not seem to fundamentally differentiate the word from *ownership*; in its case we also need to learn to use the word in appropriate situations, to distinguish appropriate uses of *This is ownership* from inappropriate ones. So maybe the difference is that spiders are directly *visible* and hence the reference can be established as a mental link between the word and an image? But if this were the crucial difference, then obviously many of our ordinary words would group with *ownership* rather than *spider* – words like *fun*, *atom*, *solution*, and so on (not to mention *very*, *over*, etc.). Hence it seems unlikely that reference can be something achievable other than through the establishment of suitable conditions of application.

Take the sentence *This is edible*. It 'follows' from pointing at an apple or a sugar cube, and it follows from *This is an apple*, *This is sugar*, or *This was eaten by my friend without any harm*. It 'entails' eating it, and it entails *This is not poisonous* or *A man can eat this and it will not kill him*. This way of talking about 'following' and 'entailing' is, to be sure, somewhat sloppy.[1] To be less sloppy we may adopt the term 'transition' introduced by Wilfrid Sellars. Sellars (1974) talks about three kinds of transitions:

(1) Language Entry Transitions: The speaker responds to objects in perceptual situations, and in certain states in himself, with appropriate linguistic activity.
(2) Intra-linguistic moves: The speaker's linguistic conceptual episodes tend to occur in patterns of valid inference (theoretical and practical), and tend not to occur in patterns which violate logical principles.
(3) Language Exit Transitions: The speaker responds to such linguistic conceptual episodes as 'I will now raise my hand' with an upward motion of the hand, etc.

Given this terminology we can say that Ross's claim that *tû-tû* is redundant amounts to the claim that if we have a *language entry transition* followed by a *language exit transition*, there is, in principle, no need to enter language at all, for we can make a direct transition from the extralinguistic states from which the entry transition starts to the extralinguistic activities into which the exit transition results.

This is true, and, indeed, it is true not just in the case of an entry transition followed by an exit transition, but in the case of *any* pair of concatenable transitions (entry + exit, entry + intra, intra + intra, intra + exit), and hence *any* term may be seen as eliminable in this sense. However, the point is that the term is used precisely to *forge* such a link in the first place, or at least to make it explicit.

2.3   Material inference

The general assumption of inferentialism is that inferential rules govern not only logical vocabulary, but also the rest of the vocabulary of natural language. Thus the meaning of any kind of word (not only logical words like *and* or *if... then ...*, and nor only 'classificatory' terms like *spider* or *fun*, but of all words whatsoever) consists in its inferential role. This, however, presupposes that our understanding of the concept of inferential rule must be somewhat broadened.

First, we must be clear about the fact that when we talk about inferential rules, we need not have in mind anything like *logical* rules. Thus, examples of inferential rules are not only:

(1) X is P
      If X is P, then X is Q
      X is Q

but also:

(2) X is a dog
      X is an animal

or:

(3)   *Lightning now*
      Thunder soon

The recognition of (2) as an inferential rule goes hand in hand with the rejection of the view that an inference of the form (2) is valid only because we see it as implicitly containing a second premise, such as *Every dog is an animal.*[2] According to our view, this inference is no less self-contained than (1). Even in the latter case we could consider an additional premise such as *If anything has a certain property, and whatever has this property has a certain other property, then the thing in question has the other property* (as articulated by Russell, 1914, p. 66). Ultimately the requirement of making every such alleged premise explicit would obviously lead to the infinite regress of the kind diagnosed already by Lewis Carroll (1895).[3] On the other hand, the additional premise is not necessary, because for the inference to hold it is enough that the meaning of *if...then...* be fixed; of course, when talking about inferences we assume the context of a specific language, with the meanings of its expressions fixed. But by the same token we can vindicate the original inference: for it to hold, we need nothing more than the meanings of *dog* and *animal* be fixed. Let us follow Sellars (1953) and call these 'extra-logical' inferential rules *material*.

The reason for taking rules like (2) seriously is that, according to Sellars, rules of this kind are not abridged versions of logical rules, and, moreover, they are in fact more fundamental than the logical rules. According to this view, nonlogical vocabulary and the rules governing it constitute the basis of language, while the single role of the logical vocabulary is allowing us to make the material inferential links explicit. (Before having expressive resources like *if...then...* and *something*, we can use the words *dog* and *animal* in accordance with rule (2), but not until we acquire these resources can we make the rule explicit in the form of the claim *If something is a dog, it is an animal.*) Brandom (2001) elaborated this into an expressivist notion of logic; we will discuss this further in the second part of the book (see esp. Chapter 9).

The recognition of (3) as an inferential rule requires, moreover, recognition of the fact that inferential rules need not be indefeasible: (3) is obviously a paradigmatic case of a *ceteris paribus* rule. This goes against the tradition that something deserves the name *inferential rule* only if it is 'bulletproof'. However, the question is whether there are any inferences that are bulletproof in this sense in natural language at all. Take (2), which is a paradigmatic example of a rule that would be taken to hold on *analytic* (though not *logical*) grounds. Would a mother telling her child that her fluffy toy dog is not an animal (and hence will not eat candy) be seen as compromised from the viewpoint of understanding the meaning of the word *dog* or *animal*?[4]

And is (1) bulletproof? It probably comes as close to being such as possible in natural language, but nevertheless it is not. Arguments to the effect that the English *if...then...* does not, as a matter of fact, generally follow modus ponens are available,[5] and even were it to follow it with no exceptions, this would still only be a contingent matter, open to disturbances by the vagaries of the English language. Hence truly bulletproof inferences in natural language are generally in short supply. (We will say more about this in Chapter 10).

The fact that there is no sharp boundary between rules that are a matter of the meanings of words and rules needing some kind of empirical underpinning is evocative of Quine's (1952) rejection of the analytic/synthetic boundary. Sellars followed logical empiricists in maintaining that to accept a conceptual framework is to accept a set of rules.[6] However, unlike the logical empiricists, Sellars did not think that this institutes a firm analytic/synthetic boundary in the sense that truths concerning the framework are analytic, whereas those concerning the content on which the framework is imposed are synthetic. In contrast to philosophers like Carnap, who believed that choosing a conceptual framework (and attaching it to our language) is a purely deliberate, conventional act, for the world can have its say only *after* we accomplish the choice (only then can it make our empirical sentences true or false), Sellars, similarly to Quine and Davidson, believed that the two processes (of choosing the framework and letting the world make its appearance through that framework) are not clearly separated. Especially, Sellars believed that the world influences our putting together of the framework, though in a very different way from how it determines the truth values of our sentences (Sellars, 1953, pp. 336–337):

> The familiar notion … that the form of a concept is determined by 'logical rules'; while the content is 'derived from experience' embodies a radical misinterpretation of the manner in which the 'manifold of sense' contributes to the shaping of the conceptual apparatus, 'applied' to the manifold in the process of cognition. … The role of the given is … to be compared to the role of the environment in the evolution of species; though it would be misleading to say that the apparent teleology whereby men 'shape their concepts to conform with reality' is as illusory as the teleology of the giraffe's lengthening neck.

Hence already the concept-forming rules, which Carnap would hold for exclusively conventional, are shaped, as Sellars put it borrowing from Kant, by the 'manifold of sense', though very differently from how empirical sentences are furnished with their truth values.

Consider natural laws. The adherents of the analytic/synthetic distinction would conclude that since they cannot be among the rules constitutive of our framework (for we accept or reject them on the basis of empirical data), they must be simply empirical generalizations, formulatable only after the terms they involve come to be furnished with concepts (by the rules of the conventional framework). However, Sellars noticed that, as a matter of fact, natural laws *do* take part in conferring roles on the terms they involve and hence that they do constitute concepts; moreover, they constitute some of the concepts that are quite crucial for us and for our dealing with the world. And he concluded that the boundary between, on the one hand, a framework that has nothing whatsoever to do with the empirical world and, on the other hand, a content that is nothing but empirical, is illusory. Every framework and every rule (perhaps with the exception of the rules of pure logic whose role is merely explicitating) is – more or less – contaminated by the empirical.

Sellars therefore insisted that laws of nature, and material rules more generally, are *both* rules capable of taking part in constituting concepts *and* empirical claims that may be accepted and rejected on the basis of empirical data. This is what endows many concepts with their empirical content – the acceptance or rejection of the rules that are constitutive of them is an *empirical* matter: 'material transformation rules determine the descriptive meaning of the expressions of a language within the framework established by its logical transformation rules' (ibid., p. 336). So we must give up the idea that *either* a rule is *conceptual* ('analytic'), and then its acceptance is a matter of nothing but convention and hence it can *create* ('implicitly define') concepts, *or* it is an empirical generalization and hence it *presupposes* concepts, and then its acceptance is an exclusively empirical matter. The acceptance of a Sellarsian material rule may (partly) be an empirical matter but it may still have its place in shaping the concepts that are used to articulate it.[7]

2.4 Empirical vocabulary

However, even if we admit that material rules take part in forming empirical concepts, the proposal that the meanings of empirical words are entirely identifiable with their inferential roles might still seem too far-fetched. Even those willing to agree that such inferentialism may work for logical (and perhaps certain other nonempirical[8]) words might doubt that it could work for empirical words; it would seem that empirical words, to be truly meaningful, must *refer* to something or *represent* something. Whereas with logical words there may be an issue over the relative merits of grasping their semantics in inferentialist or in representationalist terms, for empirical words there seems to be only the latter option.

Obviously empirical words must be somehow 'tied to the world' – the word *spider* to spiders, the word *run* to episodes of running, etc. We must ask, therefore, about the nature of the tie. We have already seen that the most usual way of establishing such a tie would be to establish a link between an observation sentence and a certain situation, prototypically a situation in which there is an object to be pointed at. The question is whether this link is sufficiently like inference to warrant being taken as part of an 'inferential pattern' that confers an inferential role on the word in question. However, before we consider this, we will indicate why even empirical words must be interwoven within the network of inferences in the standard sense. (In the preceding section we have concluded that the material inferential rule *may* take part in shaping meanings; what we want to show now is that such a shaping is indispensable for any word.)

Can an empirical word become meaningful just by being 'tied to the world' in the above sense? Can the word *dog* come to mean what it does in English in force merely of the fact that the sentence *This is a dog* becomes 'tied' to appropriate situations? Consider a cat emitting a peculiar kind of hiss when it sees a dog: the hiss, in the mouth of the cat, appears to be tied to the same situations to which the sentence *This is a dog* is in the mouth of a speaker of English. So why do we say that the latter is a meaningful sentence, a description of the situation, whereas the former is a mere *reaction* to the situation?

The reasons usually stem from the fact that the human utterer, unlike the cat, deals with language with the versatility characteristic of thinking, meaning-mongering beings like us. Her utterance is embedded within a richly structured spectrum of other utterances, hence we assume that the sentence is part of a certain network of other sentences. We may use another sentence to challenge the claim of the utterer and we assume that if her utterance was really meaningful, she will react in an appropriate way, for example that she will give some reasons for her claim. If we were to find out that the utterer follows her utterance of *This is a dog* with *Hence it lives in water*, or that her reply to our objection *But it looks more like a cat than a dog* would be *Yes, it is a dog and also a cat*, we would start to wonder whether she knew what she was talking about (or whether she was *talking* at all).

So the question of meaningfulness of a word turns on the question of its embeddedness within networks of other words, more precisely of sentences containing the word being in inferential relationships to other sentences. Therefore inferentialism embraces the proposal that what makes something an assertion, rather than just a sound, is the fact that it is a move in a certain *language game*, a rule-governed game; what makes something a *meaningful sentence* is its capability of serving as a token playable in such a game, and what makes a *word meaningful* is being part of meaningful sentences.

The links that are, according to the inferentialist, the most important have to do with the ability of engaging in the intercourses of the kind just exemplified, and more generally with practices that Brandom (1994) termed *the game of giving and asking for reasons*. One important dimension of interconnectedness of sentences has to do with the possibility of *challenging* one's claim, which calls for a defense in the form of *justification* of the claim. This amounts to the relations of incompatibility (the most primitive version of challenging a claim is to display something that is incompatible with it) and of inferability (to justify a claim is to give a reason for it, and hence to display something from which the claim is inferable). Inferentialist has bracketed the latter relation (which can be perhaps reduced to the former one, as discussed in the second part of the book) and has made the former its emblem.

So we must conclude that the contentfulness even of empirical words must be underpinned by certain inferences in the standard sense of the word. No empirical word is meaningful in the distinctively human way (particularly none expresses a *concept*) unless it is capable of taking part in complex linguistic games (and especially the game of giving and asking for reasons). A word does not express the concept of *dog* unless it can be used as part of sentences that can in turn be used for reasoning, i.e., from which other sentences can be inferred and which themselves can be inferred from other sentences. The English word *dog* would not express our concept of dog if it could not be used to reason from *This is a dog* to *This is an animal, This is not a cat* etc.

Hence the meaning of an empirical word must involve some inferences, but what about the residual part, the part which 'ties the word to the world'? Is it not here where we *cannot* make do without concepts such as *reference* or *representation* understood as irreducible to inference? How could a word like *dog* come to express the concept of dog without, at least inter alia, referring to dogs or representing dogs (or perhaps a 'doghood')? But though the word *dog* must be, no doubt, somehow 'tied to the world', the inferentialist verdict is that the concepts of *reference* and *representation* lead to a very misleading way of capturing what is going on between our empirical vocabulary and the world.[9]

As it is only *sentences* that may be used to make a move in a language game, any contact between a word and (a part of) the world must be mediated by sentences.[10] Besides this, what matters, according to the inferentialist, is not primarily what the speakers really do with the sentences, but what they take to be *correct* to do – hence the tie between language and the world is of a normative character. Thus the link between the word *dog* and the world is a matter of such facts as that it is correct to use the sentence *This is a dog* in certain situations, and incorrect in others.

It is clear that the usage of *This is a dog* may be 'noninferential' in the sense that its correctness is a matter directly of the extralinguistic circumstances, and hence the way it responds to the world is not an inference in the standard sense (from language to language), but perhaps we can talk about an 'inference', as it were, from the world to language? (Similarly, at the other 'end' of language, perhaps we can talk about 'inferences' from language to action?) By stretching the term *inference* to include this, we could directly extend the inferentialist treatment of meaning from expressions like *and* to expressions like *dog*. What are the pros and cons of such a stretching, and is it really viable?

2.5   Inferences into and out of language?

Imagine that we do broaden the sense of *inference* so that we are able to talk about inferences from situations to utterances and from utterances to actions. (Keep in mind that this broadening is to accommodate the fact that the role an expression plays within language is co-constituted by certain sentences being *correctly* asserted in certain situations, and *incorrectly* in others, and that a sentence may express a reason for some actions, though not for others. In this sense, certain normative links seem to connect situations to sentences and sentences to actions just like they connect sentences to sentences.) This makes it possible to say that the inferential role of an empirical term like *dog* consists both of (material) rules of inferences of the standard kind, i.e., rules like:

X is a dog ⊢ X is an animal
X is a dog ⊢ X is not a cat

and also of some 'inferential rules' linking types of situations to sentences or sentences to types of actions.

This would lead us to a straightforward generalization of the concept of inferential pattern from logical to empirical words, whereby just as the meaning of a logical word is conferred on the word by a pattern that is inferential in the ordinary, narrow sense, so the meaning of an empirical word is conferred on the word by an inferential pattern in the extended sense. Hence while the meaning of $\wedge$ is a matter of our already well-known pattern

$A \wedge B \vdash A$
$A \wedge B \vdash B$
$A, B \vdash A \wedge B$

the meaning of *dog* might be thought of as a matter of a pattern constituted by some rules of a similar kind plus some rules leading from dog-featuring situations to *This is a dog*, from *This is a dog* to certain actions, and so on. All of this might be helpful, for it would lead us to a unified inferentialist theory of meaning of both empirical and nonempirical words. This is what is suggested by Brandom (2007, p. 658):

> The way the Gentzen hyperinferentialist model for the semantics of logical concepts is to be extended is by taking seriously the thought

that in using any expression, applying any concept, one is undertaking a commitment to the correctness of the (in general, material) inference from the circumstances in which it is correctly applied to the correct consequences of such application. And this is so even where some of those circumstances or consequences of application are noninferential. Thus the visible presence of red things warrants the applicability of the concept red – not as the conclusion of an inference, but observationally. And the point is that the connection between those circumstances of application and whatever consequences of application the concept may have can be understood to be inferential in a broad sense, even when the items connected are not themselves sentential.

Illuminating as the stretching of the concept of inference in this way might be, the question remains whether it can be taken as more than a metaphor. We have already talked about the 'transitions' that, according to Sellars, form the backbone of every language, the 'Language Entry Transitions', 'Intra-linguistic Moves' and 'Language Exit Transitions'. What we have now done, in effect, is to substitute the term *inference* for *transition*; thus we have achieved a generalized sense of 'inference' that allows us to say that the meanings even of empirical words are inferential roles. Can we appeal to Sellars's patronage here?

Why did Sellars himself avoid the term *inference*? First, he did not think that transitions from world to language are transitions in the same sense as those from language to language, i.e., inferences in the standard sense. Thus, Sellars (1953, pp. 335–336) writes:

There is at first sight some plausibility in saying that the rules to which the expressions of a language owe their meaning are of two kinds, (a) syntactical rules, relating symbols to other symbols, and (b) semantical rules, whereby basic descriptive terms acquire extra-linguistic meaning. It takes but a moment, however, to show that this widespread manner of speaking is radically mistaken. Obeying a rule entails recognizing that a circumstance is one to which the rule applies. If there were such a thing as 'semantical rule' by the adoption of which a descriptive term acquires meaning, it would presumably be of the form 'red objects are to be responded to by the noise *red*'. But to recognize the circumstances to which this rule applies, one would already have to have the concept of red, that is, a symbol of which it can correctly be said that it 'means red'.

In an even more explicit manner, Sellars (1954, p. 209) stresses that an observation sentence is not the outcome of a move, hence that there is no such move as going from a situation to its observational report:

> Here we notice that the game involves an *initial* position, a position which one can be at without having moved to it. Shall we say that language games involve such positions? Indeed, it occurs to us, are not 'observation sentences' exactly such positions? Surely they are positions in the language game which one occupies without having moved there from other positions *in the language.*

But is this a matter of more than mere terminology? Of course, a situation in the world is not 'in the language' and if we consider only moves which are 'in' it, we exclude the extralinguistic world (by fiat). But we can envisage a more inclusive game which does encompass the extralinguistic world. It may not be the game of giving and asking for reasons, but is it not this more inclusive game that is truly crucial for *empirical* languages?

Moreover, there seems to be no reason to restrict the possible interventions of the world to the choice of an initial position; we can easily imagine an intervention happening 'inside the game'. Imagine that in a variant of chess I am forbidden to move certain pawns if it is raining. Moving one of these pawns, under favorable weather conditions, could then be seen as a response to my opponent's moves *and* to the weather (or as a response to merely the opponent's moves *mediated* by the weather). Here the external world would act as something to which our moves respond just like they respond to opponent moves; it would become, in this sense, a part of the game.

Such a modification of chess looks weird, admittedly, but it is important to realize that something of this very kind happens along the imaginary path from chess to football.[11] Here the space that is open for our operation ceases to be delimited exclusively by the rules (and thus conceivable purely *in foro abstracto*) and starts increasingly to be co-delimited by the physical laws of the real world. And it seems, as pointed out by Lance (1998), that in this respect language is much closer to a *sport* like football than to a *game* like chess. (In this book we invoke similarities between language and chess quite frequently, however here we have a basic *dissimilarity*.)

Is all this sufficient to vindicate speaking about inferences from situations to sentences? Unfortunately there is a graver problem. The relation of inference requires a specific kind of relata: for example, it makes little sense to say that an object (such as a chair) is inferable from another object (say, a table). We can infer *that* so-and-so from *that* so-and-so, hence a belief from a belief, a judgment from a judgment, or a proposition from a proposition. (Keep in mind, however, that a proposition, and consequently belief and judgment, for us, is nothing else than a certain role of a sentence; it is no self-standing furniture of the universe but rather something that owes for its form completely to our linguistic practices, especially the *game of giving and asking for reasons*.)[12]

Hence the question whether an inference can directly connect language to the world turns on the question in how far we can see 'the world' as containing something as propositions. And Sellars's answer is negative: for him the ordinary, physical world is constituted by objects interconnected by causal relations. Therefore Sellars urged that it is better to see propositions as inhabiting a kind of 'virtual world' called by him *the realm of reasons*. He thought that propositions came into being because the relation of *being a reason for* (where a necessary condition for A being a reason for B is that B is inferable from A) necessitates a specific kind of relata. The emergence of reasoning (i.e., of Brandom's game of giving and asking for reasons), of reasons and of propositions, is, according to him, intimately connected with the unprecedented step of human evolution that rendered us not only capable of *know-how* (i.e., skillful dealings with our environment, an ability we share with many other animals), but also of *know-that* (theorizing). As Sellars (1954, p. 210) puts it:[13] 'To occupy a position in a language is to think, judge, assert *that so-and-so;* to make a move in a language is to infer *from so-and-so, that so-and-so.*'

Importantly, Sellars urges us to beware of the illusion that the physical world, aka *the realm of the causal*, and the space of reasons, aka *the realm of the normative*, can be made continuous with each other. The relations constitutive of them (causal ones and normative ones, respectively) are of such different natures that it is misguided to think that they can be somehow concatenated. In fact, according to Sellars, it is this illusion that has brought about empiricism as a philosophical doctrine, for this doctrine is based on the conviction that a causal chain, delivering to us a certain sensation, can continue as an inferential chain so that the sensation, the endpoint of the causal chain, acts, construed as a 'sense datum', as the starting point of an inferential chain. This is what Sellars (1956) calls the Myth of the Given (for the initial point of the inferential chain is considered to be indisputably *given* to us just *in force* of the fact that it is at the same time the sensation brought to us by the causal chain from the outer world).[14]

Hence, according to Sellars, the causal world is not 'propositional', or, as it is also sometimes expressed, it is 'non-conceptual'. (A concept, in this context, is just a part of a proposition corresponding to a word or other subsentential part of the corresponding sentence – hence again an inferential role.[15]) This led McDowell (1994) and others to re-cast the dualism of the normative and the causal as that of the *conceptual* and the *non-conceptual*, and this terminology has become quite widespread.

These considerations suggest that stretching the term inference in the way put forward at the end of the previous section is problematic. And indeed I think that Sellars is right that understanding the talk about inferences from the world to language or from language to the world nonmetaphorically might lead us to muddy waters. There is a danger that this way of talking would obscure how our language really comes into contact with the world, which we have already started to throw light on by contraposing chess and football.

The move I make within a chess game responds exclusively to the moves made by my opponent (and perhaps my own earlier moves). It cannot respond to anything else, for there is nothing else to respond to. The pieces, board, and other equipment, strictly speaking, are not necessary; it is clear that we can play chess completely without them. Thus the rules of chess spell out a pure, disembodied structure. Football has no disembodied structure like this because its rules *must* take into account the physical properties of the ball, the goalposts, the players' bodies, etc. Consequently, the rules of football cannot be disentangled from the causal order in the way those of chess can. The rules *involve* the causal world indispensably: it is not only that what a player can do depends on more than the current score (it may also depend on the state of the world); the rules may involve also what Haugeland (1998) calls *constitutive principles* that do not concern the behavior of the players at all, but rather put some restriction on the worldly equipment engaged in the game. Similarly, the rules of language must reflect the fact that our language games are not disembodied and self-contained; they are our means of interacting with the world.

As Brandom (1994, p. 332) stresses, our linguistic practices cannot be seen as 'hollow, waiting to be filled up by things', but rather 'as concrete as the practice of driving nails with a hammer'. Hence, to understand the word *dog*, we must know not only how the sentences containing it (*This is a dog, Every dog is a mammal*...) can be correctly played within the game of giving or asking for reasons in response to utterances of other players (that *This bird is a dog* counts as a challenge to *Every dog is a mammal*, which then can be defended by *No bird is a dog* or by *But this bird is not a dog*), but, more broadly, how they are correctly used also vis-à-vis nonlinguistic circumstances (that *This bird is not a dog* is correctly played only when what one is pointing at is a bird, etc.).

Hence the relationship between language and the world, leaving aside metaphors, is, though normative in nature, not really inferential in any straightforward sense of the word. The question, then, is whether it is still substantiated to call the roles of empirical words *inferential*, and not, say, merely *normative*. I will follow Brandom in doing so, but I admit that the positive answer to this question is not something I would consider fighting for.

2.6   Spinning in the void?

I think that understanding the real nature of the interplay between language and the world, as envisaged at the end of the previous section, also alleviates the worry expressed by McDowell (1994) that the incompatibility of the causal and normative relations may undermine our ability to understand human empirical knowledge, for the knowledge seems to be precisely a matter of a relationship between an entity of the causal realm (an object, a situation, or something of this kind) and an entity of the normative one (a piece of knowledge representing or being about the object or the situation). McDowell, though concurring with Sellars in the rejection of the Myth of the Given, urges that the rejection must not lead us to a position that would render the whole notion of empirical knowledge mysterious.

The most basic problem McDowell points out may be pictured as concerning the nature of the relation between a piece of empirical knowledge and what it is knowledge of: for example, the relation between my knowledge that there is a spider in front of me and the very spider. As the piece of knowledge is a proposition and hence not an object of the causal realm, the relation cannot be causal, but as the spider is neither a proposition, nor a concept, hence not an inhabitant of the normative realm, it would seem it cannot be normative either. This leads McDowell (ibid., p. 11) to wonder whether we do not end up with a picture of our reason losing all contact with the world and hence 'frictionlessly spinning in a void'. And as we cannot, according to him, 'naturalize reason' by dragging our basic pieces of knowledge into the causal realm, our only option is to 'de-naturalize' our grasp on the world – to accept that the world is, after all, able to deliver us knowledge that is conceptual: 'The conceptual sphere', McDowell (ibid., p. 72) claims, 'does not exclude the world we experience.'

I think this worry is misplaced. I think that the normative is intertwined with the causal realm in such a way that the gap that McDowell strives to bridge should not really be opened at all. Let us return to Brandom's description (1994, p. 333):

> Thus a demolition of semantic categories of correspondence relative to those of expression does not involve 'loss of the world' in the sense that our discursive practice is then conceived as unconstrained by how things actually are. ... What is lost is only the bifurcation that makes knowledge seem to require the bridging of a *gap* that opens up between sayable and thinkable contents – thought of as existing self-contained on their side of the epistemic crevasse – and the worldly facts, existing on their side.

I think that the illusion of the 'epistemic crevasse' will overwhelm us only when we consider rules that are conceivable as entirely 'disembodied'. Such are the rules of chess. As we pointed out above, though we usually employ some tangible objects to play chess, this is in no way essential; we know that we could play it without any board or pieces. Thus, the rules of chess can be seen as existing wholly independently of the causal realm, and chess as such can be seen as purely a matter of an ideal realm disconnected from the causal one. In contrast to this, the rules of language (or, for that matter, football) are intertwined with the causal realm from the very beginning.

A further problem with McDowell's view is that it invokes the impression that the conceptual/non-conceptual divide has to do with the inner/outer divide. Despite his meticulous efforts to avoid the Myth of the Given, I think this *did* lead him into the vicinity of the muddy waters of problematic empiricism.[16] McDowell (ibid., pp. xi–xii) claims that 'a belief or judgment whose content (as we say) is that things are thus and so – must be a posture or stance that is *correctly or incorrectly* adopted according to whether or not things are indeed thus and so' and that hence 'our thinking is thus answerable to the world.' This is clearly wholly of a piece with the inferentialist position advocated here. However, he then poses the rhetorical question: 'how can we understand the idea that our thinking is answerable to the empirical world, if not by way of the idea that our thinking is answerable to experience?' and here it is that his way parts with our inferentialist one. Why replace 'answerability to the world' with 'answerability to experience'? It is crucial for inferentialism in our sense that the kind of correctness relevant for language comes from the fact that language is a public, rule-governed enterprise just as chess or football is. You do something correctly iff you comply with the publicly available rules; your personal experience is not truly relevant.[17] And I have no other explanation for McDowell's view save his implicit misguided conviction that the answerability should not cross the boundary between the inner and the outer, and hence that we must substitute our inner reflection of the world – *viz.* experience – for the world itself.

What Sellars taught us, expressed in McDowell's terms, was that the conceptual cannot be made straightforwardly continuous with the non-conceptual. McDowell is convinced that if we do not envisage an inter-face, we will be destined to see mind as hopelessly severed from nature. Hence he construes experience as something that is propositional, and hence conceptual (and thus it can act as a legitimate inhabitant of the normative realm), and yet it is not a belief, but merely a 'deliverance of the senses'. But seeing the conceptual and the non-conceptual as the inner and the outer, as mind and nature, is unwarranted. An interface between the conceptual and the non-conceptual can only be sought within our linguistic practices, where the game for giving and asking for reasons, the game that is the home of asserting and hence propositions and hence concepts, draws its materials from the world, possibly with the help of other kinds of practices.[18]

2.7   Is language dispensable?

Let us return to the introductory section of this chapter. Ross argued that his model word *tû-tû*, and by parity of reasoning the English word *ownership*, is dispensable, for it merely serves to forge the link between the conditions of its application and the consequences of its applica-tion, which can be forged directly, without the intervention of the word. Subsequently we have argued that, according to inferentialism, all words are of this kind; they forge links, either of the language-language type, or of types involving the world. Should the conclusion not be, then, that language is completely dispensable?

Consider *tû-tû* once more. Linking (1) to (2), i.e., making anybody who has eaten of the chief's food liable to being ceremonially purified, can, no doubt, be accomplished without the employment of such a word. What, then, is the word needed for? Let us distinguish two cases. In the first, the language has the means to express that somebody fulfills the condition (1) and also the means to express that somebody fulfills the condition (2). The connection between the two conditions is then a matter of the (intralinguistic) inference from the former to the latter, which can come to be practically endorsed. The introduction of the word *tû-tû* then merely encapsulates the inference into a concept.

In the second case, there are no means to express (1) and (2). Still, there might be an 'inference', as it were, from situation to action, which may come to be practically endorsed: the common practice may have come to be that if one is seen to touch the chief's bowl, he is dragged to the shaman. In this case the word is, obviously, more useful: if I see somebody lick the chief's bowl and I am not strong enough to get hold of him, the word may make it easy for me to indicate to others why they should join me in grabbing him. The situation is even clearer when there are many different conditions of application and/or many different consequences, as in the picture we borrowed from Ross's paper. As we saw, the word then serves as a junction that may reduce the number of necessary 'mental links' from $n \times m$ to $n + m$.

This concerns the situation where the word merely certifies (or perhaps also streamlines) a link that already exists. We may say that in such case the introduction of the word is *conservative*: it does not extend the set of the underlying links constitutive of our practices, merely makes them explicit and perhaps more easily manageable. But of course it may happen that a word is introduced to forge a *new* link, *extending* our practices. It may be that the emergence of the word *tû-tû* is part and parcel of the introduction of the very rule that the chief's food is untouchable.

It seems that this may well happen, and indeed it seems that a great deal of the charm of language is that it makes such extensions easier, if not possible at all. Language is clearly not a mere appendix of our practices, it is a crucial factor of such practices, a vehicle in terms of which we greatly refine, sophisticate, and streamline the practices. (We will have more to say about the development of language in Chapter 6.) Reasoning and argumentation, for example, is an all-important kind of practice, the development of which is inconceivable without the development of language.

From the inferentialist viewpoint, it is these links between sentences that can be seen as conferring meanings on words, hence especially as constituting concepts. (As Brandom, 2002, p. 87, puts it, '[For Sellars,] grasping a concept is mastering the use of a word.') This is to say that our conceptual framework, the framework by means of which we 'grasp' the world, co-develops with the establishment of these links, *viz.* with the *inferential articulation* of our words.

Notice that if words can serve as means of extending our practices, there is the possibility that they will extend them in some 'bad' ways. A case in point is the broadly discussed case of the word *Boche*, the introduction of which effects the establishment of a link between Germans and some nasty properties. Dummett (1973, p. 454) appears to indicate that the problem is that *Boche* is not conservative in the above sense; however, Brandom (1994, pp. 126ff) counters that the requirement of conservativeness for nonlogical words is unreasonable (We will see in the second part of the book that it *is* reasonable for logical vocabulary; see Chapter 9).

Note that an extension of practices, a new concept, might be conceivably 'bad' also in more serious ways. Imagine, as an extreme, that we introduce a word that would be applicable to anything whatsoever and that would license doing anything with it. The result would be an 'absolute' extension of the practices: they would pour out of any reasonable limits, and we would have a kind of practical analog of Prior's *tonk*. What would prevent us from making this disastrous move?

We have already mentioned Dummett's concept of *harmony* as a proper 'fit' between the introduction and the elimination rules of a logical constant. But Dummett's (1973) employment of the term is broader: he uses it to indicate that there is a kind of fit between various parts of linguistic practices, and hence that a new link may come to fit with them, or else it can, as it were, go counter to them. However, unless we identify harmony with conservativity (which, as a matter of fact, Dummett, 1991, is on the verge of doing[19]), no explanation of this concept is at hand. And the identification, I agree with Brandom, would then so strangle language that it would not be able to serve its important purpose: especially it would prevent us from introducing new concepts.

Moreover, I think this is not really needed. It is futile to require a formal guarantee of the impossibility of such disastrous concepts as *tonk* and the kin. They are not impossible, but we humans know better than wasting time with them. But we do not *decide* which concepts we have, we inherit them – so how we have managed to avoid them? The answer is that if there were our ancestors who engaged such kinds of concept instead of (or in addition to) our ones, we might assume that they were wiped out by natural selection. The possibility of the introduction of such concepts is as real as the possibility of cutting off one's arms, but we need not upset ourselves too much about either reality.

2.8 Summary of Chapter 2

In this chapter we have considered various aspects of identifying the meaning of a word with its inferential role. We started from the alleged *reductio ad absurdum* of the fact that some legal terms of our language have meaning, which Ross purported to carry out by showing that these terms possess nothing more than their conditions and consequences of application (and that they do not refer to anything). We envisaged inferentialism as the doctrine that embraces the fact that *no* words of our language can have anything else; in particular that the semantics of every word is given by the inferences involving sentences containing the word. We stressed that this presupposes an understanding of the term *inference* that may be nonstandard in two ways, one less and one more controversial.

The less controversial feature of our understanding of *inference* is that we give pride of place to *material* inferences, inferences that are valid not merely in force of the logical words they contain. Thus we consider the inference from *Fido is a dog* to *Fido is an animal*, or from *Lightning now* to *Thunder shortly* as acceptable just as they stand (and not because of any purported hidden second premise such as *All dogs are animals* or *If there is lightning, thunder will follow shortly*). Our reason is that material inferences take part in constituting the meanings of the words contained in them (there is no sharp dualism conceptual vs. empirical) and hence adding the surplus premise, that would, of course, presuppose that the premise is fully meaningful, would lead us into a vicious circle.

The more controversial feature is that we speak about 'generalized inferences' that may go not only from sentences to sentences (from propositions to propositions), but also from kinds of situations to sentences (propositions), or from sentences (propositions) to kinds of actions. We have stressed that it is hard to take the talk about generalized inferences as more than a metaphor, hence saying that the meanings of empirical words are inferential roles is not to be taken literally. Despite this, we concluded that the way in which empirical words are 'tied to the world' may be seen as sufficiently inference like to warrant the label *inferentialism*.

3
Meanings as Inferential Roles

3.1 Use theories of meaning

The conclusion reached in the preceding chapter is that from the viewpoint of inferentialism, meanings are certain roles (which we can call *inferential*, although this means a broadening of the concept of inference). In this way inferentialism parts company with what we called 'relational' theories of meanings and joins the theories that are usually subsumed under the broad heading 'use-theories of meaning'. It thus abandons what Quine (1969) called the 'museum myth': the traditional notion of language as a system of symbols each of which stands for something extralinguistic, being glued to it by our minds. Instead, the new theories follow Wittgenstein's advice to seek meaning in the way an expression is *used*.

In general, the basic credo of the use theories reads:

(U) *the meaning of an expression consists in the way in which the expression is used by the speakers of the relevant community.*

To prepare ground for differentiating inferentialism from other varieties of use theories of meaning, let us discuss (U) in greater detail, providing some disambiguation. First, let us notice that (U) is significantly more substantial than the prima facie similar claim:

(U*) *any meaning an expression (i.e., a sound- or inscription-type) has, it has as a consequence of the fact that it is treated in a certain way by the speakers of the relevant community.*

Few people would wish to oppose (U*): it is generally accepted that sounds or inscriptions do not mean anything *by themselves*, but only *due to us*.

One crucial difference between (U) and (U*) is that the term *use*, as employed in (U), is taken as something more specific than the term *treatment* in (U*); it amounts to treatment, as it were, *in the outer world* (as contrasted with the treatment *in the inner world of one's mind*, which we may call *conception*). Another difference is that while (U*) states that an expression has meaning *in force* of our treatment, (U) states that the meaning directly *is* the treatment (usage). Hence, to get from the generally acceptable (U*) to the more controversial (U), we must take two substantial steps:

(i) identify any meaning-conferring kind of *treatment* with (*public*) use;

and

(ii) identify meaning directly with the use.

Why should we (and should we at all) take these steps?

Let us consider (i) first. Why should we see meaning as a matter of usage rather than of conception? Why should we not say that an expression means thus and so iff the speakers conceive of it in a certain way, perhaps take it as a sign of something? The basic trouble is that as conception is a private, subjective matter (at least until it becomes manifested in behavior), it cannot serve as the foundation of the essentially intersubjective institution of meaning. As Davidson (1990, p. 314) aptly stressed, 'that meanings are decipherable is not a matter of luck; public availability is a constitutive aspect of language'.

To be sure, if an expression has a meaning within a linguistic community, then the speakers of the community *will* conceive of it in certain specific ways. However, this is not enough to establish the fact that it means what it does. An essentially private act of conception is not capable of grounding the essentially public institution of language. That people of some community mentally associate the word *spider* with a certain kind of animal is a fact of their individual psychologies not capable of establishing the fact that *spider* expresses, within their language, the concept of *spider*; what is needed alongside any private associations are some public practices that make the link between the word and a concept public and shared.

Moreover, once the practices are in place, the private associations become redundant; from the viewpoint of the institution of language they become the idle wheel whose presence or absence makes no noticeable difference. This is the point of the famous case of 'Wittgenstein's beetle':

Suppose everyone had a box with something in it: we call it a 'beetle'. No one can look into anyone else's box, and everyone says he knows what a beetle is only by looking at his beetle. – Here it would be quite possible for everyone to have something different in his box. One might even imagine such a thing constantly changing. – But suppose the word 'beetle' had a use in these people's language? – If so it would not be used as the name of a thing. The thing in the box has no place in the language-game at all; not even as a something: for the box might even be empty. – No one can 'divide through' by the thing in the box; it cancels out, whatever it is. (Wittgenstein, 1953, §293)

What Wittgenstein is urging here is that as our linguistic games are essentially cooperative, intersubjective enterprises, they cannot rest on anything that is purely subjective. If meaning were impeccably hidden within one's mind, then its presence or absence, *from the viewpoint of the language game*, would be bound to be irrelevant. (Note that this does not mean that it cannot be relevant from other viewpoints, such as that of the psychology of communication, i.e., the study of what goes on in one's mind when one communicates. Note also that what makes the contents of minds unacceptable as meanings is their inherent non-shareability; thus an alternative approach might be to develop a theory of mind which would not take mental contents to be inviolably private.[1])

What Wittgenstein wanted philosophers to relinquish was the view of meaning that for so long had held sway: the view that our signs are animated by chunks of our minds, chunks normally hidden within the mind's depths, but that we somehow managed to bring to light by sticking them to the signs. If people attach something to a word within their minds, then this is a fact of their individual psychologies being incapable of establishing the different fact that the word actually *means* something within their language. In order for it to mean something, it is not enough that each of them individually makes the association, he/she must also presume that the others do the same, that he/she can use the word to intelligibly express its meaning in various public circumstances and so forth. Language is *essentially* public, and as such it cannot rest on private associations.

Another way of expressing the same point is to say, as we saw Davidson does, that the very *point* of meaning is that it can be shared by many: that new people can always enter the realm of a language, learning the meanings of its words and then participating in the language games staged by its means. As Quine (1969, p. 28) stressed, 'each of us, as he learns his language, is a student of his neighbor's behavior' and 'the learner has no data to work with, but the overt behavior of other speakers'. Insofar as language and meaning is something essentially intersubjective, the contents of the minds of the speakers cannot be its *components*. Thus Quine (ibid., p. 29) concludes: 'There are no meanings, nor likenesses or distinctions in meaning beyond what are implicit in people's dispositions to overt behavior'.

Wittgenstein indicates what should assume the place of the representational theory of meaning in the following way:

> Frege ridiculed the formalist conception of mathematics by saying that the formalists confused the unimportant thing, the sign, with the important, the meaning. Surely, one wishes to say, mathematics does not treat of dashes on a bit of paper. Frege's idea could be expressed thus: the propositions of mathematics, if they were just complexes of dashes, would be dead and utterly uninteresting, whereas they obviously have a kind of life. ... And further it seems clear that no adding of inorganic signs can make the proposition live. And the conclusion which one draws from this is that what must be added to the dead signs in order to make a live proposition is something immaterial, with properties different from all mere signs. But, if we had to name anything which is the life of the sign, we should have to say that it was its use. ...
>
> The mistake we are liable to make could be expressed thus: We are looking for the use of a sign, but we look for it as though it were an object co-existing with the sign. (1958, p. 4)

Here Wittgenstein is arguing that, despite appearances, words may not become, and in fact are not, animated by having a chunk of mind stuck to them. We give them their meaning by *using* them in a specific way. (Thus we could say that the signs 'come to life' in our hands analogously to a puppet's coming to life in the hands of a skillful puppeteer.) If we have private associations, then what we need to establish meaning is some way of their interpersonal interconnection, some *public practices* that would make the associations public and shared. (And once the public practices are in place, the private associations become the idle beetle in the box.) In this way, a use theory of meaning was obviously forthcoming.

But here we face the question of whether by giving a word a use, we thereby already give it such kind of meaning that the words of our ordinary language have. We have many tools, tools like hammers or pencils, which have uses (some of them even quite regimented uses) without having anything like *meanings* of the kinds our expressions have, hence it seems that a word having a use is not yet it having a meaning in the sense of having a 'semantic value'. What is it that makes a word acquire a *genuine* meaning, such as those that are in play when we talk?

Wittgenstein's answer is that which I indicated in the first chapter of this book, namely that it is a certain kind of *rule-governed* employment. This is, I am convinced, why he pays such attention to the concepts of rule and rule following:

> For Frege, the choice was as follows: either we are dealing with ink marks on paper or else these marks are signs of *something,* and what they represent is their meaning. That these alternatives are wrongly conceived is shown by the game of chess: here we are not dealing with the wooden pieces, and yet these pieces do not represent anything – in Frege's sense they have no meaning. There is still a third possibility; the signs can be used as in a game. (Wittgenstein as quoted by Waisman, 1984, p. 105)

Hence Wittgenstein is driven to the standpoint that meaning is a role vis-à-vis the rules of language, a standpoint a specific variant of which we are defending in this book. More generally, the point is that meaning is not a matter of psychology, but an essentially intersubjective matter of certain social 'institutions'.

3.2   Dispositions vs. proprieties

Let us elucidate the relationship between meaning and rules from a different angle. To do this, let us return to a critical point of the usual formulations of the use theories of meaning. We want to express that meanings are a matter not of the peculiarities of the ways individual speakers put a term to use, but rather of some 'principle behind this'. We want to state that there is a relevant interconnection between the occurrences of spiders and the utterances of *Lo, a spider!*, despite the fact that only some of the speakers (in fact very few, if any), and only sometimes (in fact only exceptionally, if at all), would actually react to a spider with this very utterance. And the usual technique, adopted also by Quine, makes use of the concept of *disposition*. The sentence *Lo, a spider!* means what it does because the speakers have *the disposition* to utter it when confronted with a spider. (We have already encountered a complex elaboration of a theory of meaning based on dispositions, namely, Boghossian's causal variety of inferentialism; see Section 1.4.)

However, what is a disposition? A disposition is a property whose nature is so unclear that it must be characterized in terms of the potential behavior of the entity purportedly having the property in given situations (e.g., to say that sugar is soluble in water is to say that in the circumstance of it being put into water, we should expect it to dissolve). But how should we characterize a disposition of the above kind, e.g., a disposition to utter *Lo, a spider!* when confronted with a spider? We should be able to say something to the effect that to be disposed to emit *Lo, a spider!* in the presence of a spider is to emit it whenever there is a spider around and some further conditions are fulfilled, but which conditions? That the person in question has no reason to stay silent? That she wants to let others know? That she is not dumb, nor too lazy, nor afraid to talk, and so on? Obviously none of these approaches a fair characterization of the relevant circumstances.

We are soon led into a vicious circle. We claim that the meaning of a sentence is a matter of a disposition to utter the sentence; and we reduce dispositions to specific behavior in specific situations. In this case, however, we are unable to specify the relevant circumstances other than as those circumstances in which the relevant sentence is really uttered, hence we say, in effect, that the meaning of a sentence is a matter of uttering the sentence in those situations in which it is really uttered. Of course, proponents of the dispositional analysis will claim that there *is* a possibility – at least as a matter of principle – of characterizing the relevant circumstances explicitly (and that, moreover, the disposition is ultimately a matter of as yet unknown physical properties of the brain), but it is very difficult to imagine how such a characterization could even get off the ground.

Notice that the basic problem is not the absence of an explicit specification of the conditions of actualization of dispositions, but rather the fact that the concept of disposition, as employed here, does not have any nontrivial content: it seems to do no more work than the ill-famed concept of *dormitive power* within the explanation 'Opium makes you sleepy because it has dormitive power.'[2] I think that the dispositional elaboration of the use theory of meaning therefore leads us up a blind alley. (This makes us part our way with Quine.)

I would suggest that the relevant relationship between *Lo, a spider!* and spiders, the one which is responsible for the former to mean what it does, is of a different ilk. Inferentialism of the kind I am exposing here maintains that the correct description of the link between a sentence meaning that there is a spider around and the circumstances in which there is a spider around, is not that the speakers are *disposed* to utter the former in a case of the latter, but rather that it would be, for them, *proper* (conforming to rules of their language) to do so (and, perhaps more importantly, that it would be *improper* to utter it if there is no spider around).[3] This does *not* mean that people regularly utter *Lo, a spider!* when they see a spider, it means that doing so is immune to certain ways of criticism (unlike uttering *This is a beetle* in the same situation). Hence, whereas saying that one is *disposed* to do something amounts to predicting that given suitable conditions one will inevitably do it, to say that one would be correct in doing so does not involve any prediction of this kind. (Though it does yield certain predictions regarding certain kinds of 'disapproving' reactions of speakers to improper usages of language.)

In what respect is *propriety* less problematic than *disposition*? Can we be any more successful in explicitly spelling all the rules governing the usage of a word than we can be in explaining the disposition to use it? The basic difference is that while the term *disposition* refers to a covert mental state (and supposedly underlain by a physical state of the organism in question, which, however, nobody is able to specify), the term *propriety* refers to an overt social mechanism. We all know what proprieties, in simple cases, are; we know what it means to say that it is proper to move a chess piece thus and so, and similarly we know what it means to say that it is proper to assert a sentence in such or another situation or that it is improper to assert a sentence when we assert certain other sentences. True, in many cases the clusters of rules governing uses of expressions are so complex (and also so fuzzy) that it is difficult or impossible to spell them out. But this is a matter of the complexity of the interrelated and interwoven proprieties that are in play; it does not concern the relevant concept of propriety itself.[4]

In the following chapters we will try to illuminate the social mechanism behind the existence of proprieties; here we restrict ourselves to saying that proprieties are basically a matter of what we will call *corrective* behavior (see Section 4.3), a behavior that is a matter of the fact that we humans have developed not only attitudes to the world and to one another, but, importantly, also 'second-order' attitudes to others' attitudes and behaviors. It is this that creates space for proprieties and for the ties between language and the world that the inferentialist deems crucial.

3.3 Inferential potential and inferential significance of a sentence

The inferential structure of language is a matter of which sentences of the language are correctly inferable from which other sentences. What we will call the *inferential potential* of a sentence is the place of the sentence within the structure: it is a matter of which sentences are inferable from it and which sentences it is itself inferable from. Only sentences have inferential potentials. We can explicate the inferential potential of a sentence A, e.g., in the following way:

$IP(A) = <A^{\leftarrow}, A^{\rightarrow}>$, where
$A^{\leftarrow} = \{<A_1, ..., A_n> \mid A_1, ..., A_n \vdash A\}$
$A^{\rightarrow} = \{<<A_1, ..., A_{i-1}>,<A_{i+1}, ..., A_n>, A_{n+1}> \mid A_1, ..., A_{i-1}, A, A_{i+1}, ..., A_n \vdash A_{n+1}\}$

Thus the inferential potential of a sentence A, we said, can be characterized in terms of a pair of sets, one representing what A is inferable from (in particular containing the sequences of sentences from which A is inferable), the other representing what is inferable from A (together with possible collateral premises – in the form of triples the first two constituents of which represent the collateral premises and the third constituent a conclusion). We assume that the inferential potentials of all sentences in a language are generated by a finite set of inferential rules, for the establishment of such a set of inferential rules is what has brought the language into being (see Chapter 6).

Given some rather modest assumptions about the nature of the inferability relation, this can be simplified. Assuming the reflexivity and transitivity of the inference relation, it can be shown[5] that any of the two components of $IP(A)$ suffices in the sense that $A^{\leftarrow} = A'^{\leftarrow}$ if and only if $A^{\rightarrow} = A'^{\rightarrow}$. Hence the inferential potential of A can be represented by any of them alone. Let us try choosing $A^{\leftarrow}$ first. Accepting the indifference of the order of premises of an inference and their free reusability, we can see it as a set of finite (and perhaps, by extrapolation, also infinite) *sets* of sentences:

$\{\{A_1, ..., A_n\} \mid A_1, ..., A_n \vdash A\}$.

Such a representation may be further reduced to the set $\{X_1, ..., X_n\}$ of sets of sentences such that $X_i \vdash A$ for every i and for every Y such that $Y \vdash A$ there is an i so that $Y \vdash B$ for every $B \in X_i$. On the other hand, it can be expanded to the set of all proofs of A, whereby it would coincide with what is traditionally taken as the meaning of a sentence within intuitionist logic and consequently within what has now come to be called proof-theoretic semantics.[6]

If we now try to represent IP(A) by $A^{\rightarrow}$ (rather than $A^{\leftarrow}$), i.e., as

$$\{<\{A_1, ..., A_n\}, A_{n+1}> | \{A_1, ..., A_n, A\} \vdash A_{n+1}\},$$

IP(A) comes to relate $\{A_1, ..., A_n\}$ to A_{n+1} if one's belief A, on the background of her beliefs $A_1, ..., A_n$, warrants her belief that A_{n+1}; or that given the collateral commitments to $A_1, ..., A_n$, the commitment to A brings about the commitment to A_{n+1}. Generalizing IP so that it applies also to sets of sentences (instead of merely single sentences), so that

$$\text{IP}(M) = \{<\{A_1, ..., A_n\}, A_{n+1}> | \{A_1, ..., A_n\} \cup M \vdash A_{n+1}\},$$

we are in the vicinity of the Tarskian approach to consequence, construed as a closure operator.

This brings to the fore the (obvious) fact that the consequences of a belief one acquires are influenced by other beliefs one happens to entertain. In this sense, 'content' is essentially, as Brandom (1994) puts it, 'perspectival': the significance of the belief that *the man over there left the room with blood on his hands* has a different significance for me if I also believe that the room is an operation theatre where a doctor is trying to save human lives, than for somebody who believes it is a room in which a murder has just been committed. Chess again: though the pieces have their 'position-independent' roles that reflect their 'force' (the role of the queen makes the queen more powerful than the knight), the significance of pieces for a particular player in a particular position need not always reflect this; there are (rare) positions in which the knight is more useful than the queen.

Hence the *inferential significance* of a sentence within a particular context of collateral premises is something essentially different from its context-invariant *inferential potential*. However, having explicated the potential as the above kind of function, their relationship turns out to be quite straightforward: the inferential significance of A within the context C is the value of the inferential potential of A for C. But this should not be read as claiming that potentials are prior to significances; a sentence has an inferential potential to the extent to which the employment of A becomes invariant across contexts, i.e., to which there emerge context-independent rules (which we explicate in terms of the function).

3.4 Inferential roles

Every expression can be considered as having a kind of an *inferential role*; i.e., its particular contribution to the inferential potentials of the sentences in which it occurs. The set of rules that generates the potentials of the sentences containing the expression can be seen as constitutive of the inferential role.

But *what exactly* is an inferential role? Well, I do not think this question is answerable any more explicitly than the question *what exactly is a role in a theater play*. An item *plays a role* if it contributes, in a specific way, to a larger whole or to a plot. Roles of the items adding up to the whole or the plot are supposed to explain it, but there are alternative ways to apportion what is attributed to which item. Hence roles are products of *decomposition*, and there is no unique way of such a decomposition. Roles as such are not really objects; they lack clear criteria of individuation.

However, inferential roles can be *explicated* as objects, in various ways. The inferential role of a word *w*, IR(*w*), then, is an entity whose constitutive property is that the inferential potential of every complex sentence can be seen as the sum of the contributions of its parts, i.e., that the inferential potential of every sentence $G(w_1, ..., w_n)$ (where *G* symbolizes any kind of grammatical way of assembling a sentence from its ultimate parts – words) equals the result of some way of combination of inferential roles of $w, ..., w_n$, i.e., there is a function G* such that

$$IP(G(w_1, ..., w_n)) = G^*(IR(w_1), ..., IR(w_n)),$$ for every *n*-tuple of words $w_1, ..., w_n$ and every grammatically possible way *G* of putting them together into a sentence.

Note that this is nothing other than the celebrated principle of compositionality. Note, however, that its role here is very different from the one in which it is usually considered. If you are an atomist, in the sense that you think that words must have meanings before they can be combined to produce meaningful complex phrases, then the principle of compositionality is your way of describing how semantic parts add up to a semantic whole (as Fodor and Lepore, 2007, p. 678, put it, 'the meaning of a sentence is ontologically dependent on the meaning of its subsentential constituents.'). However, if you are, like the inferentialist, a holist, then the principle of compositionality is your tool for individuating semantic contributions of parts to semantic values of wholes.[7] Thus roles are given merely through an 'implicit definition', and just as Quine (1969, p. 45) claims that 'there is no saying absolutely what the numbers are, there is only arithmetic', we can claim that *there is no saying absolutely what inferential roles are, there are only rules of inference* (and *compositionality*).

Note that it is not excluded that two sentences sharing the same inferential potential (the same sentences are inferable from them and they are inferable from the same sentences) differ in inferential roles. This is because a sentence is not only a node in the inferential structure of language, but also a part of other, more complex sentences. In this sense a sentence has both what Dummett (1973) called the *freestanding sense* (and what we see as the inferential *potential*) and what he called an *ingredient sense* (and what we see as the inferential *role*).

The technical aspect of inferentialism can now be seen as concentrated into the problems of characterizing the roles of expressions by means of inferential patterns (on the background of the assumption that such patterns *must* obtain, for it is only via them that expressions acquire inferential roles in the first place) and perhaps finding suitable explications of the roles.[8] (Hence our earlier Quinean dictum that 'there is no saying absolutely what inferential roles are' is not to be read as implying that there is no point in *explicating* inferential roles!)

However, someone might object, the result of all this seems to be that inferential roles must be rather ghostly entities, with no sharp boundaries and no clear status. Would it not be better to steer clear of such specters? The answer to this objection would be that from her own perspective, the inferentialist is quite happy to leave them alone. What she sees as the unavoidable foundation of semantics is, to repeat, *inferential rules* and inferential patterns constituted by clusters of the rules. It Is, however, usual – simply as a matter of fact – to perceive semantics as a matter of values of individual words adding up to the semantic values of complex expressions, sentences, and supersentential wholes, just as we tend to perceive a game of chess as a matter of a conspiracy of the powers of individual pieces.[9] Hence I think we should account for this, though keeping in mind that any explication of individual meanings in the form of genuine (e.g., set-theoretical) objects is at heart an idealization, not only because it does away with vagueness, fuzziness, and the like, but also because it captures as objects something really not very object-like.

The upshot of this discussion appears to be that inferential roles of words are rather unfathomable entities. This is true in the sense that roles, as such, are not well-behaved objects, and it is not easy to get hold of them without resort to a certain 'intellectual violence'. It is, however, not so true in the sense that the role of any word would be so distributed over all kinds of sentences containing it that it would not be possible to encompass it. The fact is that once we agree on an acceptable way of explication, our prospects for gaining some insight into the roles are not so bleak.

The fact that inferential roles of words are secondary to inferential potentials of sentences should not be read so that the inferential role of a word is not determined by an inferential pattern, a restricted number of rules applying to the words. True, there is no guarantee that for every word there would be an inferential pattern fixing its meaning independently of meanings of other words (the meanings of some words may be interdependent in the sense that their meanings are co-constituted by the same inferential pattern containing both of them), but on the other hand we may assume that this does not lead to some excessive holism making any word dependent on any other.

It is certainly not the case that to understand a word, we must understand all other words of the language. True, to understand *some* words we may *sometimes* need to understand *some* other words, but it is reasonable to assume that the vocabulary of any language forms a hierarchy such that understanding words of an 'upper' level presupposes understanding those of a lower one (i.e., the inferential patterns constitutive of the meanings of the former may contain the latter), but not vice versa. This hierarchical edifice was analyzed by Cozzo (1994).

The kind of holism that is essential to inferentialism is the holism that compromises the picture of language that has come to be called 'layer-cake'. As deVries (2011) characterizes it in his reconstruction of Sellars's rejection of the picture, it is the view 'that there are three distinct levels of assertion in the empirical sciences: observation level claims of particular fact, empirical generalizations in the observation language, and, finally, claims in a theoretical language which function to systematize the empirical generalizations'.

Consider Peano arithmetic. We can see its axioms as a complex inferential pattern characterizing its basic vocabulary: 0, S, +, ·. This formulation of the rules presupposes logical vocabulary in the sense that to understand it one must already understand logical vocabulary. Perhaps there is a different, natural-deduction-like formulation of arithmetic in which each of the symbols is characterized independently of the other symbols and in which this characterization does not presuppose logical vocabulary. The existence of this alternative might provide for some logical neatness; it is, however, not the case that in its absence arithmetic would be flawed.

3.5   A toy language

Imagine, by way of illustration of the above considerations, a toy language based on the following vocabulary: terms TI, TA, JO, MA, unary predicates MN, WM, PE, and binary predicates MTHR, FTHR, CHLD. We can imagine that the words of the toy language are simplified versions of the following English expressions:

TI	*this*
TA	*that*
JO	*John*
MA	*Mary*
FTHR	*is the father of*
MTHR	*is the mother of*
CHLD	*is a child of*
MN	*is a man*
WM	*is a woman*
PE	*is a person*

The inferential rules characterizing the roles of the words include, aside from inferences proper, 'entry inferences' and 'exit inferences'. We write the rules linearly so that we do not write the conclusion under the premises and separate them by a horizontal line, but rather by the ⊢ sign. Three dots indicate extralinguistic factors: for example ... ⊢ TI FTHR TA indicates that we can 'infer' the sentence 'TI FTHR TA' from certain extralinguistic circumstances (such that there are two specific objects pointed at), while x FTHR y ⊢ ... indicates that we can 'infer' a certain extralinguistic action (perhaps treating x as somehow superordinated to y) from x FTHR y. (The lowercase letters act as placeholders for any expressions suitable for the relevant context, hence 'x FTHR y' stands for 'TI FTHR TA', 'JO FTHR MA', etc.)

1. ... ⊢ TI FTHR TA
2. ... ⊢ TI MTHR TA
3. ... ⊢ JO TI (TA)
4. ... ⊢ MA TI (TA)
5. x TI, TI p ⊢ x p
6. x r TA, y TA ⊢ x r y
7. x FTHR y ⊢ y CHLD x
8. x FTHR y ⊢ x MN
9. x MTHR y ⊢ y CHLD x

10. x MTHR y ⊢ x WM
11. x MN ⊢ x PE
12. x WM ⊢ x PE
13. x FTHR y ⊢ ...
14. x MTHR y ⊢ ...
15. x CHLD y ⊢ ...
16. x PE ⊢ ...

We can also consider additional 'metarules' (rules for deriving inferential rules from other inferential rules, where the rules that form the premises of the metarules are separated from that which acts as the conclusion by a slash and *A* is a placeholder for any sentence):

17. x FTHR y ⊢ *A*; x MTHR y ⊢ *A* / y CHLD x ⊢ *A*
18. x MN ⊢ *A*; x WM ⊢ *A* / x PE ⊢ *A*

The rules can be mastered in the order listed, or in any other order; the question is which rules we need to master in order to qualify as mastering the individual words. Take, for example, the predicate FTHR. An idea might be that to count as mastering this word we need to master the rule 1. (which is, as it were, its 'introduction' rule). But this is an idea the inferentialist would certainly deny; if this were the case then TI FTHR TA would qualify merely as a reaction to a certain situation, not as a sentence expressing a proposition.

What else must be added to 1. to make TI FTHR TA into a genuine sentence expressing a proposition? In fact we would need resources that are not available in our toy language, resources that would structure the sentences of the language into a 'logical space'. In particular, for every sentence of the language we would need something as a complement (contradictory sentence); for every two sentences we would need something as their meet (disjunction) and join (conjunction) and so forth.[10] As this is not the case, the sentences of our toy language do not really express propositions, do not have genuine meanings, but we can perhaps say that the toy meaning of FTHR, adequate to the toy language, is conferred on it by 1., 7., 8., 13., and perhaps the 'metarule' 17. Similarly, we can say that the toy meaning of MTHR is constituted by 2., 9., 10., 14., and perhaps 17. Mastering 1., 2., 7., 8., 9., 10., 13., 14., 15. and 17. may count as amounting to mastering FTHR, MTHR, and CHLD, which presuppose mastering TI and TA and which is a presupposition of mastering MA, WM, and PE. (Note that these claims to the effect what inferences count as necessary for mastering a word and which word presupposes other words are purely hypothetical; they all depend on the way hypothetical speakers of the language treat those who fail to master the individual rules.)

Hence, although for inferentialism a certain kind of holism is essential (as Brandom, 2002, p. 361, puts it, 'on the inferential account of distinctively conceptual articulation, grasping a concept requires mastering the inferential connections between the appropriate use of some words and the appropriate use of others'), the kind of holism that is necessary is not the universal, all-encompassing kind. What is essential is that an 'empirical' part of language is not taken as independent of the 'theoretical' part; in our case, for example, we cannot take the rules 1. – 4. as constituting a self-contained sub-language in which the words TI, FTHR, and so forth acquire fully fledged meanings of the kind of their English counterparts *this, is the father of, ...* . But this does not mean that the meaning of every word is dependent on that of every other word.

3.6   Which inferences determine meaning?

Fodor and Lepore (2001) argue that if meaning is to be a creature of inferences, then we must specify of *which* inferences, where the only reasonable answer appears to be *analytic* inferences, and as *analytic* is nothing other than *in virtue of meaning*, we have a vicious circle: meaning is constituted by those inferences that hold in virtue of meaning. And the authors suggest that Brandomian inferentialism is trapped in this very circle since in order to avoid *all* kinds of inferences being constitutive of meaning, it must draw a boundary between *analytic* (meaning-constitutive) and *synthetic* (empirical) inferences.[11]

In a more recent paper, Fodor and Lepore (2007, pp. 680–681) present a more elaborate version of this objection:

We're also not clear what Brandom [2007] thinks about the status of utterly contingent inferences like 'If it's a plant in my backyard and it's taller than 6 feet, then it's a tree'. He does apparently endorse the idea that '[the concept constitutive inferences] must include...those that are materially [sic] correct' (p. 657). But what he gives as examples are two he borrows from Sellars: 'A is to the East of B' → 'B is to the West of A' and 'Lightning is seen' → 'Thunder will be heard soon'. We find this puzzling since the first of these strikes us as arguably conceptually necessary (whatever that means) and the second strikes as arguably nomologically necessary (whatever that means). So even if we granted that both are concept constitutive, we would still want to know whether clear cases of purely contingent hypotheticals are too; and, if they aren't, how Brandom proposes to do without an analytic/synthetic distinction.

On the basis of this, they conclude (pp. 681–682):

> The basic problem in this area isn't, however, the holism that Brandom's suggestions invite; it's rather that he seems to want to be on both sides of the analytic/synthetic distinction at the same time. On the one hand, he would like to agree with Quine that there's no principled difference between empirical and conceptual truth; but, on the other hand, he wants to endorse the idea that nomological necessities are concept constitutive. His problem is that the kind of necessities that a notion of conceptual content underwrites are, ipso facto, conceptual necessities; and nomological necessities aren't conceptual.

My purpose here is not to speak for Brandom whom Fodor and Lepore directly address, but rather to defend the version of inferentialism advocated in this book; however, clearly the objection is much more general than to affect only Brandom himself. From this viewpoint, it is crucial to remind ourselves that inferential roles – and hence meanings as construed by the inferentialist – are constituted by inferential *rules*, not by *inferences*. Far from every inference I may carry out corresponds to a rule.

As we will see in greater detail in later chapters, a rule exists where there are normative attitudes; hence there is an inferential rule in force for a given language if the speakers of the language tend to see some inferences that violate the rule as incorrect ('whatever this means', one would like to paraphrase Fodor and Lepore – but in fact we will expand upon this in the following chapters). Hence there is an important distinction between inferences that comply with a rule, and those that do not. This preempts the main thrust of the objection, for it alleviates the worry that we would have to take any kind of inference, actually carried out by any speakers, as meaning-constitutive.

Here it is crucial to keep in mind that rules are not merely 'in the eye of the beholder'. They are a matter of normative attitudes and these are detectable as certain behavioral patterns. True, there is far from *always* a decisive yes/no answer to the question about an existence of a rule (there may be all kinds of intermediary stages between the complete absence of a rule and the existence of clear-cut and unmistakable normative attitudes), but this does not mean that there are no cases where there *is* a decisive answer, or that the fuzziness of the non-decisive cases would be a matter of a vacillation on the part of the person who articulates the rules – the fuzziness is a (nonsurprising) characterization of the corresponding social situation.

Can we say that it is the rules that constitute the analytic (meaning-constitutive) part of language (as contrasted with the synthetic, empirical part)? In fact, as should be clear from the discussions of the previous chapter, not really. And this, admittedly, makes Fodor and Lepore's objection resurface at other places of even our inferentialist setting, though in a somewhat weakened form.

The first shape in which the objection resurfaces might be that it is not clear what is a rule and what is not. Is, for example,

$$\frac{X \text{ is a dog}}{X \text{ chases cats}}$$

a rule that is in force for English (and which is co-responsible for the meaning of *dog*, or perhaps *cat*)? Obviously, there is no univocal answer to such questions. Unlike the case of chess, the rules of natural language (also due to the fact that they are mostly implicit, as we will discuss it in our next chapter) range from those that are undoubtedly in force to those that have only a trace of this status. And discovering which are in force and which not is an empirical matter.

There is an (inconclusive) test, based on the fact that rules are a matter of our normative attitudes: some kinds of inference are such that if somebody turns out to be ignorant of them, we tend to see this as a shortcoming in their knowledge of the language, while others are such that this is not the case. Thus, if they were to doubt that dogs are animals, we would probably become suspicious about their mastery of the words *dog* and *animal*. On the other hand, were they ignorant of the fact that dogs chase cats, this would probably not compromise their mastery of English in our eyes (though we might question their general knowledge of the world).

The fact that the set of rules of a natural language has no sharp boundary obviously entails that inferential roles, and hence meanings as construed by inferentialists, are fuzzy. This should not surprise us; it is the lesson Quine taught us long ago. We concluded this already in our previous chapter and it is nothing capricious; it is not a shortcoming of the inferentialist approach, it is merely a reflection of the nature of natural languages.

Another version of the same objection is that not all the rules that can be said to be in force for English are relevant for meaning to the same extent. Hence it would seem that a version of the analytic/synthetic boundary needs to be drawn somewhere in the middle of the rules (perhaps with the inference from *X is a dog* to *X is an animal* falling to the analytic side, while that from *X is a dog* to *X chases cats*, if this obtains the status of rule, to the synthetic side).

What distinguishes meaning-constitutive ('analytic') inferential rules from other ones? We have seen, in the previous chapter, that material rules may be both (partly) meaning-constitutive and (partly) empirical, in particular that to be a 'conceptual' truth and to be a 'nomological' one (in Fodor and Lepore's terminology) are not mutually exclusive properties. Hence material rules range from those that are (almost) purely meaning-constitutive to those that are (almost) purely empirical, and meaning-constitutiveness is not a yes/no matter. It is true that if we want to explicate meanings as sharply delimited, we must draw a sharp boundary, but this is like with any other explication: we replace, deliberately, fuzzy boundaries with sharp ones.

However, should the fact that there is no sharp dividing line between the 'meaning-constitutive' and the other rules related to a word (or, as it is sometimes expressed, between the dictionary and the encyclopedia) not lead us to conclude that this distinction makes no sense whatsoever? We must keep in mind that, as a matter of fact, we tend to see individual words as having meanings, and insofar as we do this, we divide rules we learn regarding the employment of that word into general, sine-qua-non rules and more casual rules that we may fail to know without being rendered ignorant of the word's meaning. We tend to see some rules as related to dictionaries rather than to encyclopedias and others the other way around. In short: we distinguish between strategic, context-independent rules, which have more to do with meanings, and tactical, context-dependent ones that do not concern meaning so much. Drawing the sharp boundary, then, merely does justice to this natural tendency.

3.7   Are inferential roles compositional?

Fodor and Lepore (2001) argue that inferential roles are not good candidates for the explication of meanings because they are not compositional. But we have shown that compositionality is an *inherent* feature of inferential roles, inherent to such an extent that they could not exist, as individual entities, without it. Hence, far from not being compositional, compositionality is, if not directly their *modus existendi*, then clearly their *modus individuandi*. They are contributions that individual expressions bring to the inferential potentials of the sentences in which they occur; and it is only the principle of compositionality that makes it possible to individuate such contributions.

The point is that understanding contributions as individual, and individually explicable objects, makes sense only against the background of their adding up to the potentials – hence of a picture informed, from the very beginning, by the principle of compositionality. (However, we must not forget that the inferentialist never sees this picture as showing meanings of wholes as composed of those of the parts in the sense that the latter would be *prior* – 'ontologically' or in whatever other way – to the former.[12]) Hence the principle of compositionality is so deeply embedded within the inferentialist explication of inferential roles that their compositionality is just trivial.

Again, in their more recent paper, Fodor and Lepore (2007, p. 679) elaborate on their previous point:

> In fact, we think that the (radical) interpretation/translation of languages...probably is sentence-first; that language learning may be; and that understanding sentences is probably a complex mixture of both. But, in our view, none of this bears at all on the direction of the ontological dependency between sentence meanings and constituent meanings.... Here's what we take to be the ground-rule: Brandom has to show that (and how) word meanings might be ontologically dependent on sentence meanings (rather than vice versa) in a language that's productive and systematic.

Here the biggest problem is that there seems to be no room for such an 'ontological dependency' in the inferentialist picture of language. From the essentially pragmatist viewpoint of the inferentialist, the only thing that is there when it comes to language are people exchanging sounds and reacting to one another's sounds so that the reactions involve what we call normative attitudes. These attitudes constitute a 'space' that endows the sounds with certain specific significances (just like the wooden pieces become rooks, bishops, or knights if they are put into the 'space' of the rules of chess). These significances, i.e., the inferential potentials of the sounds, then get distributed to the basic building blocks of the system of sounds as their inferential roles. There is a clear dependency of the roles of words on the potentials of sentences. (Is this dependency ontological? I confess I have no idea what this is supposed to mean.)

But, of course, then the most obvious question is how we can endow sentences, the number of which is unlimited, with meanings other than by composing them from those of a finite vocabulary. The answer is that it works as described by Quine under the label of 'analogical synthesis'. We are first acquainted with a limited number of sentences from which we extract the ways in which individual words function, and then we start to use the words analogously to compose new, hitherto unheard, sentences.[13] The process seems no more mysterious than the process of learning to use a hammer to drive hitherto unseen nails after having initially been taught to drive some prototypical ones.

Fodor and Lepore further argue that the basic problem for inferentialism is that ' "knowing how" doesn't compose':

> You can know how to recognize good examples of pets (in favorable circumstances) and how to recognize good examples of fish (in favorable circumstances) without having a clue how to recognize good examples of pet fish in any circumstances (for example, because the conditions that are favorable for recognizing fish may screen the conditions that are favorable for recognizing pets; or vice versa).

However, it is hard to see how this example is to bear on the compositionality of inferential roles. If functioning within *pet fish* is part of the functioning of either *pet* or *fish* (and if we see *pet fish* as an atomic idiom, we do not see it as containing either of the words as its parts), then mastering such word *involves* mastering its functioning within *pet fish*.

It is again helpful to invoke the analogy with chess. The king 'normally' moves in its own way (namely, one square in any direction), and the rook has its own way, neither of them being allowed to jump over another piece. But there is an exception: the two pieces, under precisely defined circumstances, can castle: one of them 'jumps over' the other. What does the role of the king consist in (and hence what does understanding what a king is involve)? Just that it moves one square in any direction? It seems obvious that it involves also that it can castle. Hence castling may be said to be 'noncompositional' only in the metaphoric sense in which this means that castling makes the king move in an 'unusual' way, not that it would make it do something that would not be part of the role of king. And, similarly, *pet fish* makes *fish* function in an unusual way, not do something that is not a matter of its meaning *fish*.

3.8   Are there inferential roles, really?

Probably the ultimate kind of objection we may face is that inferential roles, as envisaged here, are rather ghostly entities, which we delimited indirectly, just by stipulating that they do justice to certain desiderata of semantic theory. The way, for example, we have coped with the principle of compositionality may seem to be too easy to be attractive. We should, so the objection would go, present some nontrivial examples of inferential roles. Then we can see them in action and, among other things, check, in a nontrivial way, whether they are consistent entities and whether they are compositional.

A version of the objection is also present in the paper of Fodor and Lepore discussed above. Fodor and Lepore (2007, p. 689) remind us that 'there isn't, so far, any known candidate for an inferential role analysis of any concept; not, anyhow, one that meets reasonable constraints on accounts of concept possession and individuation'. This is somewhat unfair. The fact is that *any* complex analyses of concepts are short in supply. (Personally I would very much like to put my hands on, for example, a token in the language of thought that pretends to be a concept!) Inferentialism by itself, of course, does not claim any advances in empirical semantics (i.e., it does not claim to reveal any hitherto unrevealed semantic features of concrete terms). What it claims is that it is able to even up the offerings of the various rival theories, and that it can raise the bid: the explanations of meanings given by the rival theories can be 'translated' into the inferentialist idiom, while the inferentialist explanations go deeper than the rival ones.

Let us return to our toy language:

1.   ... ⊢ TI FTHR TA
2.   ... ⊢ TI MTHR TA
3.   ... ⊢ JO TI (TA)
4.   ... ⊢ MA TI (TA)
5.   x TI, TI p ⊢ x p
6.   x r TA, y TA ⊢ x r y
7.   x FTHR y ⊢ y CHLD x
8.   x FTHR y ⊢ x MN
9.   x MTHR y ⊢ y CHLD x
10. x MTHR y ⊢ x WM
11. x MN ⊢ x PE
12. x WM ⊢ x PE
13. x FTHR y ⊢ ...

14. x MTHR y ⊢ ...
15. x CHLD y ⊢ ...
16. x PE ⊢ ...
17. x FTHR y ⊢ *A*; x MTHR y ⊢ *A* / y CHLD x ⊢ *A*
18. x MN ⊢ *A*; x WM ⊢ *A* / x PE ⊢ *A*

Let us write ||E|| for the explication of the inferential role of the expression E. Consider the word FTHR. One part of the inferential role of FTHR can be seen as constituted by the rule 1. It can be accounted for by letting ||FTHR|| be a set of situations each with a pair of 'highlighted' individuals, or, if we disregard any context-dependence, simply by a set of pairs of individuals (possibly relativized to possible worlds, but for simplicity's sake we consider the simplest, extensional case). The other inferential rules constitutive of ||FTHR|| can now be accounted for in the following way:

7.: $||\text{FTHR}||^{-1} \subseteq ||\text{CHLD}||$ (where R^{-1} is the relation inverse to R, i.e.,
    $R^{-1} = \{<y,x> \mid <x,y> \in R\}$);
8.: $D(||\text{FTHR}||) \subseteq ||\text{MN}||$ (where D is the domain of a relation, i.e.,
    $D(R) = \{x \mid <x,y> \in R\}$)
17.: $||\text{FTHR}||^{-1} \cup ||\text{MTHR}||^{-1} = ||\text{CHLD}||$.

In this way the explication of inferential roles comes to be almost indistinguishable from a version of the standard model-theoretic semantics. Thus our inferentialist approach is not incompatible with such approaches, it merely changes the way we look at the model-theoretic denotations: from the inferentialist viewpoint we see them as encapsulated inferential roles. I discussed this aspect of inferentialism at length elsewhere (see Peregrin, 2001, Chapter 8).

However, our account so far has disregarded one of the rules constitutive of the inferential role of FTHR, namely the rule 13. Taking it into our account may mean a certain deviation from the usual model-theoretical explication, for it may be not easily incorporated into it. The rule 13. may say that if x FTHR y, then x has some kind of rights and duties over y, e.g., rights to punish and reward y and the duty to take care of y. These normative statuses are not something that would be easily representable as an object. However, if we introduce a representation of this (normative) relationship, call it RD(x,y), then the rule can be incorporated into our explication so that ||FTHR|| will be no longer a relation between individuals, but rather a function that maps those pairs <x,y> that are in this relation on RD(x,y).

Taken thus, model-theoretic (or, for that matter, any other) denotations of expressions are interpreted as explications of their inferential roles. Thus, if an explication of a predicate, say *dog*, is a function from possible worlds to classes of individuals, then this is interpreted as explicative of a rule stating which kinds of entities (in factual as well as contrafactual circumstances) could be correctly 'pointed at' (literally or metaphorically) when saying *This is a dog*. (If this is the case, then it follows that not every function from possible worlds to classes of individuals is a reasonable denotation.) Or if the meaning of *dog* is somehow based on a prototype of dog, then from the inferentialist viewpoint this tells us something about the nature of the rules tying sentences of the kind of *This is a dog* to reality. (Inferentialism, moreover, clarifies what the role of such a prototype should be: the substantial role does not consist in the prototype being associated in the minds of speakers with the word, but rather in the role that such a prototype would play in the public practices of the speakers and in the assessments of correctness of their linguistic displays.)

In which sense does inferentialism generally aspire to presenting a deeper explanation of meanings and of meaningfulness than rival theories? Take the thesis that the meaning of *and* is the usual truth table, or that the meaning of *dog* is the function from possible worlds to sets of individuals. This is no ultimate explanation. If we learn this, we must further ask: and what does *this* mean? (Surely the thesis cannot be construed as saying that our ancestors once christened the functions by the words, but if not this, *what* does it say?) The inferentialist answer is that such functions, or other artifacts of semantic theories, should be understood as explications of inferential roles, which the words have acquired by being subjected to inferential rules that emerged as governing our language games.[14]

Can we give an example of nontrivial inferential roles? Fodor and Lepore (2007, p. 680) write:

> What, for example, is the 'introduction rule' for 'tree'? (We do hope it's not some procedure for identifying trees as such since we're a bit tired of verificationism.) Correspondingly, what is the 'elimination rule' for 'tree'? (We do hope it's not something like a conceptually sufficient condition for being a tree since we doubt that there are any conceptually sufficient conditions for being a tree (except, of course, question-begging ones like 'x is a tree if, and only if, x is a tree').)

It is not part and parcel of general inferentialism that the rules governing a word must be divisible into 'introduction' and 'elimination' ones. (It is the contention of logicians following Gentzen that the rules constitutive of logical constants should be so divisible.) Anyway, the rules that come closest to introduction ones (Sellars's *language entry transitions*) would most probably be rules for using *tree* in observational sentences of the kind of *This is a tree.* (One would wonder what is the relevance of the authors' being tired here. ...) Rules that would be closest to the elimination rules (Sellars's *language exit transitions*) would concern rules for dealing with trees resulting from their status as such (for example, not chopping them down at will.) And in between them there would be a number of *intralinguistic moves*, i.e., inferences (in the narrow sense) involving the word *tree* such as inferring from *This is a tree* to *This is a plant*, or from *This is a tree* to *This is not an animal*.

It is easy to show inferential roles of expressions of most formal languages (and this holds by far not only for the hackneyed ∧; see Peregrin, 2006d); it may be possible to show those of expressions of some regimented natural languages (Francez, Dyckhoff, and Ben-Avi, 2010; Francez and Ben-Avi, 2011). It is much more complicated to explicate an inferential role of an expression of a raw natural language: even the English counterpart of ∧, *and*, is semantically, and hence inferentially, not entirely simple. And the ways we use most of the words of English, and hence their inferential roles, are fantastically complex. Inferentialism, just like any other philosophical theory of meaning, does not have the ambition to describe and anatomize concrete cases; its ambition is to provide a framework within which we can accommodate relevant empirical findings.

3.9   Summary of Chapter 3

In this chapter we have continued to inspect the question of what it takes to explicate meaning as an inferential role. We have stated that this explication falls within the range of use theories of meaning that for the last three or four decades have been flourishing in philosophy of language, but that inferentialism differs from many other kinds of such theories in that it urges that it is not what we actually do with language that determines meaning, but rather the rules we take to (implicitly) govern our usage of language.

We have analyzed the concept of inferential role and distinguished the *role* from inferential *potential* (which is a matter of what a sentence is inferable from and what is inferable from it) and from inferential *significance* (which is a matter of the inferential consequences of a sentence in a particular context). We have concluded that in natural language inferential potentials (and hence inferential roles) are not sharply delimited entities; nevertheless they may be usefully *explicated by* sharply delimited entities, such as various set-theoretical constructs.

We have also addressed two objections raised against the identification of meanings with inferential roles, namely the objection that it leads us into an untenable holism and that it precludes us from accepting the principle of compositionality. We have stated that given that inferential roles derive not from actual inferences carried out by speakers, but from inferential rules accepted by them, the first problem reduces to an acceptable indeterminacy, whereas the second simply vanishes, because the principle of compositionality is built into the very constitution of inferential roles as individual entities. The problem that pertains is that inferential roles are vague, fuzzy, and difficult to fathom, but this, we argued, is not a problem of inferentialism, but a characteristic feature of natural language.

4
The Rules of Language

4.1 Implicit rules?

We have already indicated that what is peculiar about the rules of language and what makes their study an enterprise very different from the study of rules of football or chess is that they are largely merely implicit within our linguistic practices, rather than explicitly formulated. All of them *cannot* be explicit, on pain of a vicious circle. We can have explicit rules of chess or football; we cannot, however, have explicit rules for using language – at least not generally. The reason is that to have an explicit rule we already *need* (a) language. To have an explicit rule means to have something that must be interpreted, hence to be able to follow this rule we need some rule for the interpretation, which leads us into an infinite regress. Wittgenstein (1953, §85) analyzes the situation in the following way:

> A rule stands there like a sign-post. – Does the sign-post leave no doubt open about the way I have to go? Does it show which direction I am to take when I have passed it; whether along the road or the footpath or cross-country? But where is it said which way I am to follow it; whether in the direction of its finger or (e.g.) in the opposite one? – And if there were, not a single sign-post, but a chain of adjacent ones or of chalk marks on the ground – is there only one way of interpreting them? – So I can say, the sign-post does after all leave no room for doubt. Or rather: it sometimes leaves room for doubt and sometimes not. And now this is no longer a philosophical proposition, but an empirical one.

Hence the key problem in making sense of language as a rule-governed practice is to make sense of the very concept of implicit rule.

It might seem that the notion of an 'unwritten rule' is not an especially problematic one; after all, there seems to be a lot of such rules around. To indicate the depth of the problem tabled by Wittgenstein, let us consider a way in which such an 'unwritten rule' can be grasped. The following definition is due to Bicchieri (2006, p. 11), for whom a prototypical 'social norm' is precisely the unwritten kind of rule which is contrasted, on the one hand, with a 'codified rule', and, on the other, with a mere 'recurrent behavior':

Conditions for a Social Norm to Exist

Let R be a *behavioral rule* for situations of type S, where S can be represented as a mixed-motive game. We say that R is a social norm in a population P if there exists a sufficiently large subset $P_{cf} \subseteq P$ such that, for each individual $i \in P_{cf}$:

Contingency: i knows that a rule R exists and applies to situations of type S;

Conditional preference: i prefers to conform to R in situations at type S on the condition that:

(a) *Empirical expectations:* i believes that a sufficiently large subset of P conforms to R in situations of type S;

and either

(b) *Normative expectations:* i believes that a sufficiently large subset of P expects i to conform to R in situations of type S;

or

(b′) *Normative expectations with sanctions:* i believes that a sufficiently large subset of P expects i to conform to R in situations of type S, prefers i to conform, and may sanction behavior.

A social norm R is *followed* by population P if there exists a sufficiently large subset $P_f \subseteq P_{cf}$ such that, for each individual $i \in P_f$ conditions 2(a) and either 2(b) or 2(b′) are met for i and, as a result, i prefers to conform to R in situations of type S.

This definition makes sense if we construe R as an *articulation* of the rule in question (such as *One drives on the right side of the road* or *One should pay one's debts*) and if what is in question is whether the rule thus articulated is in force. But we have seen that not every rule can be explicitly articulated, so this construal does not seem to be acceptable; hence we must ask what R in Bicchieri's definition *is*, in the first place?

Notice that if we tried to read Bicchieri's definition as a delimitation of what her R is, it would be hopelessly circular: it defines R in terms of 'i knows that a rule R exists', 'i prefers to conform to R', and so forth. Our concern is what exactly it *is* that i knows to exist, prefers to conform to and so on. If R cannot generally be a linguistic item, then what is it? A proposition in a Platonist heaven? A regularity of behavior?

The trouble is that whatever we take as a materialization of the rule, we will not fully rid ourselves of the Wittgensteinian problem. For suppose that R is whatever token representing, expressing, or envisaging the rule. Now, any such token, to yield us a rule, must be *interpreted*, and to lead us to the role it is supposed to materialize or express, it must be interpreted *in a particular way*.[1] Hence taking the attitude to the token as the attitude directly to the rule presupposes that we interpret the token in the *correct* way. In other words, either we need a rule to follow a rule, which leads us into a regress, or we can have the ability of doing correct things without thereby following a rule.

Hence we cannot get a real grip on the concept of rule, and especially not on the rules underlying semantics, by taking our conscious attitudes to the rule for granted. Of course the problem would be solved if we identified rule with a *regularity*: a regularity is (or is not) there independently of anyone's attitudes.[2] But we feel that a rule is more than a regularity; we do not want to admit that there is no difference of principle between a car driver following the rules of traffic and a stone following the law of gravity.

At this point a rule might start to appear as something utterly mysterious: it can be identified neither with the corresponding regularity, nor with a symbol or a symbolic representation. Hence the aim of this chapter is to show how a rule can steer clear of both the Scylla of what Brandom (1994) calls *regularism* ('rule = regularity') and the Charybdis of what he calls *regulism* ('rule = explicit rule').

Let us say, as a first approximation, that a rule is a matter of a certain cluster of interlocking behavioral patterns. Does this mean that a rule is a regularity, though some very complex regularity, after all? The answer to this calls for some delicacy. A rule *can be looked at* as such a complex regularity; but it is important to see that even so the rule that one ought to X can never be seen as merely a matter of doing X regularly, it must involve other kinds of regularities, especially regular attitudes to those who do not do X, and so forth. Moreover, and this is crucial, apart from being *observed* matter-of-factual behavioral patterns, rules can be *accepted*, *endorsed*, or *participated in*, and this aspect makes them into something *more* than mere regularities of behavior.

In this way the concept of rule, without being in any sense 'supernatural', may enable us to get a grip on phenomena that elude straightforwardly naturalistic accounts: phenomena like human language, meaning, or reason. Rules are connected with the fact that we humans have mastered a specific kind of speech act that we accomplish by means of normative vocabulary. It is special in that it envisages, on the one hand, what we tend to think of as our *rationality*, and, on the other, what we tend to call our *freedom*. As Sellars (1949, p. 311) puts it, 'To say that man is a rational animal is to say that man is a creature not of *habits*, but of *rules*.' This led Brandom (1994, p. 33) to conclude, 'For brutes or bits of the inanimate world to qualify as engaging in practices that implicitly acknowledge the applicability of norms, they would have to exhibit the behavior that counts as treating conduct (their own or that of others) *as* correct or incorrect.'

4.2   Following rules vs. bouncing off them

The role of rules within human (not only) linguistic conduct is often obscured by the conviction that no engagement of rules is compatible with the obvious spontaneity that the conduct displays. Human thinking, speaking, and acting, so the story goes, is spontaneous, creative, and unpredictable; indeed this is what distinguishes humans from machines, which are restricted to following the rules that are hard-wired into them, and hence are bound to be automatic, rigid, and predictable.[3] And indeed it is hard to think of a rule we could be said to be following when thinking or talking; it would seem self-evident, for example, that when we actually reason, we *cannot* be seen to follow the rules of inference we find in logic textbooks!

It is crucial to see that all of this hinges on the kind of role rules are supposed to play. I am afraid that the post-Wittgensteinian 'rule following discussion' (fanned especially by Kripke, 1982), concentrating on the problem of 'going on as before', tends to lead us astray here. On the pages of *Philosophical Investigations* that have come to the fore in this way, Wittgenstein was concentrating on the problem of finding a regularity in a number series: of 'getting' the rule to follow in the sense of being able to produce numbers that the rule tells us to produce. This makes us think that, generally, *following a rule* amounts to doing what the rule tells us to do, and hence that following a rule we cannot act freely or spontaneously. But if we are now to concentrate on the kind of 'rule following' that is crucial with respect to meaningful talk, it is best to shelve this model case. Indeed it is best to shelve the very term *rule following*, for what is really important here is more aptly termed *bouncing off rules*.

The point is that the crucial role of rules with respect to our linguistic conduct is not *prescriptive* in the narrow sense of the word in which rules dictate what to do, but rather *restrictive*; rules tell us what *not* to do, what is *prohibited*. Though the difference between prescriptions ('commands') and restrictions ('constraints') is in no way clear cut (and in one sense they are interdefinable), we can say that whereas the former do not tend to leave us much space for a deliberate choice, the latter do. This is connected to what Sellars (1992, p. 76) terms the distinction between 'rules of doing' and 'rules of criticizing'; we can say that inferential rules are basically the latter. They delimit a space of what is appropriate by trimming off – by way of criticism – the inappropriaties; they restrict the space in which we may operate by discouraging us from leaving it. If you assert that Fido is a dog, you are not obliged to assert that Fido is an animal, but you are obliged not to deny it; if you do deny it, you are a legitimate target of criticism.

This is also closely related to the Sellarsian 'dialectics' of *ought-to-do* (commands to carry out a specific action) and *ought-to-be* (statement of the desirability of a state). Sellars (1969, p. 508) writes:

> Now ought-to-be's (or *rules of criticism* as I shall also call them), though categorical in form, point beyond themselves in two ways. In the first place they imply (in some sense of this protean term) a *reason*, a *because* clause.... In the second place, though ought-to-be's are carefully to be distinguished from ought-to-do's they have an essential connection with them. The connection is, roughly, that ought-to-be's imply ought-to-do's.

Thus, whereas an *ought-to-do* in a sense directly *is* also an *ought-to-be* (and hence a rule of criticism directly piggybacks on every rule of doing), an *ought-to-be* bears an *ought-to-do* via a kind of 'practical syllogism' (see Sellars, ibid., p. 507): via the conviction that we ought to do what brings about that which ought to be. But, of course, as *ought-to-bes* are rules of *criticism*, they will usually bear, as in the case of inference, 'ought-not-to-bes'.

It is important to realize that many objections to the claim that meaning is normative that can be found in the literature (Glüer and Pagin, 1999; Boghossian, 2005; Hattiangadi, 2006) assume that *being normative*, in this context, amounts to *being prescriptive in the above narrow sense of the word.* Here is where I think the malicious influence of the Kripkean revival of Wittgenstein's rule following considerations makes its appearance: many readers of Kripke have gained the errant impression that the question of normativity of meaning reduces to the problem posed by Kripke, and consequently the problem of what it is that prescribes to us how to proceed. It is important to realize that the reasons that lead the inferentialist to claim that meaning is normative are quite different.

Looking at rules in their restrictive, rather than prescriptive, capacity allows us to see that through *limiting* us in what we may do they also *delimit* some new spaces for our actions. Think about chess: it is only thanks to the fact that we 'follow' the rules of chess (i.e., consider violating them as incorrect) that we are able to enter the space of chess games. In this space I can *attack the opponent's king, take his pieces, defend myself from his attempts to checkmate me*, and so forth – things that I cannot do outside of this space. And the idea is that rules may have similar effects in general; they open up new spaces in which new kinds of actions become possible.

Thus the rules of language also open up a new space: the *space of meaningfulness* (which is only a different name for Sellars's *space of reasons*). It is only within this space that we can communicate in our distinctively human way, apply concepts and reason. The space is so realistic that we tend to see its constituents as solid objects (meanings, propositions, pieces of information) which we then try to locate within the physical world.[4] But this is a different dimension of reality, a dimension that some people might want to say *supervenes* on the physical one, but a new one nevertheless.

This, I think, is a reason for rejecting the claim that a *constitutive* rule cannot be a rule that *guides* us. It does, and its capacity of constituting something, on a higher level, is parasitic precisely upon its capacity of guiding us on an underlying level, of making us bounce off it. Thus if Glüer and Pagin (1999, p. 207) claim that 'rules that *can* determine meaning...i.e., rules that can be regarded as *constitutive of* meaning, are not capable of guiding speakers in the ordinary performances of speech acts', then our diagnosis is that this is correct only in the sense that the rules of semantics do not dictate to us what to say. (And, of course, they do not!) They *constrain* us: if we want the sounds we emit to count as meaningful utterances, these rules dictate to us to avoid certain ways of using them. (It is only insofar as I follow the rule that this piece of wood moves only diagonally that the piece is a *bishop*.)[5]

4.3   Rule following as a behavioral pattern

We have claimed that a rule is more than a regularity, but that it is not always a matter of linguistic articulation. It is time to explain the mechanism by which 'unwritten rules' may be sustained throughout human communities. Imagine, first, that we are studying an alien community and we want to find out whether members of this community follow some rules. How can we do it?

As a first step we would certainly look for regularities. If the members of the community display a specific regularity of behavior for which there seems no other explanation, this behavior may become, in our eyes, a candidate for a behavior that is rule-governed. But as a regular behavior *need not* be rule-governed, how could we find out whether it is; to which further test should the candidates be subjected? We have already indicated that an essential ingredient for rule following is *normative attitudes*: the fact that people perceive behavior conforming to the rule as correct and behavior violating the rule as incorrect. How can we find out whether such attitudes are present?

Normative attitudes are, of course, also manifested in behavior. Wittgenstein writes (1953, §54):

> One learns the game by watching how others play. But we say that it is played according to such-and-such rules because an observer can read these rules off from the practice of the game – like a natural law governing the play. – But how does the observer distinguish in this case between players' mistakes and correct play? – There are characteristic signs of it in the players' behaviour. Think of the behaviour characteristic of correcting a slip of the tongue. It would be possible to recognize that someone was doing so even without knowing his language.

Let me call the kind of behavior aimed at rectifying others' behavior *corrective*. The species of corrective behavior are punishments, sanctions, or corrections (and in an extended sense also rewards, praise, or encouragement that may be directed to those who behave in accordance with the rule). And, of course, if the community we are studying has a language that we are able to interpret, at least tentatively, then we may learn about rules by listening to people and querying them: they may directly *tell* us what is correct or incorrect and what rules are in force.

In sum, then, the existence of a rule may be documented by three kinds of behavioral regularities:

(1) complying with the rule (e.g., avoiding chief's food);
(2) correcting those who do not comply (e.g., beating those who do not avoid chief's food);
(3) explicitly endorsing the rule (e.g., saying that one should avoid chief's food).

However, it must be kept in mind that no single one of the regularities is strictly speaking *necessary* for the rule to be in force. As for (1), an individual may, for example, never occur in any situation that would require the complying behavior. As for (3), we have already stressed that we must admit rules that are not explicitly articulated, hence we cannot expect that every normative attitude be explicitly endorsed. The closest to a necessary condition is (2), but its lack can be compensated by the other two. (If everybody behaves in the correct way, there is no behavior open to correction, whereby (2) is again rendered vacuous; but there may be some detectable attitudes of 'approving of' the correct behavior.) Nevertheless, though any of the three kinds of regularities may be absent, not all of them can.

The existence of a rule is thus, even on the behavioral level, more than the regularity that corresponding to what the rule requires; the existence of an implicit rule that one ought to avoid chief's food is thus more than a mere regularity consisting in the members of the society usually avoiding chief's food (though it *can* be seen as a matter of a more complicated system of regularities, including the members ostracizing those who do not avoid chief's food, etc.).

In Section 3.2 we stated that what, in other kinds of use theories of meaning, is accounted for in terms of *dispositions*, we explain in terms of *rules*. The interconnection between the assertion *Lo, a spider!* and spiders is not a matter of the disposition to emit the former in the presence of the latter, but rather of the fact that it would be *correct* to do so, i.e., that there exists a rule authorizing this. However, the fact that now we are seeing rules as behavioral patterns might suggest that we are ending up with a dispositional account after all, only at a higher level. Does assuming a normative attitude to something reduce to being disposed to behave in a certain way with respect to this something?

In a sense, the answer may be positive. Invoking a suitable concept of disposition, anything that a human subject does can be said to be a matter of dispositions. (This would amount to simply saying that everything one does can be traced back to a cause or a motive.) But even if we accept this way of looking at things, the concept of disposition necessary to account for normative attitudes is much thinner, and hence less problematic, than that necessary to account for our linguistic behavior. The point is that displaying normative attitudes is a behavior much more automatic and less flexible than talking, hence the underlying dispositions (if we choose to talk this way) are far more reliably realized in suitable circumstances than linguistic utterances. Whereas there may be great unclarity over how to specify the circumstances which would block the actualization of the disposition to utter *This is a spider* in the presence of a spider, the disposition to voice the disapproval that we would feel if somebody uttered this while pointing at a car is probably detectable already on a physiological level.

Added to this, our account of linguistic practices based on the concept of rule, which might be seen as ultimately also resting on certain dispositions, differs from directly dispositional accounts for the practices in more important respects. We must realize that, as we already indicated, a *rule* (or, for that matter, *propriety*) is a very different kind of entity. Unlike a disposition, it exists in the intersubjective, public, space. What we call a rule is nothing psychological or physiological; it is a matter of a social setting. Nevertheless, this intersubjective, social pattern is carried by certain psychological and physiological substratum; ultimately anything anybody does is a matter of some motives that may be called dispositions.

Learning to live in our natural world crucially involves learning what the 'limits' of this world are: what one should not do if one wants to avoid the world 'striking back'. And learning to live in our *social* world involves something very similar, in this case not only learning where there is a threat of the society literally striking back, but also recognizing the 'social friction' that indicates when our ways do not smoothly fit into our social milieu and there is a prospective danger of some 'striking back'. Learning language involves learning to sense just this kind of social friction, and the relevant normative attitudes are, in this case, the means of inducing it.

4.4 Normative attitudes

Now that we have characterized rule following *as a* kind of behavioral pattern, we may ask whether following a rule simply *is* displaying this behavioral pattern, i.e., whether the previous section may be read as a straightforward naturalization of rules and of normativity. And the answer is negative; there is a reasonable sense in which rules amount to more than behavioral patterns.

Compare the following two claims:

(1) Doing this would take us 10 minutes.
(2) Doing this would be wrong.

Both can be seen as assertions that express certain classifications: they classify a certain action from a certain viewpoint. But whereas (1) uses a classificatory criterion that is wholly independent of the classification and can thus be read as objective in the most straightforward sense, things are different with (2). Though it can perhaps be read in the same objective and hence disengaged way, the important point is that it can be read also in a rather different way, where its aim is not only to classify, but at the same time to uphold the criterion that is employed, to declare one's allegiance to it. Hence the two sentences, though their grammatical structure is the same, may be used to accomplish dissimilar speech acts.

I have already introduced the description of the situation in terms of an 'internal space' that some systems of rules have the ability to constitute. From outside of the space we can only report on the fact that the rules are in force for the insiders, but once we join the insiders, they start to be in force *for us* and hence be in force (full stop), and claiming this does not amount to stating a fact (or an alleged fact); it is a different speech act. Hence, let me call the former reading the 'outsider' reading and the latter the 'insider' one.

Thus claims to the effect that something is correct or that something ought to be done (I will call them *normatives*, for short), on the insider reading (I will call them *genuine* normatives), are simply speech acts different from assertions or reports. They do not report that something is the case, they point out that something *ought to be* the case, and hence they always involve the utterer's taking a rule for being in force, her endorsing it. In this respect, they are similar to oaths of loyalty: they always involve one's decision to assume a certain status, namely to bind oneself by a rule, and in this sense they *institute* something (a certain social link) rather than *report* it. However, the case when the institution happens in a single instant (as in the case of signing an oath) is only a very special case; more generally, binding oneself with a rule is more like the case of loyalty that is not formally established with an instant oath, but is continuously testified by one's performances and declarations. Normatives of this kind involve instituting and upholding – or, as the case may be, amending or contravening – a rule.

This means that genuine normatives are what Kusch (2002, p. 67) calls 'communal institution-creating performatives':

> Institutions and statuses need not be created by the speech-act of a single individual; they may well be created by the speech-act of a community. Such speech-act has the form 'We hereby declare it right to greet people known to us'. The individual subject is replaced with a communal one. Of course, such communal speech-acts are fictitious; we do not create social institutions by speaking in chorus. What happens instead is that the communal institution-creating performative testimony is typically *fragmented and widely distributed over other speech-acts*. The communal performative is never explicitly made; it is only made implicitly or indirectly. It is carried out by people when they do other things: when they talk about greeting their colleague on the way to work; when they actually greet their colleague; when they criticize others for not having greeted them back; or when they chastize others for not having greeted them first. All these other speech-acts – most of which are in fact constatives – 'carry' the relevant communal performative.

In this way genuine normatives make explicit our *normative attitudes* toward something, the fact that we hold something for correct or for incorrect. In the most interesting case the something is a kind of people's behavior. I do not think that the attitude of *holding-correct* is explainable in any simpler terms (in this way it is merely a more general version of Davidson's [1973] attitude of *holding-true*). On the other hand, we *can* see holding-correct, from 'outside', as a matter of a behavioral pattern.

What kind of states, from the psychological viewpoint, are normative attitudes? Definitely they cannot be *generally* propositional attitudes, for propositional attitudes are made possible by a certain normative framework constitutive of propositions, and hence *presuppose* certain normative attitudes. Though in a developed society many normative attitudes *may* be propositional attitudes, these must bootstrap themselves into existence via some kinds of attitudes that are *not* propositional. (And many normative attitudes undoubtedly persist in this form even in the developed societies.) We can speculate that these nonpropositional normative attitudes might be of the kind of Gendler's (2008a; 2008b) *aliefs*, but what I think may be the most illuminating description would be in terms of something like the *absorbed coping* of Dreyfuss (1999), in which the conduct of the agent is unreflectively responsive to the behavior of others and produces norms 'by a response to a gestalt tension that need not be symbolically represented or even representable'.

Hence the conclusion is that an implicit rule is the result of resonating and interlocking normative attitudes. The existence of an implicit rule that one ought to avoid chief's food is thus more than a mere regularity consisting in the members of the society usually avoiding chief's food, and also more than the complex system of regularities including the members ostracizing those who do not avoid chief's food and so on. The surplus consists in the fact that it creates a space for me to enter and to dwell in; it creates, that is, a social context in which I can bind myself with rules, thus limiting my possibilities for the purpose of delimiting new kinds of actions.

4.5   Is meaning normative?

The upshot of the previous sections can give rise to the slogan *meaning is normative*. From the inferentialist viewpoint, just like a piece of wood becomes *a bishop* solely by means of being assigned a role vis-à-vis the rules of chess, a type of sound or an inscription becomes *a word meaning thus and so* solely by means of being assigned a role vis-à-vis the rules of our language games. Hence meaning is normative in the sense that to say that a word means thus and so is to say that it is *correctly* used thus and so (which amounts to a genuine normative).

However, this slogan has been a target of fierce objections (Wikforss, 2001; Boghossian, 2005; Hattiangadi, 2006, Glüer and Wikforss, 2009; etc.). It seems that though all of the critics agree that the employment of language involves a sort of correctness (to say that *This is a dog* when pointing at a dog is correct, whereas to say the same thing when pointing at a cat is not), they reject that this can provide for a normativity of meaning. One version of the objection has already been dealt with: namely the objection that if meanings were to be the product of rules, then these rules would spend their normativity on constituting the meanings and would not be able to be normative in a 'deeper sense'; they would not be able to 'guide us'. (We have concluded that the constitutive rules *do* guide us by restricting us to stay in the space within which the constituted items persist.) Another version is that semantic correctness is a 'non-normative species of correctness', correctness that does not signal the presence of rules and does not have any normative consequences. A third version of the objection is that the rules of semantics can wield a normative force only via some additional rule or rules, such as the rule that we should aim at truth, and that no such rules are in force.

The objection that semantic correctness does not provide for a genuine normativity has been articulated by Glüer (2000, p. 460; my translation from German):

> 'Correctness' in the sense of only semantic correctness thus does not yet mean anything more than that utterances can be *conceptually categorized.*, i.e., here that they can be *sorted out* into true and false. This talk of 'correctness' appears thereby deontically wholly innocent; to show that a use 'correct' in this sense is at the same time already a prescribed use, we must answer the question about the source of the prescriptive force, i.e., the question why we *should* do the 'correct'.

Similarly, Glüer and Wikforss (2009, p. 36) write:

> If I mean green by 'green', then 'green' is true only of green things, and if I say 'That is green' while pointing at a red object, I have said something false. But it does not immediately follow that I have failed to do what I ought to do – not even from a merely semantic point of view. There are non-normative uses of 'correct', and this is one of them. The relevant notion of correctness in this context is that of semantic correctness. ... Semantic categorization is non-normative in precisely this sense: it has no direct normative consequences.

It is hard to imagine that the authors might want to divorce the meaning of *correct* from any *ought to* and any *normativity* whatsoever. It seems to me to be impossible to deny that *some kind* of *ought to* is constitutive of the very meaning of *correct*. Saying that *This is a dog* is correctly asserted when pointing at a dog is just another way of saying that *This is a dog* ought to be asserted (only) of dogs. Hence the point appears to be that this is not *genuine* normativity.

Why is this normativity not genuine? It seems that the reason is that it does not really *make us* do anything. It does not make us say *This is a dog* on any particular occasion. However, we have already concluded that the nature of normativity instituted by the rules of language is usually of a *restrictive* nature; in this particular case it averts us from claiming *This is a dog* when pointing at, say, a car. (And it *does* make us do something after all: it makes us display corresponding corrective behavior.)

But is this really so? It seems that often I can assert *This is a dog* when pointing at a car not only with impunity, but sometimes perhaps even to some useful effect. (I can make a good joke, for example.[6]) Is there, then, really any restrictive force in play? It is important to realize the subtle character of sanctions connected with an activity such as speaking a language. The cost of an isolated violating of the rules is infinitesimal; it is only when I commit this regularly that I may bear significant consequences.[7] If I make frequent and regular errors, my fellow speakers may well start to wonder whether I really *do* speak the language or whether I qualify as a responsible assertor. The ultimate punishment then is exclusion from the community of speakers.

What does it take, in general, for a classification to have normative consequences, to imply an *ought*? Consider the claim that killing is wrong. What argument can we bring for *it* having normative consequences? Aside from an appeal to intuition (usually not very helpful), we can point out that if a society adopts this norm, then when a member of the society *does* kill somebody, he will suffer exclusion from the society (he will not only be despised, but excluded literally by being jailed, if not losing his life), and if not immediately, then surely upon recidivating he will be excluded from the society permanently. What does it mean to say that moving a rook diagonally is wrong has normative consequences? Well, whoever moves a rook in this way will be excluded from the chess game in progress, and recidivating will, sooner or later, bring about his permanent exclusion from the community of serious chess players. And, in a very similar way, whoever uses English words incorrectly repeatedly will be excluded from the community of English speakers; the sounds he emits may continue to sound like English words but they will not be taken seriously as English pronouncements.

Of course these cases differ in respect to the kind of sanctions involved. There are norms whose violation may cost you your life and there are those that you can violate with only mild consequences. But in all cases you risk exclusion from a circle of adherents of the corresponding norm, be it a whole society or a smaller circle, such as that of chess players or of the speakers of English. Hence the claim of Glüer and Wikforss that only some of these cases concern genuine, prescriptive correctness lacks clear substantiation.

I suspect there is one more (and perhaps the most decisive) reason for the 'anti-normativists' rejecting the view that semantics involves genuine normativity. This reason is clearly spelled out by Hattiangadi (2009, p. 60):

> Both 'right' and 'wrong' have non-normative uses. For example, to give the right answer to a question, or in an exam, is to give the

answer that is true or otherwise satisfies the expectations of the questioner or examiner. To say that an answer is right is not to say that it is the answer that you ought to give. If 'right answer' just meant 'answer that you ought to give,' it would sound odd to say 'you should not give the right answer,' or 'you should give the wrong answer.' However, these are perfectly reasonable things to say in some situations – for example, if by answering truthfully you will incriminate a friend you know to be innocent.

Why would it sound odd to say *You should not give the right answer* if we were to read the *right* 'normatively'? Obviously, on Hattiangadi's construal it is not possible that one kind of (genuine) correctness is trumped by another kind; if this is possible, then it is no genuine correctness at all. But why should this be the case? I think that there are always many levels of correctness, some of them quite easily able to trump others, others being able to constitute much less easily resolvable conflicts. As Davidson (1970, p. 34) puts it, not even in the narrower realm of *moral* norms, where the expectation to find absolute norms would be the strongest, is this expectation justified:

> The situation is common; life is crowded with examples: I ought to do it because it would save a life, I ought not because it would be a lie; if I do it I will break my word to Lavina, if I do not, I will break my word to Lolita; and so on...principles, or reasons for acting are irreducibly multiple.

From our perspective, 'normative absolutism' makes little sense because the only possible source of normativity is society, and there is nothing that could prevent society (or societies, for one need not be a member of only one) from issuing conflicting norms. True, one is not automatically bound by all the norms that are around, but on the other hand one is never immune to conflicts that may result from binding oneself (willingly or unwillingly; consciously or unconsciously) by norms that are actually incompatible.

Let us now consider the objection that though semantics can have genuinely normative consequences, it is only thanks to some surplus, genuinely normative rule, such as the rule that one ought to speak the truth, i.e.,

One ought to assert that p only if (she is convinced that) p.

Thus, Boghossian (2005, p. 212), calling the surplus rule 'the normativity thesis', claims:

> To put the matter concisely, the linguistic version of the normativity thesis, in contrast with its mentalist version, has no plausibility whatever; and the reason is that it is not a norm on assertion that it should aim at the truth, in the way in which it is a norm on belief that it do so. Thus, the only imperatives that flow from attributions of linguistic meaning are hypothetical imperatives.

Hence what Boghossian claims is that while there is a norm that we should *believe* the truth, there is no norm that we should *assert* the truth. The inferentialism defended here entails the contrary. The rules governing the game of giving and asking for reasons – the home of the speech act of assertion – cannot concern belief for, as we have already noted, such rules can concern only what is social and publicly accessible. (Another thing is that since one is not free to decide what to believe,[8] we cannot say that one ought to believe the truth simply because *ought* implies *can*, and of course also *need not*.[9]) On the other hand, I think that the norm that we ought to assert the truth follows from the fact that *truth* is nothing other than a nickname for a correct[10] assertability (cf. Sellars, 1992, p. 101).

Boghossian also seems to suggest that the hallmark of *genuine* normativity is entailing some nonhypothetical (categorical?) imperatives, and he is convinced that the only imperatives connected with 'attributions of linguistic meaning' are hypothetical ones. This may be related to the defeasibility issue discussed above, but we have concluded that the hallmark of normativity cannot possibly be *indefeasibility*. Could the requirement that imperatives are nonhypothetical do any better? It is not at all clear what is to be understood by imperatives being nonhypothetical here (surely, rules of language do not entail anything as Kant's categorical imperative, but what does?).

However, what is most important is that, from the inferentialist standpoint, the fact that one ought to assert only what is true (pace Glüer and Wikforss, 2009, p. 38) is *not* a pragmatic principle over and above semantic principles. For the inferentialist, truth is nothing more than a nickname for a status certain sentences have vis-à-vis the rules of the game of giving and asking for reasons, hence the result that one ought to assert only true sentences is nothing over and above unpacking the concept of truth.

Consider a parallel argument against there being a norm of asserting the truth, due to Wikforss (2001, pp. 205–205):

> Consider the case where I misperceive and utter 'That's a horse' of a cow. What semantic norm do I then violate? I see the animal, believe it to be a horse and, consequently, utter 'That's a horse'. Although I have made a false judgment, I have not broken any semantic norms.

But what if I say, 'Suppose I misperceive and move a rook as if it were a bishop. What rule of chess am I then violating? I see the piece, believe it to be a bishop and, consequently, move it diagonally. Although I have made a move that is not admissible, I have not broken any rule of chess.'

Williamson (1996) put forward the notion of assertion as a move in a rule-governed game, which is of a piece with the view entertained here; however, he went on to propose that the crucial rule governing the activity of asserting is of the kind *assert P only if you know that P*. It is crucial to realize that this is a view very different from the Brandomian one put forward here. According to Brandom (1983), the kind of game constitutive of assertion (just like any other language game) is a 'social behavioral game'. This means that following the rules is necessarily socially observable and monitorable, and hence the rules cannot turn on what the players know. (Can they turn on what is true; hence can we have the rule *assert P only if P(is true)*? This depends on how we construe the concept of truth; unless truth is something we can get a grip on in the course of the language game, it fares no better than knowledge.) The difference between Williamson's 'epistemic' construal of rules constitutive of assertion and Brandom's 'social behavioral' becomes obvious if one considers a version of chess in which rules depend on what the players know or think: for example, moving a rook diagonally would be legitimate provided that the player who moves it is convinced, albeit mistakenly, that it is a bishop.[11]

In any case, the inferentialist analysis of meaning reveals a *deeper* source of normativity than the alleged norm that we should assert the truth: meaning, according to the inferentialist, is normative in the sense that when I say that an expression means thus and so, then what I say does not amount to stating a fact, but rather invoking a propriety: it is stating that the expression is *correctly* used thus and so. (Hence the inferentialist rejects Boghossian's claim that to derive 'a should or an ought from the mere attribution of meaning' we need an additional premise, such as his 'normativity thesis'.) True, on one of its readings, this may still be read as stating a kind of fact, namely that an activity or a community is – as a matter of fact – governed by certain rules (hence on this reading we treat the propriety in question *as a fact*); however, there is a second and crucial reading in which this is not the case (this is the reading in which it becomes what we have called the *genuine normative*), for the claim does not amount to a declarative statement at all; it is rather an *endorsement*. As Sellars puts it in his letter to Chisholm,

> My solution is that
>   '...' means ---
> is the core of a unique mode of discourse which is as distinct from the *description* and *explanation* of empirical fact, as is the language of *prescription* and *justification*. (Chisholm and Sellars, 1958, p. 527)

Is it true, then, that, as Boghossian claims, 'the only imperatives that flow from attributions of linguistic meaning are hypothetical imperatives'? Well, if we read the attributions of meaning in the first of our two ways, then it is: it follows merely that you should use the expression thus and so *in the case that you want to speak a certain language, or to belong to a certain community*. But on the second reading, and this is crucial, the qualification drops out; it follows simply that the expression should be used thus and so (full stop).

4.6   Normativity and human practices

Lance and O'Leary-Hawthorne (1997) discussed in detail the conception of normativity that is, I think, needed to underlie the picture we have drawn above. According to them, we have to steer clear both of the Scylla of the 'transcendental conception' (in which stating somebody ought to do something is reporting a robust normative fact) and the Charybdis of the 'attributive conception' (in which saying this is spelling out a contingent rule the person follows). The authors think that to arrive at the correct conception of normativity we must take a middle course, and they build their conception around the concept of *social practices*.

What the *attributive conception*, according to Lance and O'Leary-Hawthorne, gets right is that issuing a normative is possible always only in the context of some practices that are already rule-governed. However, what it gets wrong is that it simply reports the rules as they stand. A crucial point, for them, is that rule-governed practices are always, by their very nature, 'open'. Rules in this sense of the word can be challenged (or, alternatively, reinforced), but, and this is even more important, they are open also in the sense that they can be further developed: extended into areas previously untouched, and refined or resolved for cases where the outcome of their application was unclear. Hence the claim that somebody ought to do something, aside from being anchored in the existing practice, also either reinforces, or challenges, or extends this practice.

Lance and O'Leary-Hawthorne elaborate on Sellars's suggestion that issuing a normative is a speech act that is sui generis in the following way (ibid., pp. 202–203):

> Normatives are in many ways just like ordinary declaratives. They take their place in the game of giving and asking for reasons, serving as premises and conclusions in reasoning. In some respects then, normatives have criteria and consequences of application that are like declaratives; they follow from certain claims and certain claims follow from them. ... But in another crucial respect their consequences of application are like imperatives. Like a declarative, one of the consequences of application of a normative is entitlement to certain other claims. But unlike declaratives, one of the direct, and widely stable, consequences of application of a normative is the appropriateness of some act: to commit oneself to a normative is *ipso facto* to commit oneself to the propriety of some act.

We can say that normatives may contain something that can be called a 'descriptive component' (corresponding to its anchor in the existing, established practices) and it contains an 'imperative component' (expressing my insisting on going on as I put forward). Lance and O'Leary-Hawthorne point out that normatives are like declaratives in that they may be justified (and hence they are among the legitimate participants of the enterprise of giving and asking for reasons), but are like imperatives in that they create, aside from the commitments and entitlements common to assertions, also different and more specific kinds of commitments and entitlements.

Part and parcel of this is also the fact that our linguistic practices possess a kind of 'retroactive' dimension. When I claim that something is correct, I do not simply report, I take part in establishing (reshaping, extending) a rule, whereby I may institute a certain correctness as not coming into being together with the institution of the rule, but rather as being there already earlier, perhaps ever before (and ever after).

This may sound weird for it seems to suggest an utterly voluntarist conception of correctness. Is it so that we can make anything correct (and, moreover, make it having been correct already always) by simply proclaiming it as such? Surely not. Proclaiming something as correct must be continuous with the relevant practices of the community in question, and insofar as it goes beyond them, it always counts merely as a proposal that must be subsequently either reinforced or refuted.[12] Correctness is thus, from this viewpoint, merely a transient moment of a dynamics of practices. But, on the other hand, what is built into the concept of correctness is a certain stability, nontransience, which implies the retroactivity. Though the correctness did not exist before my act, my act instituted it as already existing before.

Compare this with the Platonist construal of mathematical objects. On the one hand, it is clear that, for example, sets were invented by Cantor and his followers. The 'invention' was an organic continuation of a certain prior development of mathematics; nevertheless from this viewpoint it makes clear sense to say that sets did not exist before Cantor. On the other hand, once mathematicians accepted sets, they accepted them as abstract, ideal entities, of which it makes no sense to say that they 'came into existence at a particular time'. Hence we may say that their introduction into mathematics involved a certain retroactivity; their introduction involved the introduction of the notion that they have already always existed (more precisely that it does not make sense to say that they started to exist). Therefore, if we want to avoid misguided disputes, we must always distinguish between two different 'time frames'. the historical frame, within which it makes sense to say that sets came into being thanks to the effort of Cantor, and the Platonist frame that came into being together with them, and that gave them their way of existing without ever having been brought into being.[13]

Now the retroactivity connected with a rule is similar to this. Many normative attitudes not merely uphold a rule, but also give it a more definite shape than it had before, and giving it this shape they make even some previous actions accountable to it. Thus it may happen that we can say that we were wrong before, although up to now there was no relevant rule and hence no relevant concept of correctness around. But just as we can say that there were sets already for our ancestors to grasp, only they never managed to discover them, we can say that our ancestors were wrong measured by a rule we have only now managed to establish, or that they were using a rule that we have since discovered was wrong.

Lance and O'Leary-Hawthorne (ibid., p. 206) once more:

> Though judgments about how to go on from here require a prag-
> matic understanding of where here is, no descriptive characteri-
> zation of existing or future practice completely determines the
> correctness of such judgments. One is neither describing a mysti-
> cally grasped platonic norm, reporting past practice, nor predicting
> future practice at any level of description. One is, rather, proposing
> an explicit standard which one hopes to have added to the complex
> corpus of explicit and implicit social constraints upon activities
> within the practice in question, a standard which though explicit
> is not understandable except in the context of the underlying
> implicit practice.

We have already seen that genuine normatives are vehicles of *communal performatives*, of normative acts that are 'fragmented and widely distributed' over individual people. Hence I think the prototypical job of the
speech act of the genuine normative is to contribute to the establishment and sustaining of social norms, and thereby to the establishment
of various social 'virtual spaces' in which we humans live our lives. This,
I think, is closely connected with the fact that we humans have developed a very peculiar way of augmenting our environment: not only do
we reshape, rebuild (and sometimes unfortunately also devastate) our
natural environment, but we also erect our own normative, institutional
reality atop it.

4.7   Inside and outside of the rules of language

Part and parcel of the conception of rules exposed in this chapter is
the claim that rules act, in a sense, like walls. Walls restrict us, prevent
us from walking through them, but precisely thanks to this they can
constitute a house, an inner space that we humans find so useful and
enjoyable. And what I have suggested is that rules, in force of preventing
us from doing certain things, can likewise constitute a kind of 'inner
space'; a space, of course, somewhat dissimilar to the inner spaces of
houses (unlike the case of solid walls, you can get bumps from being
bounced off the limits of language only in the Wittgensteinian sense).[14]
Constituting such a space is, of course, not the work of a single rule;
such a space can be created only by way of cooperation of an interlocking system of rules, such as that of the rules of language. We will
address how this is managed in the next chapter.

Rules have an inner and an outer face. From the outside they, and the spaces they create, can be simply *described*: we can report on complicated linguistic practices that are going on within a community allowing members to use 'signals' to achieve complicated things. However, from the inside the spaces can be *inhabited*: we can *accept* the rules, making them into virtual 'walls' of a 'dwelling' we share with other people. Unlike a normal dwelling built from stone or wood, the walls of this one stand and fall with the attitudes of its dwellers. This creates the need for specific kinds of acts in order to support them.

It is, I think, precisely this ability of our rules to vault over inner spaces that distinguishes us from other animals. We are not only able to detect constraints due to which we are *not able* to do something, we are also able to grasp and accept constraints due to which we merely *ought not* to do something. And, unlike the former, which are completely external to us, the latter constraints are of our own making; it is we who not only bring them into being, but also keep them there. This was noticed by H. L. A. Hart (1961) in the context of systems of law:[15] he realized that law does not act as merely an external factor, such that people obey it merely because they want to avoid punishment; many subjects obey the law (partly or wholly) simply because of their allegiance to it. Hart (ibid., pp. 55–56) writes:

> A social rule has an 'internal' aspect, in addition to the external aspect which it shares with a social habit and which consists in the regular uniform behaviour which an observer could record. This internal aspect of rules may be simply illustrated from the rules of any game. Chess players do not merely have similar habits of moving the Queen in the same way which an external observer, who knew nothing about their attitude to the moves which they make, could record. In addition, they have a reflective critical attitude to this pattern of behaviour: they regard it as a standard for all who play the game. Each not only moves the Queen in a certain way himself but 'has views' about the propriety of all moving the Queen in that way. These views are manifested in the criticism of others and demands for conformity made upon others when deviation is actual or threatened and in the acknowledgement of the legitimacy of such criticism and demands when received from others. For the expression of such criticisms, demands, and acknowledgements a wide range of 'normative' language is used. 'I (You) ought not to have moved the Queen like that', 'I (You) must do that', 'That is right', 'That is wrong'.

Hence Hart (ibid., p. 86) summarizes:

> When a social group has certain rules of conduct, this fact affords an opportunity for many closely related yet different kinds of assertion; for it is possible to be concerned with the rules, either merely as an observer who does not himself accept them, or as a member of the group which accepts and uses them as guides to conduct. We may call these respectively the 'external' and the 'internal points of view'.

What does the upholding of the walls of the inner space amount to, speaking nonmetaphorically? How does a community uphold the rules it accepts? In the simplest case, of course, a rule is made explicit and instituted; paradigmatically, this is the way of the coded law. Here the rules are carefully written down and a sophisticated system of social institutions is erected to ensure that people comply with them. Penalties, as we know, may be drastic.

But, as we also know, the idea that the law can be codified such that its application is mechanical and hence an unproblematic process is an illusion. The most basic problem is that the rules are written down in a language and that language must be interpreted, and we can always consider alternative interpretations. Some interpretations are obviously correct or incorrect, but then there is a gray zone of interpretations whose correctness is unclear. The fact that there is a correctness with respect to interpretations implies that the codified law, and indeed any rules expressed in language, presuppose other rules, which means that not all rules can be explicit, on pain of a vicious circle. We have already seen that this implies that there must be the possibility of rules underpinned simply by normative attitudes; of rules that are 'unwritten' not only in the shallow sense of not being *codified*, but in the deeper sense of lacking any explicit articulation at all.

What is crucial is that dwelling inside 'inner spaces' vaulted over by rules has become our *modus vivendi* to such an extent that the idea that we might be able to assume a disengaged viewpoint by moving wholly outside such spaces is utterly illusory. This is what made Sellars (1962) insist that the *scientific image* of the world (i.e., its image as a web of causal laws, devoid of any normativity), though in a sense our most advanced picture, cannot be the only picture we use to steer clear of the cliffs of our world; it must be coupled by the complementary *manifest image*, thanks to which nature becomes populated by *thinking, rational* persons *talking meaningfully* and *acting responsibly*.

4.8   Summary of Chapter 4

In this chapter we turned our attention to the nature of the rules that are constitutive of the semantics of natural language. First, we concentrated on the important fact that these rules, unlike the rules of chess or football, are mostly implicit to our linguistic practices. We have claimed that they exist mostly through *normative attitudes* which speakers assume to the utterances of other speakers (and of themselves). Therefore, what is crucial for the existence of implicit rules is that the members of a society not only display 'first-order behavior' towards the world and toward one another, but display also 'second-order' – especially 'corrective' – behavior toward one another's first-order behavior.

We claimed that a form of such a 'second-order behavior' are utterances that we have called *genuine normatives* and the vehicles of which are sentences stating correctness or stating what ought to be or ought not to be done. These utterances are so close to assertions that we tend to see them as true or false, but the fact is that they involve a 'performative' component, rendering them irreducible to ordinary assertions. Due to their closeness to assertions they can be seen as expressing facts, but if we see them thus, we must realize that the facts expressed by them are *institutional facts* and that genuine normatives help to bring them into existence and keep them there.

This has brought us to a certain vindication of the slogan that meaning is normative, but the sense in which this slogan gets vindicated is not quite the same as that in which it has been recently attacked by a host of philosophers of language. These philosophers often assume that normativity of meaning is claimed to consist in the fact that there is a rule to assert the truth, or to assert what one knows, and hence it is this view they fight against; however, the kind of normativity urged by inferentialism is of a quite different kind: it renders meaning normative because meaning ascriptions are usually genuine normatives.

We have invoked an illuminating metaphor: rules, and especially the rules of language, are capable of taking part in the constitution of certain 'inner spaces'. From outside of the space, we can describe the rules being in force as a fact, while when we are inside, when we *endorse* the rules, we need the genuine normatives to express them. And we cannot live otherwise save inside some systems of rules.

5
Our Language Games

5.1 From meaning to linguistic practices

In the previous two chapters we discussed the kind of rules that can be expected to underlie our linguistic practices and the kind of normativity that is inherent to them. The upshot of these considerations was that certain rules are capable of constituting 'inner spaces' providing for new spectra of actions, and especially that the rules of language constitute *the space of meaningfulness* aka *the space of reasons*. This constitution requires a conspiracy of a plurality of rules: an inner space comes into being only when all the voussoirs interlock appropriately to form a solid vault – when the rules interact with one another in a specific, fruitful way.

Take chess; it is only thanks to the very special way its rules are balanced against one another that the game is interesting and that nobody can find a winning strategy. Tampering with the rules might easily destroy this equilibrium; not every assortment of rules would yield such a fascinating game. With this in mind, we should consider not only the nature of individual rules (as in our previous chapter), but also how these rules are capable of interlocking to form systems that afford inner spaces, especially the space of meaningfulness. Following the Wittgensteinian tradition, we use the term *games* for the activities governed by such systems of rules.

The concept of *language game* rose to take center stage in philosophical discussions during the latter half of the twentieth century, being connected with the fundamental shift of focus (discussed in Chapter 3) toward use theories of meaning. It came to be no longer taken for granted by many semanticists that the investigation of our linguistic conduct must be preceded by an explanation of meaning. Instead, they started to prefer to first explain our conduct, leaving any need for an explanation of meaning to emerge subsequently (and were it not to emerge, then perhaps the whole concept of meaning might even be superfluous). They felt that to persist in seeing the quest for meanings as necessarily *underlying* and prior to any explanation of language games was to make ourselves hostage to a certain specific, and perhaps ill-founded, view of the nature of language.

This shift of focus represents what can be termed the 'holistic' turn of semantics, but it was largely part and parcel of the broader kind of turn that is sometimes called *pragmatic*[1] and that has also fostered the boom of interest in use theories of meaning (discussed in the previous chapter). Thus language games, the subject of this chapter, found their way to the introductory sections of semantic textbooks instead of lurking in foot- notes and appendices. The meanings of individual expressions ceased to be seen as the basis that must be fully explained before we can move to the explanation of the workings of language as a whole; the meanings began to be seen as explainable only within the context of the working of the whole language, *viz.* our language games.

Needless to say, the term *game* is being used somewhat metaphorically. Also, emphasis is being laid on an aspect of the Wittgensteinian usage different from the aspect that has often been brought to the fore. What has frequently been assumed is that the moral of Wittgenstein's meta- phor is to stress the heterogeneity and elusiveness of our linguistic prac- tices (this is the point of departure for those who, like Lyotard (1979), want to see Wittgenstein mainly as a prophet of postmodernism), whereas what we are stressing, in contrast to this, is the constitutive role of the rules with respect to the games.

True, rules may not always be crucial for everything that can be called a game. When considering, for example, 'the game little children play of throwing a ball in any direction and then retrieving it' (Wittgenstein, 1969a, §32), no rules that would be essential for it spring to mind. But, despite this, the stress on rules does not seem to be distorting the Wittgensteinian view. After all, the considerations focusing on rules and on how we find out 'how to go on' constitute a substantial part of *Philosophical Investigations*, which indicates that the language games Wittgenstein was especially interested in were essentially governed by rules.

Hence, though Wittgenstein certainly urged us not to see language as something simple and homogeneous, serving a unique purpose, and to accept that what we do with language is tantamount to playing different kinds of games, I do not think that his urging was meant to be a conclusion, but rather a starting point for his research into language and meaning. It is clearly the entering wedge into the host of problems he discusses in *Philosophical Investigations*, including the problem of rule following (discussed in previous chapters). I think that, with some oversimplification, we can say that the statement of the heterogeneity of the games we play with language stimulated Wittgenstein to consider what it takes to play a *language* game, and that the concept of rule turned out to be a principal characteristic.

What is important for us now is the broadening of our focus from an individual rule to the interplay of rules. Earlier we rejected the idea that a meaning can be seen as a chunk of mind-stuff (or, for that matter, of any other kind of stuff) glued to an expression. We also rejected the idea that it can be a matter of a single rule (such as a rule that it is correct to assert *This is a dog* when pointing at a dog): it is only a complex edifice of rules that can yield meaning of our, human, kind. And though we may think that the pattern of rules governing a single word may be relatively restricted, we must add that this is possible only on the background of a much larger formation of rules.

Before we begin scrutinizing the nature of such formations, it is worth noting that although Wittgenstein's *language games* provided for the emblematic metaphor characteristic of the turn – and the holism implicit in it – it was not due to Wittgenstein alone. A similar perspective had always been natural for many pragmatists, and in Wittgenstein's time this perspective was revived by neopragmatists like Quine.

We have already seen that Quine holds that to discover what meaning is, we must study how we acquire meanings, in particular which aspects of human behavior an adept of language must observe to learn what a word means. Concentrating on this issue led Quine to develop his much discussed thought experiments with 'radical translation', the situation where a linguist faces an utterly unknown language and must learn what its words mean by studying the behavior of its speakers. Quine is fascinated by his discovery that the task of assembling a translation manual from the language to be deciphered to the translator's language is unlikely to have a unique solution, the root of his personal holistic turn. But this, I think, is not the most important lesson (in fact, as I will try to indicate later, such an outcome is not so surprising given the pragmatic nature of the turn); a more important lesson of the whole pragmatic turn is that meanings, as traditionally conceived, are perhaps less crucial for semantic theory than previously thought.

Some of the philosophers who turned their focus from meanings of individual expressions to linguistic practices concluded that this shift in perspective should result in utterly dumping the concept of meaning. Quine (1992, p. 56), for one, claims: 'I would not seek a scientific rehabilitation of something like the old notion of separate and distinct meanings; that notion is better seen as a stumbling block cleared away.' But, as I have already pointed out, I find this conclusion too hasty: I do not think that the fact that meaning loses its foundational role in semantics should make us conclude there is no place for meanings in semantics whatsoever. I think that to 'make sense' of our linguistic practices we need to see them as an interplay of contributions of individual expressions, although we know that the individuation of the contributions is partly deliberate.

Before continuing, let me indicate, by way of digression, how this turn brings about the Quinean indeterminacies. If the meaning of a word were a mental content, then it would appear reasonable to try to discover it by taking the word in isolation and searching out the links leading from it into the mind. (The same would be the case, for that matter, if meanings were conceived as elements of the real or of a Platonist world christened by expressions.) However, if the meaning is rather the *role* of the word within our language games, then the only way to grasp it is to investigate the word's interaction with other words and with the world within the relevant games. Thus, while the mentalist conception of meaning led to the atomist view of language ('we find out meanings of individual words and thereby explain language and its workings'), the interactive conception leads instead to the holistic view ('we must capture the workings of language and meanings will come out as spin-offs').

From this viewpoint, the indeterminacy thesis should not be surprising at all. In fact, once we accomplish the pragmatic turn, it is forthcoming: it is a matter of the leeway we have when individuating the contributions of individual parts to a 'semantically self-standing' whole. And it is important to see that the indeterminacy *of individual meanings* is not an indeterminacy *of semantics*: semantics is a matter of the ability of our linguistic tools to serve as various kinds of vehicles of various language games, and though such an ability is vague in the sense that it is usually not a yes–no matter, it is not indeterminate (indeed it is not even clear what it would mean to call it so). On the other hand, furnishing individual words with values that would compositionally add up to the determinate abilities of the significant wholes (as we discussed in Chapter 3) can surely be done in more than one way, hence meaning assignment in this sense is indeterminate almost trivially.

5.2 Game-theoretical perspectives

Accepting Wittgenstein's urge that we should see the enterprise of language as a game or a motley of games, and accepting that it is the normative structure of the games, the rules constitutive of them, that is crucial about them, can we envisage a paradigmatic game we play with language? What does winning and losing in such a game amount to? We have seen that Wittgenstein would say that the ways of language are so multifarious that it is not clear that it makes sense to talk about a 'paradigm' here at all. However, it is likely that some of our language games are central, and others only marginal; some are essential and others optional; some are more and others less important. We have already seen that for Brandom such a central game is the *game of giving and asking for reasons*. Could we, then, get a grip on the nature of language by pinpointing such *most crucial* language game or games? But the most crucial in which of all conceivable respects?

Let us now, for a moment, restrict ourselves to logical vocabulary. Just as we saw logical constants as the easiest kinds of words to tackle inferentially, it may be the logical vocabulary of natural language which may be easiest to apply a 'game-theoretical' perspective to. Hence are there any results of logic that can indicate what kind of semantically crucial game(s) we play with language?

An early attempt to represent the basic part of standard logic in game-theoretical terms, and also to account for what Wittgenstein had in mind when speaking about language games, was presented by Jaakko Hintikka (1973).[2] What he did was that with each formula of standard logic (i.e., the first-order predicate calculus) he associated a game of two players, called *I* and *Nature*, so that the formula in question is valid iff *I* have a winning strategy, and it is contradictory iff *Nature* has a winning strategy. (For a fully interpreted language, the winning strategy of *Me* coincides with truth and that of *Nature* with falsity; in the case of a logical calculus there are, of course, many formulas with no winning strategy for either of us.)

For the first order predicate calculus, the games, compared with the standard truth definition, look as follows:

Traditional truth-definition	The associated game
$R(i_1,...,i_n)$ is true iff the objects denoted by $i_1,...,i_n$ are in the relation expressed by R; otherwise $R(i_1,...,i_n)$ is false	*I* win the game associated with $R(i_1,...,i_n)$ iff the objects denoted by $i_1,...,i_n$ are in the relation expressed by R; otherwise *Nature* wins
$\neg A$ is true iff A is false	the game associated with $\neg A$ starts with *I* and *Nature* swapping roles and continues as the game associated with A
$A \wedge B$ is true iff A is true and B is true	the game associated with $A \wedge B$ starts with *Nature* choosing either A or B and continues as the game associated with the chosen formula
$A \vee B$ is true iff A is true or B is true	the game associated with $A \vee B$ starts with *I* choosing either A or B and continues as the game associated with the chosen formula
$\forall x A[x]$ is true iff for every element i of the universe, $A[x]$ is satisfied by i (where $A[x]$ is a formula with zero or more occurrences of x)	the game associated with $\forall x A[x]$ starts with *Nature* choosing an element i of the universe and continues as the game associated with $A[x]$ with i in the role of x
$\exists x A[x]$ is true iff there is an element i of the universe such that $A[x]$ is satisfied by i	the game associated with $\exists x A[x]$ starts with *I* choosing an element i of the universe and continues as the game associated with $A[x]$ with i in the role of x

Let us consider an example: a sentence of the form $((A{\rightarrow}B){\rightarrow}A){\rightarrow}A$, or, which is equivalent in classical logic, $A\vee\neg(A\vee\neg(B\vee\neg A))$. How would the associated game proceed? Do *I* have a winning strategy?

1. As the sentence is the disjunction of A and $\neg(A\vee\neg(B\vee\neg A))$, it is *My* move and *I* must choose one of the disjuncts. Distinguish two cases: If A is true, *I* may, of course, choose it; and I win. Let us therefore suppose that A is not true; in such a case I choose $\neg(A\vee\neg(B\vee\neg A))$. (Let me remark that of course *I* do not need to know whether A is, or is not, true, and so *I* may come to choose wrongly and consequently lose even if there is a winning strategy for *Me*. However, what interests us is not whether *I* am really able to follow *My* winning strategy, but rather if such a strategy exists.)
2. As now we are facing a sentence that is a negation, our roles are swapped and we continue with the game associated with $A\vee\neg(B\vee\neg A)$.
3. This is a disjunction again, and hence again *I* would have to choose one of the disjuncts, but as the roles are swapped, it is *Nature* who chooses. *Nature* is thus to choose one of A and $\neg(B\vee\neg A)$. As we have

assumed that *A* is false, if *Nature* chooses it, she loses (she would win if the roles were not swapped, but unfortunately for her, they are), so let us assume that she chooses the second one.
4. The roles are swapped again (so that they are back to normal now) and we continue with the game associated with *B*∨¬*A*.
5. *I* choose one of *B* and ¬*A*, and of course *I* choose the second.
6. The roles are swapped and we continue with the game associated with *A*.
7. It is *Nature*'s turn, and as *A* is false and the roles are swapped; I win.

Hence we have shown that *I* have a winning strategy for every *A* and *B*; in other words, we have shown that the formula $((A{\to}B){\to}A){\to}A$ (Peirce's law) is a tautology.

In this way we see that the rules of logic can also have an 'interactive' reading; we can read them not as describing the truth or satisfaction conditions for various kinds of sentences, but rather as spelling out rules of a language game. In this way, the concept of truth gives way to the concept of *winning strategy*, thus making the assertion of every sentence a game of its own, a game that the assertor wins if she is able to defend the truth of the assertion.

Hintikka's achievement was that he showed how the logicians' activities of capturing the 'logical backbone' of language could also be seen as describing an *interaction*. However, it was not the interaction of the kind we are after, an interaction among users of language. His games are duels of a solitary individual against the world, not a social game. Are we able to do better in this respect?

Games more closely resembling social practices were presented by Paul Lorenzen and his fellow German logical constructivists. They saw their *dialogic logic* (Lorenzen, 1955; Lorenzen and Lorenz, 1978) as predominantly a tool to elucidate the semantics of logical constants for their games were devised to capture the most basic semantic operations that characterize the constants. Their approach, however, received relatively little international attention – until its rediscovery in the course of the recent boom of game-theoretic semantics.

Here the games are not those of *Me* against *Nature*, but games among participants of an argument. Arguments are seen as the putting forward, challenging, and defending of theses. The *Proponent* asserts a sentence and the *Opponent* tries to challenge it by attacking the asserted sentence or its parts. He does so by means of asserting other sentences, which can in turn be challenged by the *Proponent*. The *Proponent* wins if she deflects all the attacks and if there is no other way for the *Opponent* to attack her.

The rules specifying what counts as an admissible attack and what as a defense against it are summarized in the following table (note that though prima facie one may defend oneself by asserting even something unwarranted, this would be of no help, for whatever one asserts becomes a legitimate target of a further attack):

Sentence	The way(s) of attacking it	The way(s) of defending it against the attack
$A \wedge B$	challenging A challenging B	asserting A asserting B
$A \vee B$	challenging	asserting A or asserting B
$\neg A$	asserting A	–
$A \rightarrow B$	asserting A	asserting B
$\exists x A[x]$	challenging	asserting A[i]
$\forall x A[x]$	challenging A[i]	asserting A[i]

The games within the framework of dialogic logic are then subject to some further restrictions which do not concern individual types of attack but the overall structure of the game. Standardly, the following constraints are in force:

(a) The *Proponent* can assert an atomic sentence only after it was already asserted by the *Opponent*.
(b) It is possible to defend only the sentence last attacked.
(c) Only one response to an attack is possible.
(d) An assertion of the *Proponent* may be attacked only once.

The loser of the game is then the player who can make no further legitimate move.

Let us return to our example $((A \rightarrow B) \rightarrow A) \rightarrow A$. (Within this framework, it is *not* equivalent to $A \vee \neg(A \vee \neg(B \vee \neg A))$ – which indicates that we are deviating from classical logic.) The game would now proceed as follows:

1. The *Proponent* asserts $((A \rightarrow B) \rightarrow A) \rightarrow A$.
2. The *Opponent* attacks by asserting $(A \rightarrow B) \rightarrow A$.
3. The *Proponent* cannot defend her assertion against this attack (for she would have to assert the atomic sentence *A*, which is forbidden by (a)); however, she may counterattack and challenge the *Opponent*'s assertion. Hence she asserts $A \rightarrow B$.

4. If the *Opponent* were to defend it by asserting *A*, the *Proponent* could use this to repeat this assertion and thereby eventually defend her original assertion; the *Opponent* is thus left with a counterattack, which, by chance, again amounts to asserting *A*.

5. This is the end of the *Proponent*, for her defense would amount to asserting *B*, which is not possible due to (a). Moreover, she is no longer able to reassert *A* to defend her original sentence, for this would break law (b). The *Proponent* thus has no move left and loses.

In this case, in contrast to the previous one, there is *not* a winning strategy for the *Proponent*. This means that the set of sentences for which there is a winning strategy for the *Proponent* within this type of game does not coincide with the set of those in which there is a winning strategy for *Me* within the previous one. What is remarkable is that, as it turns out, this set coincides with the set of sentences that are valid within intuitionist logic (a conclusion that is of a piece with the verdict we will reach in Chapter 9 with respect to the most 'natural' logic of inference).[3]

Anyway, here we have a *social* rendering of the interactive aspect of the logical backbone of our language: a game consisting in defending one's claim against possible challenges. We can imagine that it is precisely this kind of game that may be seen as the basic building block of our everlasting meaning-conferring games.

5.3 The builders' game

Games like the Lorenzenian ones concern exclusively logical vocabulary, which is not, from our viewpoint, the truly interesting part of language. (Some do extend also to mathematical vocabulary,[4] but not to empirical vocabularies.) To explore the roots of our language games and of the space of reasons which gets erected together with their elaboration requires a return to fundamentals. Consider, for this purpose, Wittgenstein's (1953, §2) example of a rudimentary language game:

> Let us imagine a language for which the description given by Augustine is right. The language is meant to serve for communication between a builder A and an assistant B. A is building with building-stones: there are blocks, pillars, slabs and beams. B has to pass the stones, and that in the order in which A needs them. For this purpose they use a language consisting of the words 'block', 'pillar', 'slab', 'beam'. A calls them out; B brings the stone which he has learnt to bring at such-and-such a call. Conceive this as a complete primitive language.

The role of each of the four words within this game is different – hence insofar as we want to call the roles *meanings*, each of them means something different. They do not seem to have any *inferential* role for there do not seem to be any inferential rules in play. (But there *are* rules in play: B *should* bring a slab, rather than a block, a pillar, or a beam if A calls out *Slab!*.)

Hence we have a language game in which words have (sort of) meanings, but these meanings are of a kind different from meanings of words of our normal, natural languages. The meaning of *block* in this language is very different from that of *block* in ordinary English. Now Wittgenstein's 'game-theoretic' turn is meant to prevent us from seeing the situation in such a way that the difference between the former *block* and the latter one is that between a mere 'differentiated yell' and a *truly* meaningful word – *viz.* a word with a chunk of mind-stuff glued to it. Wittgenstein wants us to see what we do with English (or, for that matter, with any other natural language) as only a much more intricate version of the above game. Hence the difference, he indicates, is merely a matter of degree.

However, in the previous chapters we described the doctrine of Sellars and Brandom as yielding a different view, a view that though our language games are indeed merely more intricate versions of the builders' game, there still *is* a qualitative difference. The point is that as the rules of the game become more elaborate (in the 'right' way), they reach a point at which they cross an imaginary threshold beyond which our sentences come to produce *propositional* content and some of our words come to express *concepts*, the threshold that lets us into the *space of reasons*. What is the threshold?

Return to the builders' game. Imagine that the builder comes to encounter situations in which he needs either a block or a slab (either will do), or situations in which he needs either a pillar or a beam (again either will do). He may introduce the words *brick* for the former case and *post* for the latter. In this way the language comes to display a rudimentary kind of structure: there is a specific kind of relation of either *block* or *slab* to *brick* and similarly of *pillar* or *beam* to *post* (a relation of 'subordination').

Now consider an elaboration of the game. Imagine that at some point of the game the builder and the assistant take a break, and the assistant 'takes stock' of the remaining building-stones; he points in turn at the individual stones, and when pointing at a given stone he pronounces a word that he assumes the builder would call out to make him bring this very stone. The builder observes him and when he thinks that the assistant pronounced a 'wrong' word, he protests – shows some kind of dissatisfaction.

Imagine that the words that the assistant uses are not the original words *block, pillar, slab,* and *beam,* but rather the additional words *brick* and *post.* Imagine that the builder then reacts using the *original* words. Now some pairs of the pronouncements would be 'incompatible', e.g., *post* and *block.* (Calling out these two words, in contrast to the words *brick* and *block,* cannot be satisfied by bringing one and the same stone.) Hence some of the builder's pronouncements count as *challenges* to the assistant's: if the assistant says *brick* and the builder replies *beam,* then the assistant cannot simply go on. He must either 'correct' himself, or insist on his pronouncement, thus challenging the builder, perhaps by using the more specific name, *block.*

The last pronouncement rests on the fact that to call a stone *brick* is appropriate whenever it is appropriate to call a stone *block.* Hence claiming that something is a block may be considered as giving a rudimentary *reason* for this being a brick. In this way we have not only rudimentary incompatibilities (*block* × *slab, brick* × *post,* etc.), but also rudimentary inferences (*block* → *brick, beam* → *post,* etc.)

Now imagine that the number of kinds of blocks would be too big to have a separate name for each. There would be stones of different shapes, sizes, and colors. This would engender a different kind of structure (a 'compositional' one). Note that while previously each word could be directly related to the independent work that it was suited for, now the work in question would be performed by compounds of words (*big + blue + pillar*) and hence the role of each word would now have to be construed as the way it contributes to the work performed by the compounds into which it enters. (And this would amount to the rudiments of natural languages' word/sentence distinction.)

We may imagine many further elaborations, some of which were considered already by Wittgenstein himself (1953, §2):

> Let us now look at an expansion of language (2). Besides the four words 'block', 'pillar', etc., let it contain a series of words used as the shopkeeper in (1) used the numerals (it can be the series of letters of the alphabet); further, let there be two words, which may as well be 'there' and 'this' (because this roughly indicates their purpose), that are used in connexion with a pointing gesture; and finally a number of colour samples. A gives an order like: 'd – slab – there'. At the same time he shews the assistant a colour sample, and when he says 'there' he points to a place on the building site. From the stock of slabs B

takes one for each letter of the alphabet up to 'd', of the same colour as the sample, and brings them to the place indicated by A. – On other occasions A gives the order 'this – there'. At 'this' he points to a building stone. And so on.

An important outcome of such expansions of the language would be the 'opening' of the set of its expressions in the sense of introducing rules that would be recursively applicable and thus capable of producing ever longer expressions. At this point the expressions of the language cease to be presentable in terms of a list, they start to form merely a potential, infinite list.

Now let us imagine that the assistant and the builder want to discuss the ways they use their vocabulary, in particular the rule according to which everything they call *block*, they are also prepared to call *brick*. (This may happen, e.g., when a new delivery of stones arrives, containing a new sort of stone, which appears to invite the label *block*, but not really the label *brick*.) In order to do so, they must have a way of expressing this. This way would not have to be overtly metalinguistic (it would not have to involve names of their words or talk about employing the words), but what they would need, to begin with, would be something like *if…then…*: *If block, then brick*. And if the language in question already has the means to provide for giving and asking for reasons, the negotiation of this principle can begin.

Thus we can progress from Wittgenstein's example of a simple language game not instituting the kind of roles, and hence meanings, that the words of our everyday languages have, toward something closer to our natural languages with sentences expressing propositions and words expressing concepts. What happens along the way? (Somewhere near its beginning we may pass the toy language we introduced in Section 3.5.) The following list (though not claiming to be exhaustive nor fully systematic) gives some of the most important milestones:

- The praxis comes to involve a specific way of displaying expressions ('asserting'), such that displayed in this way they can be challenged and backed up;
- The stock of expressions of the language becomes unlimited in that the rules governing their formation become recursively applicable; only some of them ('sentences') come to be usable as assertions;
- The inferential structure of the language becomes so rich that backing up an assertion may lead to a complicated praxis of giving reasons, and also challenging may obtain a more complicated structure;

- The inferential structure comes to be made explicit by means of specific logical vocabulary.

5.4   The space of reasons and the game of giving and asking for reasons

The previous section gave us a hint of what it takes to enter the space of reasons. Let us now look at the space more closely. Does it have a peculiar topology? What makes it so sophisticated as to create room for the flourishing of human reason? And why are we using the metaphor of 'space' in the first place?

What we normally call *space* comprises an unlimited number of locations (what is crucial is not an infinity in some metaphysical sense, but merely vastness vis-à-vis our human perspective) arranged into a multidimensional (namely three-dimensional) 'array'. Space is also crucially characterized by our being situated *inside* it and able to move *within* it. Moreover, it is not only *us* who are inside space: space contains a vast number of 'objects' mutually interacting according to laws that natural scientists have been trying to pin down for centuries. (Sometimes it is claimed that it is preposterous to see space as something *over and above* the interactions of the objects, within which the interactions take place, as a *container* for them; that space is better seen as an aspect of the interactions. And, indeed, for an analogy with the space of reasons, this view of the physical space may be more fitting.) So which of these features does the space of reasons – literally or metaphorically – share?

Of course, not everything. We cannot be *in* the space of reasons in the very sense in which we can be in physical space. But we have already seen that it may be illuminating to look at systems of rules as something that constitutes an 'inner space', so that we can be 'inside' them. Likewise, in the case of the space of reasons we as if traverse the space by moving from reason to reason, during the game of giving and asking for reasons.

The basic elements of the space of reasons, then, are propositions, which are principally the kind of entities that can serve as reasons. It is them and the relationships between them that constitute the topology of the space. The basic relations that give the space its structure are the relations of *inference* and *incompatibility*. These two relations are essential from the viewpoint of the game of giving and asking for reasons: to *ask for* reasons for a claim means to challenge the claim (in a suitably broad sense of *challenge*), and challenging a claim consists in displaying a claim that is *incompatible* with it (again in a very broad sense). To *give* reasons is to display claims from which the given claim is correctly inferable (and which are, in the present context, more readily acceptable).

The two relations are not utterly independent; there are ways of reducing one to the other, though the views on in how far such reductions are unproblematic differ. Reducing inference to incompatibility may be carried out along the following lines:

B is (correctly) inferable from A iff whatever is incompatible with B is incompatible with A.

Conversely, the well-known way of reducing incompatibility to inference is:

B is incompatible with A iff everything is (correctly) inferable from A together with B.

Both these reductions crucially depend on the richness of the underlying language: if we toy with artificial languages, then, of course, it will be easy to produce 'languages' for which such reductions will seem inappropriate. But if we keep to natural languages, the possibility of finding anything that could serve as a counterexample is much less clear.

Hence it seems that from the viewpoint of natural language, it is *either* inference or incompatibility that may be taken as the relation that lays out the topology of the space of reasons. It is also remarkable that traditional logical operators, especially those that may be called 'inferentially native' (see Chapter 9), can be defined solely in terms of the inference relation. In particular, the names of such operators can be construed as marking certain features of the structure geared up by the relation. Thus negation of a given proposition can be seen as its *minimal incompatible* (i.e., the minimal proposition that is incompatible with it), the conjunction of two propositions as their *inferential supremus* (i.e., the minimal proposition that is inferable from the two of them together) etc.[5]

The Lorenzenian games we tackled in Section 5.2 may serve as (very idealized) examples of the (simplest) kind of games that we may be seen as playing with language, and which are responsible for the meanings of our (logical) words. To pass over to the game of giving and asking for reasons, which sustains the space of reasons, we must realize that these games are rather like what are called 'games' in tennis, i.e., each of them is only a small part of what we perceive as the truly significant game – the whole match consisting of several sets with each of them consisting of several games. (It is, however, worth noticing that the distinction between a part of a game and the whole game is often context-dependent: sometimes a single set or perhaps a single tennis game could constitute the whole match, while sometimes even a match could be a part of a bigger venture, such as, in the case of tennis, the Davis Cup.) And what is 'the whole match' to which the games envisaged in the previous section add up?

What happens if an assertor does not manage to defend his assertion against challenges? It depends on many circumstances, but in most cases the consequences are not substantial. However, repetitive losing in this kind of game would mean, in the long run, descending the ladder of trustworthiness to the point of being wholly excluded from the range of people whose assertions (and perhaps other activities too) are to be taken seriously (cf. Section 4.5). This indicates that people need to keep track of their peers' victories and defeats. How do we do it? Do we store some mental lists of people around us with red and black points?

The problem of 'scorekeeping in a language game' was probably first explicitly tackled by David Lewis (1979). Brandom's version of the story is based on the assumption that what we keep track of are not directly any points (or victories and defeats) of our fellow language-users, but rather their *commitments* and *entitlements*. If somebody asserts, say, that flat taxation is the way to prosperity, we ascribe them a commitment to justify this claim (and also a default entitlement to it), and we register the general entitlement to repeat this claim deferring its justification to the assertor (which may be actual, e.g., when the original assertor is an expert in the field). Subsequently, if somebody else claims that flat taxation is the way to impoverishment, we expect the original assertor to fulfill her commitment, and if she cannot, we retract her entitlement to it, provisionally granting it to the new assertor with the commitment to defend *his* claim.

Is it theoretically possible to produce a table explicitating the rules of the game of giving and asking for reasons similarly to how the table in Section 5.2 explicitates those of the Lorenzenian game? Not really. For a start, notice that the table for the Lorenzenian game does not tell us how to play any one game associated with any one sentence (with some trivial exceptions), it gives rules for reducing games associated with logically complex sentences to games associated with its parts. Thus it explains the working of logical vocabulary, which, we saw, merely helps make underlying rules explicit.

It is the underlying rules that are crucial and that are constitutive for the 'content' of the game of giving and asking for reasons. But the quantity of rules is immense and they are quite intricate and intertwined in various perplexing kinds of ways. In a sense this situation is the direct opposite to the simple, orderly, and perspicuous situation of the rules of logic. Hence, beneath the compact and tidy cover of the rules of logic there simmers a wild mélange of material rules.

This is not because natural language must be, by its nature, chaotic or underdeveloped. I suspect that the opposite is the truth: across the millennia of natural selection it must have become quite perfected, but perhaps not in the way we may tend to imagine. It accomplishes a maximal flexibility and versatility with a minimum of tools and methods, thus often assigning one and the same tool many very distinct functions, reusing byproducts and so forth.

Daniel Dennett (1996) points out that with respect to animal organisms, the design that is the most effective from the viewpoint of evolution need not be the neatest (at least, not for the standards of 'neatness' we usually employ):

> It is important to recognize...that the cheapest design may well not be the most efficient, or the smallest. It may often be cheaper for Mother Nature to throw in – or leave in – lots of extra, nonfunctioning stuff, simply because such stuff gets created by the replication-and-development process and cannot be removed without exorbitant cost. It is now known that many mutations insert a code that simply 'turns off' a gene without deleting it – a much cheaper move to make in genetic space....It costs almost nothing to keep the old code along for the ride, and it might come in handy some day. Circumstances in the world might change, for instance – making the old version better after all. Or the extra copy of the old version might someday get mutated into something of value. Such hard-won design should not be lightly discarded, since it would be hard to re-create from scratch. As is becoming ever more clear, evolution often avails itself of this tactic, reusing again and again the leftovers of earlier design processes.

There is no reason to think that things are too different with our languages, hence it seems that what we might expect to apply as a standard of orderliness to them would not render them very orderly. (In fact, the situation is not so totally different with respect to logic, if what we take to be logic is the logical vocabulary of a natural language, rather than its purified, regimented simulacrum such as that targeted by Lorenzen.)[6]

To sum up: since we humans recognize each other as potential bearers of commitments and entitlements, we continuously do deal with one another as players of various commitment/entitlement games (social practices), especially of the game of giving and asking for reasons. And this game is inextricably integrated with language, not only because it uses language as its crucial equipment, but because it is this very game that makes language into what it is by providing for its expressions to acquire their meanings.

5.5   The 'embodiment' of the game of giving and asking for reasons

Let us return to our analogy between language and chess and let us first summarize in which respects (the rules of) our language *are* like (the rules of) chess. The following table, listing some features of chess side by side with the corresponding features of language, is designed to illustrate especially:

- That a language is *constituted* by rules;
- That the rules have the character of *constraints* and that hence they do not *command* us how to speak;
- That meanings are utterly a matter of rules of language and hence of the normative attitudes which sustain the rules;
- That we need not have meanings *before* we set up the rules, but rather that setting up the rules *is* setting up meanings, and hence
- That the question whether it is the chicken of meaning or the egg of inferential rules that comes first is misguided.

(1) One can play chess *rightly* (or *wrongly*). But one can do so in two senses: not only in the sense of playing skillfully and beating one's opponents, but also in the more fundamental sense of accepting the rules. It is the latter sense that is constitutive to the very game of chess – it is the *rules* of chess which make it possible to play chess at all (hence to play chess wrongly in the second sense means not to play it at all; to play either rightly or wrongly in the first sense presupposes playing rightly in the second sense.)	(1) One can speak English *rightly* (or *wrongly*). But one can do so in two senses: not only in the sense of successfully achieving desired goals in the social environment of English speakers, but also in the more fundamental sense of accepting (crucial) rules of English. It is the latter sense that is constitutive to the very language of English: it is the *rules* of the language which make it possible to speak English at all (hence to speak English wrongly in the second sense means not to speak *English* at all; to speak English either rightly or wrongly in the first sense presupposes to speaking rightly in the second.)

Continued

(2) Rules of chess do not tell us how to move pieces in the sense of advising us what to do at any particular moment of the game (with the singular exception of a *forced* move, i.e., of the situation when there is merely one admissible move left). They tell us what *not* to do: what is a legitimate move and what is prohibited.

(3) It is the rules of chess that make a piece used to play the game into a *pawn*, a *bishop*, a *king* etc. It is not its makeup, but exclusively the role conferred on it by the rules according to which we treat it that provides the piece with its 'value'. It makes no sense to say that what we subject to rules are *already* pawns, bishops etc. – the pieces acquire the values *via* being subjected to the rules. As to accept a rule is to treat some moves as correct and some as incorrect, we can say that the rules, and consequently the values of the pieces, are a matter of the players' normative attitudes.

(4) When I say that I should move a chess piece thus and so because it is, say, a bishop, what I say is not that it must have been a bishop *before* it could be subjected to the relevant rules; rather I say that as the piece is governed by such-and-such rules, my move is a permissible one.

(2) Rules of a language do not tell us how to use words in the sense of advising us what to say at any particular moment. They tell us what *not* to say: what is a legitimate move and what is prohibited.

(3) It is the rules of language that make a kind of sound/inscription displayed by the speakers into *a name of a certain person, a conjunction connective,* or *a predicate expressing the concept of dog.* It is not the way it sounds, but exclusively the role conferred on it by the rules according to which we treat it that provides the sound/inscription with its meaning. It makes no sense to say that what we subject to rules are *already* meaningful words – the words acquire the meanings *via* being subjected to the rules. As to accept a rule is to treat some moves as correct and some as incorrect, we can say that the rules, and consequently the meanings of the words, are a matter of the relevant speakers' normative attitudes.

(4) When I say that I should use a sound/inscription thus and so because it is, say, a conjunction connective, what I say is not that it must have been a conjunction connective *before* it could be subjected to the relevant rules; rather I say that as the sound/inscription is governed by such-and-such rules, the use is a permissible one.

Continued

(5) The values of the pieces are exclusively a matter of the rules to which the pieces are subjected, and the rules are the matter of our treating some moves as right and others as wrong. Hence the value of a piece and our normative attitudes to the way it is treated are two sides of the same coin; it makes no sense to say that something is, say, a king independently of the attitudes: to be a king *is* to enjoy these attitudes.

(5) The meanings of the words are exclusively a matter of the rules to which the words are subjected, and the rules are the matter of our treating some moves as right and others as wrong. Hence the meaning of a word and our normative attitudes to the way it is treated are two sides of the same coin; – it makes no sense to say that something is, say, a conjunction connective independently of the attitudes: to be a conjunction connective *is* to enjoy these attitudes.

(6) It makes no sense to say 'What you can *check* is obviously a *king*, not a mere piece of wood, hence you cannot formulate rules of chess unless you have pieces that already *are* kings, pawns, bishops. ... ' The concepts of *check* and *king* are established in mutual interdependence.

(6) It makes no sense to say 'What you can *assert* is obviously a *meaningful sentence*, not a mere meaningless sound/inscription, hence you cannot establish rules of language unless you have expressions that already *are* meaningful.' The concepts of *assertion* and *meaningful sentence* are established in mutual interdependence.

However, we have also seen that in some important respects language is *not* like chess. Unlike chess, it must have at least some of its rules merely implicit in our practices rather than explicitly articulated. In the previous section we saw that the rules of language differ from those of chess by their complexity, intricacy, and their, at least prima facie, disorder. It has been pointed out, too, that language is unlike chess in that it is less disembodied (in this sense it is more similar to a sport like football than to a game like chess). There seems to be no counterpart of the empirical/nonempirical distinction in chess, and indeed chess seems to be 'self-contained' in the very sense in which language, due to its empirical dimension, is not. Let us now focus on this last point.

Notice, to start with, that we usually play chess with some equipment: two sets of pieces (usually little wooden statues) and the board. Hence each player has some equipment that belongs to him (the pieces) and then there is some shared equipment (the board). Notice also that given the rules for using the equipment, individual pieces assume specific roles. The role of a piece and the rules that govern its correct employment are simply two sides of the same coin, neither of them existing independently of the other.

However, we saw that what is peculiar to chess is that we do not really need the physical equipment; in principle it is possible to play chess without any material items. Other games, and especially sports, are not like this. Take, for instance, table tennis. Here we again have two players (possibly four), each of whom has his own piece of equipment (the bat), and there is the shared equipment (the table, net, and ball). However, in this case there is no way of making do without the equipment.

We should also realize that we need two varieties of rules. There are the rules proper, delimiting what the players are obliged and permitted to do, and there are also prescriptions for the equipment. Haugeland (1998) talks about *regulations* in the first case and about *standards* in the second; and we will respect with this terminology. (Thus the rules of football include prescriptions determining the parameters of the playground, the ball, etc.) Hence playing the game is not only a matter of accepting the regulations, but also finding equipment that complies with the standards.

Next, imagine a sport for not just two players or teams, but for a host of competitors, each trying to win. Take, for example, what cyclists call a *points race*. Again, there is the personal equipment (the bike) and the shared equipment (the track). But now a bunch of riders sprint for points at the end of each points lap. At the end of the race, the rider with the most points in total is the winner. Hence it is necessary to *keep score* with respect to each rider.

To move further in the direction of language, we must now leave the realm of existing sports and start to fantasize. Imagine, first, that we have both a host of contestants, as in a points race, and also structured personal equipment, as in chess. Imagine, moreover, that also the shared equipment is richly structured. There is a large assortment of items that a player may be confronted with, each item being governed by a complicated collection of standards and thus displaying a sophisticated kind of 'behavior'. (Imagine, for example, something like the balls of Potterian *quiddich* which are supposed to have their own intelligence; or imagine what in role-playing games like Dungeons & Dragons are called *non-player characters*.) Now imagine that the personal equipment of the players is not a set of persistent things (like the chess pieces), but rather some inexhaustible stock of various tokens that can be played at various stages of the game. Playing a token is a move that may alter the score of the player who played it as well of as some other players. The possibility of playing it may also in various complicated ways depend on the shared equipment: playing a certain kind of token may, for example, bring about a change of the score only under a certain constellation of the equipment.

Before continuing, let us pause and make a few notes. We should realize that playing a game is not (only) a matter of theoretical knowledge (of the rules), it is a *skill*. In fact, we may distinguish, following Haugeland again, two kinds of skills: one related directly to the rules, the other to the 'world' shaped by the rules. To be able to play a game, we must be able to display a certain practical mastery of the rules, we must be able to see which moves are correct and which violate the rules. Haugeland calls this kind of skill *constitutive*; we can also use our terminology and talk about normative attitudes. However, it is crucially important to realize that it is not necessarily so that we first learn the rules, in a theoretical way, and then go on to turn this theoretical knowledge into practical mastery. It may be that the practical mastery is the only thing that is there – then the rules exist exclusively via our normative attitudes and are, in this sense, implicit to our practices.

The other kind of skill that we need is connected with finding our way within the 'world of the game'. Playing chess, we not only *know that this piece of wood is a bishop*, but we *see it not as a piece of wood, but as a bishop*. In this sense the game means a truly new world opening up for us, a world whose topology and whose ways we must figure out to become real players.

Now it is important to realize that in the case of our language games, the whole world is our (potential) shared equipment. Just as when playing chess we are not moving pieces of wood, of which we know that they play the roles of rooks and bishops, but are playing directly with the rooks and bishops, so when playing our language games we are living among the things constituted by these games. We structure the world by means of concepts cast in the mold of the game of giving and asking for reasons into the shapes of parts of propositions. This is not to say that these things are 'imaginary' or 'unreal' – no more than rooks and bishops are unreal. It is to say, though, that they are what they are only in the context of our language games. And insofar as we are 'inside' the games, this is what they are *ultimately*.

Language extends far beyond the words in the sense that most of its rules are 'sportish' in that they involve extralinguistic equipment. Language cannot be contraposed to the world as a mapping toolkit providing for a disengaged drawing of maps. Our language games are, on the one hand, inextricable from the world, being, on the other hand, inextricable from the 'game' of our life – from the human way we act within our society and the rest of our environment.

Moreover, if we are to subscribe to the story of language as told by Brandom, interaction with the world is at its very *heart*. Though there cannot be any self-standing purely logical language (i.e., language with only logical vocabulary), there can be a self-standing purely *empirical* language. Logical vocabulary presupposes inferentially structured nonlogical sentences, but a language (protolanguage?) consisting of only empirical sentences can exist as a matter of principle without this explicitating superstructure.

In our previous chapter we invoked the concept of *practices*. I would now like to suggest that important kinds of practices are ongoing games like the embodied game of giving and asking for reasons, games that do not aim at a final victory and defeat, but rather merely yield a fluctuation of various kinds of statuses that are not separable from the game itself.[7] Practices are important because it is their complex structure that bears normativity: they involve not merely habitual courses of action, but courses the sidestepping of which invokes corrective behavior that is in its turn potentially susceptible to later, retroactively influential corrections. Hence practices institute 'tracks' of behavior a deviation from which counts as an error.

As we pointed out in the previous section, such practices need not be only abstract or linguistic (such as the Wittgensteinian continuation of number series, and such as chess); they may also essentially involve the extralinguistic world. As Rietveld (2008, p. 985) puts it, they may be 'situated' (while at the same time essentially normative):

> Given that normativity is constituted by the communal custom in which the individual's performance is embedded, mistakes by the skilled individual are possible. Thus, even though in unreflective action a performance is not undertaken for any explicit reasons, it can fail. It is thanks to this complex context that the skilled individual's unreflective performance, which typically is, in a sense, nothing but a 'blind' response to relevant affordances (namely the individual's being moved to respond by them), is normative nevertheless.

Hence we want to avoid seeing practices in the way Glüer and Wikforss (2009, p. 58) do:

> A practice, after all, is a regularity in behaviour (social or individual) and this notion cannot be employed to secure the distinction between

merely acting in accordance with a rule, acting in regular ways, and being guided by a rule.

Though a practice *can be seen* as a 'regularity in behavior', this does not yet mean that this concept cannot help us make the differences we claim: we must distinguish between the regularity of the very behavior regulated by the rules (e.g., drivers driving mostly on the right side of the road with respect to the corresponding rule of traffic) and regularities of a much more broader behavior centered around the basic regularity, i.e., in addition, regularities in the behavior of those who react to the behavior that is not regular in the above way, regularities in behavior of those who react to these reactions and so forth (e.g., the behavior of policemen who fine those who are not driving on the right side, newspapermen who criticize the policemen for being over- or under-reactive, etc.). Moreover, the behavioral patterns will display complicated feedback loops (corresponding to the fact that a rule is always 'in the making' and can wield a retroactive force as discussed in Section 4.6). This is what makes a practice *such a complicated* behavioral pattern (a motley of patterns?) that any attempt to capture it in the idiom of natural science (even from the 'outsider' perspective) appears foolhardy.

Moreover, we may be content with saying that a practice is a regularity of behavior if we are content with staying disengaged. But what we call *practices* are often such behavioral patterns with respect to which we do not intend, and sometimes even are not able, to stay disengaged. Though what we do when we express them in words may look like a description, what we are really doing involves, due to their essential 'openness', extrapolative proposals.

Rouse (2007, p. 49) characterizes the relationship between practices and normativity in the following illuminating way:

A normative conception of practices makes normativity irreducible but not inexplicable. There are at least three crucial aspects to its explication of normativity. First, the bounds of a practice are identified by the ways in which its constitutive performances bear on one another, rather than by any regularities of behavior or meaning that they encompass. One performance responds to another, for example, by correcting it, drawing inferences from it, translating it, rewarding or punishing its performer, trying to do the same thing in different circumstances, mimicking it, circumventing its effects, and so on. ... A second crucial feature of practices, normatively conceived, is that these patterns of interaction constitute something at issue and at stake in their outcome. ... Normative practice theories, however, take the issues and stakes in practices to be not merely subject to epistemic uncertainty, but perspectively variant or opentextured, and this amounts to a third crucial feature of their conception of practices.

Rouse also invokes the terms 'mutual accountability' and 'diffraction' for the way in which the components of the practices bear on one another, producing the normative effects. Practices involving normative attitudes, and thus instituting correctness, are indeed 'diffractive' – they are a matter of interaction among moves, counter-moves, counter-counter-moves, and so forth, such that counter-moves not only push themselves off the moves to which they react, but at the same time push these moves to make the whole system interdependent in all kinds of dimensions.

5.6   Meaning and truth

What, then, about the concept that is usually taken to be, besides the concept of meaning, another pillar of semantics, namely the concept of *truth*, which we have not tackled so far? We saw that the inferential structuring of our language is correlative to its ability of serving as a vehicle of the game of giving and asking for reasons. What is crucial about the rules of the game is that they state when it is *correct* to make an assertion. And though in the most straightforward sense in which I am *correct* in making an assertion is when I can justify it (i.e., when I can infer it from some agreed upon premises), there are other, related senses, e.g., the sense in which my assertion is correct if *there is* a justification (though I am not in its possession), and such senses yield our concept of truth. As Dummett (1991, pp. 166–167) puts it:

> What do we need the concept of truth for, and where do we get it from? Without doubt, the source of the concept lies in our general conception of the linguistic practice of assertion. It is fundamental to this practice that an assertion may be judged as correct or incorrect: it may be accepted as correct, or rejected as incorrect, by a hearer; the speaker may subsequently be compelled to withdraw it as incorrect, or the hearer to acknowledge it as correct. ... The root notion of truth is then that a sentence is true just in case, if uttered assertorically, it would have served to make a correct assertion.

It is usual to reduce the concept of inference to that of consequence (inference as a rule-based approximation, or a *criterial reconstruction*[8] of consequence), and the concept of consequence to the concept of truth (consequence as truth-preservation). The concept of truth then requires a substantial explanation; it holds the whole edifice of traditional semantics on its shoulders. (We will expand upon this in the second part of the book.)

Inferentialism, we saw, inverts this order of explanation, using as the very foundation the concept of inference (or that of reason, which is nothing else than a specific kind of inference taken backwards). We will see, in the second part of the book, that we can consider consequence as a 'loosely-criterial' inference: as what becomes of inference if we allow for rules of the kind of the infinitistic omega rule (which cannot be actually applied, of the potential application of which, we can, however, reason). As a result, the concept of truth becomes unloaded; no longer must it support the rest of the semantic scaffolding. This has led some inferentialists, notably Brandom, to 'light' theories of truth: Brandom's theory is a version of the deflationary theory of truth, namely the pro-sentential one. It does not take truth as a substantial property.

However, must the inferentialist give up the appealing idea that consequence, and hence also inference, is truth-preservation? I do not think so; the only view that she must relinquish is the reading of this relationship according to which the concepts of consequence and inference are reducible to that of truth. But there is, I think, no reason not to embrace the relationship read conversely: instead of saying that consequence is a relation of truth-preservation, we can say that truth is that property that is preserved by consequence, i.e., by our loosely-criterial inference. We may perceive the moves of the game of giving and asking for reason as a matter of handing down, by means of sentences, a specific stuff – *the truth*. (Just like in the tag game, where although the point is simply to touch another person rather than to give them anything, it is very natural to perceive it as the handing down of something, 'the tag'.)

5.7   Summary of Chapter 5

In this chapter we turned our attention to the fact that rules may come in bundles and that it is only bundles of rules that have many of the effects discussed in our previous chapters. In particular, the virtual spaces that, as we urged, are constituted by rules – especially the space of meaningfulness, constituted by the rules of our language – emerge only when a large number of rules appropriately interlock. We discussed how what we do with language can be seen as rule-governed games; we surveyed some proposals for how to account for our logical vocabulary in game-theoretical terms; and we indicated how this would have to be extended to cover also nonlogical vocabulary.

Then we turned to the systematic assessment of the comparison of language and chess (exploited by many theoreticians). We stated that this comparison can help us see language as a rule-governed enterprise in many ways, and especially help us forego the tendency to think that meanings must be extant before we can formulate the rules. We also pointed out certain essential differences between language and chess, seeing, in the end, that the case of language differs significantly from the case of chess. Briefly we tackled the concept of truth, concluding that within the inferentialist framework, it is secondary to the concept of inference.

6
Rules and Evolution

6.1 Rules and cooperation

The previous chapters were largely devoted to the concept of rule, especially inferential rule. One more aspect that might help us get a grip on the concept is an inquiry into how rules manage to come into being. And, indeed, evolutionary biologists are nowadays preoccupied with phenomena that seem intimately connected with rules, namely with the phenomena of cooperation and altruism. Why do people do things that seem to be beneficial for their peers rather than for themselves? Why do they bind themselves with rules that may sometimes divert them from the trajectory dictated to them by their apparent needs, the following of which is hammered into their genes by natural selection?

We have seen what it takes, from the viewpoint of behavioral patterns, to *follow a rule*. If we assume that evolution shapes individual organisms into a shape in which they follow the trajectory that is optimal from the viewpoint of their reproduction, then the existence of a rule presupposes, in the prototypical case, the occurrence of some systematic deviations (or seeming deviations) of members of a community from such trajectories, namely deviations that are beneficial to their peers and which are also more or less 'demanded' by the peers (i.e., they are rewarded, whereas avoiding them is sanctioned).

Why do such deviations persist? Is it not so that those who systematically do not follow trajectories that are optimal for them will be wiped out, in the course of evolution, by those who do? And if it is the sanctions and rewards that keep the deviations going, surely those who impose these sanctions and rewards must also be deviating from their optimal trajectories? The fact that rules exist and flourish seems to suggest that it is only a *seeming* deviation: if evolution works as we think it does, then there must be an explanation according to which the seeming loss of fitness effected by a rule is compensated by some gain. And we are all acquainted with many rules that are good at this: at various times in our lives we often find ourselves forced, by rules, to do things which cost us something, but which usually gain us some benefit in the end. So perhaps we see following rules as deviation from the trajectories maximizing our fitness only because we have not been able to see through their complicated import.

Things are, however, not so simple. To account for the *emergence* of rules from the viewpoint of evolution, every intermediary stage of the process of this emergence must be shown to be beneficial for the participants. And here we face obstacles very similar to those which crop up in the heavily discussed topic of the emergence of cooperation. No wonder; rules and cooperation are intimately connected: from what has been said so far it should be clear that any rule-following is a form of cooperation, and what we are going to argue for is that rule-following represents a form of cooperation that is crucial for human communities.

So how is cooperation possible, if helping anybody at my personal expense seems to reduce my fitness and hence not to be a form of behavior that should spread? Several answers to these questions have already been proposed. Once Dawkins (1989) had convinced his colleagues to replace *individual* in the center of the evolutionary picture with *gene*, the explication of altruism with respect to one's kin was forthcoming. Meanwhile, several biologists have tried to explain other versions of altruism as a matter of *tit-for-tat* (Trivers, 1971; Axelrod, 1984; 1986). We do good to our peers, they proposed, because we have reasons to believe that they will do good to us later, and that the final account will be profitable for us. Hence the idea is that altruism is a profit-making investment.

Now imagine two creatures (call them *hunters*) confronting each other over a killed animal, whose meat amounts to, say, six of some energetic units. Assume that each of the hunters may be disposed in either of two ways: to fight for the whole supply of meat, or to resign the fight. Altogether, then, there are four possible cases: if both go for a fight, each of them will, in the end, get his three units (assuming their physical dispositions are comparable and average out over multiple cases), but both will lose some energy through the fight, say two units. If only one of them is ready for a fight, whereas the other withdraws, the first will get the whole six units, but being unable to consume them all at once, he will have to save part of the meat for the future, making his final energetic gain less than six – hence, say, five – units (storing will cost some energy, and the storage itself may reduce the energetic value of the meat).

The withdrawing hunter, of course, will get nothing. If neither wants to fight, they may share the meat and each of them will get three units.

A	B	Fight	Resign (cooperate)
Fight		A: 1, B: 1	A: 5, B: 0
Resign (cooperate)		A: 0, B: 5	A: 3, B: 3

This suggests that, from the global viewpoint, sharing would be the most profitable strategy, for it maximizes the gross number of energetic units distributed among the members of the hunter community. The trouble is that from the viewpoint of an individual hunter, the situation looks different; indeed from his viewpoint the unambiguously most profitable strategy is fighting. If his peer wants to fight, fighting will secure him at least one unit (whereas withdrawal none); if his peer does not, then fighting will secure him five units (whereas not fighting would secure him only three). Expressed in terms of game theory (Maynard Smith, 1982), which models the situation just envisaged in terms of the so-called *Prisoner's Dilemma* (Poundstone, 1992), not fighting is what is called a *strongly dominated strategy*: whatever the opponent does, fighting turns out to be more profitable than not fighting.

Note that the above table may be well seen as characterizing general rule-following. The point is that, as we already noted, if a rule is to be effective, it must at least sometimes divert its adherent from the trajectory that would be optimal from the viewpoint of his personal fitness. Hence there is a cost, say a. The point of the rule is, however, that, in the simplest case, the cost brings about a benefit b for somebody else, such that $b>a$, and if the other also endorses the rule, then sooner or later the situation inverts, and both players end up with the gain of $b-a$. (If, however, only one of the players cooperates, he gets all of b, whereas his fellow player loses a.)

The above table can be seen as an instance of this general situation for $a = 2$ and $b = 5$. For assume that the rule is a *Share your spoils!*, and the possibilities are to either act in accordance with it and leave half of your meat to your fellow hunter, consequently gaining only three points, or to keep all the meat for yourself, thus gaining five points. If you are disposed to act in the former way, and your fellow hunter later reciprocates, each of you ends up with six points instead of the five you would have if both of you were disposed to act in the latter way.

Hence we may see the problem as consisting in the fact that a rule cannot be operative unless it is endorsed by many people. ('I would happily give a share of my meat to my comrade, if I knew that he would give me a share of his some time in the future, but how can I be sure?'[1]) From this point of view the ideas of *reciprocal altruism* and *tit for tat* can be accommodated only if we change the settings, in particular if we assume that the dispositions of the hunters do not concern strategies with respect to individual encounters, but rather to series of such encounters. (It seems that there is no reason to suppose that it could not be the entire series together that wields evolutionary pressure.) Also, of course, fighting and resigning are not the only available strategies – we could adopt *mixed* strategies such as 'start to cooperate, but go on cooperating only with those who reciprocate'. Some such strategies may be viable (see Lehmann and Keller, 2006, for an overview).

Besides these, there are other dispositions that may foster cooperation, i.e., make the member of the community stick to cooperating rather than fighting. One of them is the disposition toward so-called (*altruistic*) *punishment* ('chastise those who are not willing to cooperate', Fehr and Gächter, 2002). Many theoreticians argue that starting on the journey to a stable social order as we know it from our communities requires more than becoming cooperative or altruistic (a community of cooperators is vulnerable to an invasion of 'parasites' who want to profit from cooperation without contributing anything themselves, as individuals with such devious, parasitic dispositions are always bound to appear, as a result of mutations). What is needed, in addition to cooperation, is penalizing those who are not willing to cooperate. Moreover, it seems that there might be a need for a third level of behavior: not only to be altruistic oneself, and to make others be altruistic too, but also to make others make others be altruistic ('chastise those who are not willing to chastise those who are not willing to cooperate', Heckathorn, 1989). Besides punishment, another significant factor may be selectiveness with respect to cooperative partners ('not only do not cooperate with those who do not reciprocate, but try to completely avoid them'). This creates special 'social networks' where cooperation may flourish (Woodcock and Heath, 2002).

6.2 Why rules?

These evolutionary stories are instructive and important, and we will return to them shortly. But at this point I want to suggest a change in visual angle. My conviction is that connecting the general idea of a norm or a rule too closely with the ideas of cooperation and altruism may be misleading, it may obscure another important role of rules. If we take a look at these matters from a less usual viewpoint we may see an important aspect of the phenomenon of rules which is currently eluding us.

Let us notice that what the evolutionary stories explain are especially 'heavyweight' rules, rules that have to do *directly* with our survival and the violation of which may cost us, if not directly our lives, then at least something else that truly matters to us (these are the rules of the kind of the *moral* ones in the narrow sense, from *You shall share your spoils!* to the legendary *Thou shalt not kill!*). But what about the rules of, say, football? This question may seem preposterous. Are not rules of football something utterly different from moral norms? It does not seem to be difficult to explain the existence of games and sports from the evolutionary perspective (a training for the struggle for survival ...), but the emergence of games seems minor to the problem of the emergence of altruism!

However, the question is not why we have games, but why we have games *governed by rules*. (After all, children are happy playing without using any true rules, or at most only rudimentary ones.) And what I want to suggest is that the difference between the rules of football and the rules of morals is not so grave that we could not try to see all these varieties of rules as species of a single kind. I think that asking the general question about why we have this very kind of institution might bring about the desirable stimulating change of visual angle. This suggestion is backed by the conviction that, though clearly there are many deep differences between morals and football (between, to put it in the form of an aphorism, *Thou shalt not kill!* and *You shall not touch the ball with your hands!*), there are also many important features that both these enterprises share.

So what essentially differentiates the rules of morals from those of football? There seem to be at least two fundamental differences: first, moral rules are incomparably *more important*, and, second, whereas moral rules seem to be *categorical* (applicable unconditionally, i.e., in force always and for everybody), football rules are *hypothetical* (applicable only conditionally, i.e., in force only, e.g., for those who choose to pursue some goal). As for the first difference, it seems indisputable that whereas the rules of morals lie in the very foundations of human sociality, the rules of games or sports concern something more parochial and dispensable. But though the difference is obvious, it is far less obvious that it cannot be construed as one of *degree*, rather than of *kind*. (Some of the rules that we might classify as moral surely hold less importance for our present society than those of football – deciding whether something was a violation of a rule of football: for example, may sometimes mean incredible sums of money changing hands.)

As for the second difference, we have tackled it already in Section 4.5. Again, it seems clear that whereas the moral rules are binding for everybody, the rules of football apply only to those who elect to be part of the game. But this difference is perhaps even less resolute than the previous one. In fact, just as the rules of football delimit what it is to be a football player, the rules of morals delimit what it is to be a human being. We do not apply them to individuals of other species: a tiger killing another tiger is not considered as violating any moral rule. Moreover, and this is important, they need not be applicable even to all humans: if a group of biological humans were to live totally amorally (without in any way interfering with us), our decision might be simply not to consider them true members of the 'human race' and leave them alone. This indicates that the term *human* related to the principles of morals may not be a biological one, but one *constituted* by the principles of morals. Hence it would seem that it is not too far-fetched to say that just as the rules of football delimit the arena of football, so the rules of morals delimit the arena of humanity.

Once we see the differences between the various kinds of rules as not totally alienating, we can see the common core. Rules regulate human conduct; they are applicable only to creatures that we hold to have a free will (which, from the viewpoint of evolution, may only refer to the vastness of behavioral patterns available to these creatures). Something is a rule only insofar as those governed by it are not incapable of doing otherwise than prescribed by it. Rules make people behave in certain ways, enforce behavioral patterns.

But to understand the consequences of enforcing behavioral patterns by rules, let us consider how else this would be possible. A behavioral pattern can be wired into a human brain (or, for that matter, into the brain of another animal) by natural selection. But this, of course, is not the only way for such a pattern to come into being. A person may get conditioned by being rewarded for behaving in accordance with the pattern and penalized when not. Why would the person's peers do this rewarding and penalizing? Perhaps *they* have this 'normative' behavior wired in their brains by natural selection? (Remember the concept of altruistic punishment.)

But this seems strange. Why would evolution enforce the pattern in such a detoured manner, producing its 'enforcers' forcing it upon 'enforcees' instead of making the enforcees display it right away? And would this kind of enforcement not lead to a selective advantage for those with an inborn adherence to the pattern, thus wiping out the others and soon enforcing the pattern directly after all?

Well, imagine that what the enforcers of the patterns would be capable of doing would be not only to make the enforcees display it, but also to make them make others display it; hence not only to become adherents of the pattern, but also its enforcers. If this were possible, the pattern would become capable of a purely 'cultural' promulgation, and would need no wired-in support. In this way the promulgation of behavioral patterns standardly effected by evolution would bear another level of such promulgation, piggybacking on it but going its own way.

The idea that at some stage the standard genetic replication bears a higher-level, 'cultural' descendant (which, though piggybacking on it, may assume a pace and a trajectory largely independent of those of its carrier) is surely not a new one. In Dawkins's (ibid.) path-breaking book about evolution, it received a suggestive shape centering around the concept of *meme*, and gave rise to the proposal that memes, the cultural analogues of genes, are replicated by imitation, fighting for survival in their abstract milieu just as genes fight for their survival in their concrete one. But Dawkins told us very little about memes and the mechanism of their spreading; in fact the only mechanism he talked about was *imitation*.

However, it would seem that what makes us humans unique, what makes our antics, in contrast to those of other species, warrant the specific name of *culture*, is precisely that we are able to go *beyond* imitation; rather than *copy* ideas (memes) of our peers, we engage in highly complicated interactions in the course of which the 'memes' get upgraded. Dawkins tries to account for this in terms of *imperfections* in the way we copy memes: people, according to him, often fail to entirely imitate one another, imitating only imperfectly. (Thus, Dawkins, for example, claims to replicate, in his book, some memes of other authors, but to replicate them imperfectly, by which he means that he does not merely repeat them, but elaborates on them and advances them). But this sounds rather odd: *imperfection* is a very inadequate word to characterize the difference between mere imitation and the way of upgrading that is really going on.

Moreover, it is problematic to see the upgrading as the matter of an individual. Upgrading ideas is usually teamwork, and ever more so. This is not to say that to get upgraded an idea must change hands more than once, but it is to say that memes are essentially distributed. They do not exist via individual humans, but via networks of human interaction within human societies.

6.3   Sellars on rules and pattern-governed behavior

Sellars (1954) realized that our language games provide for an example of an activity that is neither *merely conforming to rules* ('doing *A* in *C*, *A'* in *C'* etc. where these doings "just happen" to contribute to the realization of a complex pattern'), nor fully fledged *obeying of rules* ('doing *A* in *C*, *A'* in *C'* etc., with the intention of fulfilling the demands of an envisaged system of rules'). In the first case, language games would fall into the same category as any regular happenings, such as things falling down in conformity with the law of gravity or planets circling the sun in their wholly regular manner, which seems to be simply unacceptable. Meanwhile, in the second case, assuming that any linguistic action presupposes the comprehension of some explicit rule would lead us to the vicious circle discussed in previous chapters, for we would have to comprehend the corresponding rule *correctly*, and hence would need to follow the appropriate rule of interpretation.

In this way we return to a general version of the problem of steering clear of both the Scylla of regularism and Charybdis of regulism, which we discussed in the context of rules of language in Section 4.1. On the general level, Sellars envisaged a middle way between the two extremes; he urged that in between the rule-conforming and the rule-obeying behavior there is another important kind of behavior, which he calls 'pattern-governed'. This kind of behavior is unlike the merely rule-conforming one, for there is a sense in which we can say that it is done 'because of the system', but on the other hand it is also unlike the rule-obeying behavior, for it does not involve an explicit comprehension of the system. Sellars (ibid., pp. 207–208) gives two examples of such behavior, i.e., of behavior that is done because of a system, but not because of the comprehension of the system, and both concern evolution.

The first example runs as follows:

> Interpreting the phenomena of evolution, it is quite proper to say that the sequence of species living in the various environments on the earth's surface took the form it did because this sequence maintained and improved a biological rapport between species and environment. It is quite clear, however, that saying this does not commit us to the idea that some mind or other envisaged this biological

rapport and intended its realization. It is equally clear that to deny that the steps in the process were interrelated to maintain and improve a biological rapport, is not to commit oneself to the rejection of the idea that these steps occurred because of the system of biological relations which they made possible. It would be improper to say that the steps 'just happened' to fit into a broad scheme of continuous adaptation to the environment. Given the occurrence of mutations and the facts of heredity, we can translate the statement that evolutionary phenomena occur because of the biological rapport they make possible – a statement which appears to attribute a causal force to an abstraction, and consequently tempts us to introduce a mind or minds to envisage the abstraction and be the vehicle of its causality – into a statement concerning the consequences to particular organisms and hence to their hereditary lines, of standing or not standing in relations of these kinds to their environments.

The second example follows:

> What would it mean to say of a bee returning from a clover field that its turnings and wigglings occur *because* they are part of a complex dance? Would this commit us to the idea that the bee *envisages* the dance and acts as it does by virtue of intending to realize the dance? If we reject this idea, must we refuse to say that the dance pattern as a whole is involved in the occurrence of each wiggle and turn? Clearly not. It is open to us to give an evolutionary account of the phenomena of the dance, and hence to interpret the statement that this wiggle occurred because of the complex dance to which it belongs – which appears, as before, to attribute causal force to an abstraction, and hence tempts us to draw upon the mentalistic language of intention and purpose – in terms of the survival value to groups of bees of these forms of behavior. In this interpretation, the dance pattern comes in not as an abstraction, but as exemplified by the behavior of particular bees.

Finally, Sellars gives us direct instructions how to apply these evolutionary examples to 'the phenomena of learning':

> Indeed, it might be interesting to use evolutionary theory as a model, by regarding a single organism as a series of organisms of shorter temporal span, each inheriting disposition to behave from its predecessor, with new behavioral tendencies playing the role of mutations, and the 'law of effect' the role of natural selection.

This instruction, as it stands, may be puzzling, for what is essential for selection is the competition among an abundance of alternatives, whereas Sellars speaks merely about a succession of organism-stages, but I think it is not difficult to see what Sellars has in mind. Obviously, what he means by 'regarding a single organism as a series of organisms' is seeing an organism as a trajectory over an often branching tree of possibilities concerning behavioral patterns. At each point, only one kind of pattern, the one most appropriate to the pressures of the environment, survives and then gets us to the further branching point with further possibilities of its further development.

What is going on, then, is the selection of certain behavioral patterns from an offer of many possible alternatives, a selection that, in the end, allows us to say that the organism makes something because of the pattern, but not because of its comprehension of the pattern. How does this selection proceed? Of course, by the coercion of the teachers, but this coercion is the result of Sellars's (1969) dialectics of *ought-to-do*'s and *ought-to-be*'s we already discussed (in Section 4.2). *Ought-to-do*'s are simply commands, prescriptions that an agent is to do so and so. To comprehend them, the agent has to possess relevant concepts, concepts that make up the *ought-to-do*'s. They may be thought of as imperatives. *Ought-to-be*'s, in contrast to these, are not construable as commands, as they are not explicitly directed at an agent. Rather, they mark a state as desirable. They *may* lead to actions, because they bear *ought-to-do*'s via a specific kind of generic 'practical syllogism': *If something ought to be, and doing A is likely to bring it into being, then do A!* Again, one must comprehend the relevant concepts to use the *ought-to-be* to carry out this syllogism.

But aside from being an *agent* following *ought-to-do*'s and endorsing *ought-to-be*'s, a person may also be a *subject* of an *ought-to-be*. And, according to Sellars, there is a grave difference between *X should do A*, which requires *X* to be an agent able to understand what it takes to do *A*, and *X should be in state φ*, which does not involve any such requirement; in the latter case *X* may be any kind of thing. The latter is rather a 'free-floating' norm which is up for grabs for *any* agent and comprehender (including, possibly, *X* herself). And Sellars's (ibid., p. 512) claim is that language learning is moving from the position of a subject of certain *ought-to-be*'s to the position of their endorser:

> [T]he members of a linguistic community are *first* language *learners* and only potentially 'people', but *subsequently* language *teachers*, possessed of the rich conceptual framework this implies. They start

out by being the *subject-matter* subjects of the ought-to-be's and graduate to the status of agent subjects of the ought-to-do's. Linguistic ought-to-be's are translated into *uniformities* by training.

This indicates that if teachers of a pupil X accomplish what *ought to be* according to the prescription *One should be in a state φ*, then they cause, in the long run, not only X being in the required state φ (via following the commands of the form *Do so as to make X be in state φ!*, which they derive from *X should be in state φ*, which is in turn derived from the original *One should be in state φ*). Moreover, they cause also X's comprehension of the relevant *ought-to-be* (and his consequent deriving commands of the form *Ddo so as to make Y be in state φ!*). In short, when educating humans (or adepts of humanity), forcing behavioral patterns results not only in the patterns' coming into being, but also in the patterns being endorsed as *ought-to-be*'s.

How can this happen? Well, we may conjecture that a human agent being forced into a preconceived pattern inevitably comes to reflect and represent the pattern, and comes to represent it as something that is desirable. Perhaps this can be seen as the biological correlate of humans being 'normative beings': we tend to understand a certain kind of coercion as a manifestation of an *ought-to-be*. This is what brings into being the evolutionary mechanism envisaged above: the enforcement that makes the enforcees not only become adherents of the pattern enforced, but also its enforcers.

This appears to be precisely what makes up, from the viewpoint of the behavioral patterns, a *rule*: a general desideratum concerning members of a community, the implementation of which involves also implementation of its desirability. In other words, certain ways of forcing you to do A, rather than B, in certain circumstances, make you not only do A in the circumstances, but also construe A, and not B, as being *proper* in those circumstances, the consequence of which is that you will force others to do A, rather than B, in the given circumstances. It is in this way that the rule comes to perpetuate.

If we now return to the game-theoretical models of cooperation, we can see that it is precisely this aspect of rules that makes for the factors diagnosed as crucial for the stabilization of cooperation, such as altruistic punishment. Once I take a state as desirable, not only do I behave so as to bring about and sustain the state, but I also try to make others bring it about and sustain it.

Hence rules institute the very kind of circle that, as we indicated above, is *reproductive* in the sense that it provides for a kind of 'evolution in evolution' – for the 'cultural' spreading of 'software' behavioral patterns piggybacking on the 'natural' spreading of the 'hardware' ones. The relevant patterns are forced upon us not (directly) by natural selection, but by the ongoing demands of our peers. A *rule* is a lever necessary for putting to work the exclusively human kind of forming and maintaining of patterns of behavior; it is 'an embodied generalization which to speak loosely but suggestively, tends to make itself true' (Sellars, 1949, p. 299).

6.4   Integrative vs. standalone rules

Wittgenstein (1969a, pp. 184–185) pointed out the distinction between two kinds of rules:

> Why don't I call cookery rules arbitrary, and why am I tempted to call the rules of grammar arbitrary? Because I think of the concept 'cookery' as defined by the end of cookery, and I don't think of the concept 'language' as defined by the end of language. You cook badly if you are guided in your cooking by rules other than the right ones; but if you follow other rules than those of chess you are playing another game; and if you follow grammatical rules other than such and such ones, that does not mean you say something wrong, no, you are speaking of something else.

Rules of cooking – as well as many other rules of the same kind[2] – are determined by the end of cooking: to cook correctly simply means to prepare various kinds of edible and tasty meals. On the other hand, the rules of chess are not determined by the end of chess. In comparison to the previous ones they give us a dimension of freedom; there is nothing that would force us to accept a rule that bishops move diagonally analogously to how we are forced to accept the rule that meals should not contain too much salt!

Does it mean that it is the rules of Wittgenstein's latter kind where human freedom and human spontaneity come into the open? As a matter of fact I think it does, but we should be careful not to misconstrue the situation. Does the arbitrariness of the rules of chess, or of language, mean that chess or language have no purpose? Does it mean, for example, they have no evolutionary explanation?

I do not think this is the case. However, I do think that evolutionary explanations for either chess or language must be explanations of the whole enterprises, not of the individual rules. Though any individual rule is arbitrary, what they make up together is no longer such. The arbitrariness derives from the fact that there may be many ways to do justice to the purpose of the whole thing; as the plentitude of natural languages testifies, there are many equally good ways to accomplish what English or German or Turkish accomplish in their ways.

This institutes a crucial holism characteristic for these kinds of rules. We have already encountered what could be called an 'interpersonal holism': 'a rule cannot be operative unless it is endorsed by many people'. (This kind of holism was responsible for the clash of the collective perspective, from which the rules of cooperation were unambiguously profitable, and the individual one, from which one always depends on the goodwill of others.) Here there is an additional dimension of holism, a kind of 'internormative holism': 'a rule cannot be operative unless it is endorsed together with many other rules'. Let us call the rules displaying this additional holistic dimension *integrative*.

This perspective, I believe, may throw some new light on the distinction between Brandom's theory of normativity and those theories that try to explicitly account for normativity in terms of evolution, such as Millikan's (2004) *teleosemantics*. Millikan insists that any rule worth its name is a matter of 'natural purpose', of 'what a biological or psychological or social form has been selected for doing, through natural selection' (Millikan, 2005, p. 65). Dennett (2008), who appears basically to share this attitude with Millikan, duly points out that Brandom, in contrast to this, sees error not as a case of 'faulty design', but rather of 'social transgression' (Dennett adds: 'Roughly, it is the difference between being stupid and being naughty.') Does this mean that Brandom would rather see the norms as coming from elsewhere than as emerging from a natural development?

I do not think so (though I can understand Dennett's frustration by Brandom's total ignoring of questions concerning the source of the norms). I think that what should reconcile the views of Brandom and Dennett might be the admission, on Brandom's part, that language, as well as other integrated systems of norms, does have an evolutionary purpose, and the recognition, on the part of Dennett, that such systems have a purpose as *wholes*, so that there is a sense in which individual norms are arbitrary: the holistic nature of the whole system enables it to be constituted in different ways. (This would converge to the thesis that some errors do amount to 'being naughty' rather than to 'being stupid', but we can always say why it would be stupid not to chastise people 'being naughty' in this way.)

6.5 Virtual spaces again

We have seen that from the viewpoint of evolution, it is the 'heavy-weight' rules, especially rules of morals, that are crucial. Other rules, like the rules of football, can then perhaps be seen as their 'parochial simulacra' (football as 'morals of the playground'); we simply remove some weight of the moral rules and gain 'lightweight' rules that do not trouble us unless we are bored enough to want to play. And rules of language, though surely not so easily evitable as those of football (we cannot help playing our language games), belong with the lightweight ones; it would be hard to lose one's head or property for not respecting the rules of English.

In other words, the usual way of thinking about rules and evolution is that at some point of evolution, 'altruism' or 'cooperation' or 'collective action' became profitable and the emergence of rules is due to the fact that rules are somehow able to implement just this. But we have already suggested that what distinguishes the rules of morals from those of football may be less important than what these two kinds of rules share. Perhaps rules and altruism are not so intimately connected as we tend to think; perhaps what is crucial is not that rules allow us to cooperate and make reciprocal altruistic investments, perhaps the truly crucial thing rules bring us is something else.

Hence my suggestion, in the form of an aphorism, is that in the sense under discussion, football is no less basic than morals. Perhaps, that is to say, lightweight rules are not secondary to the heavyweight, moral ones. And as among the things that are driven by the lightweight rules we find language, the emergence of such rules would mean not only the possibility of playing prehistoric football, but also the possibility of talking. And this is not something that is in itself lightweight, even from the viewpoint of evolution.

But if cooperation is not the most basic achievement rules are involved in, what is? We have already given part of the answer: rules are the material from which we humans build our niches and which thus become our modus vivendi. Our ability of turning raising behavioral patterns into something that ought to be is also the 'metapattern' that underlies the cultural spreading of behavioral patterns. It provides for patterns that can be passed down not only as such, but including the comprehension of their desirability, which causes them to be perpetuated. Let us now complete the answer.

Success in evolution is a matter of fitness *with respect to an environment*. (It is trivial that being fit with respect to one kind of environment may well be being unfit with respect to a different one.) Now, once our predecessors started to form communities, part of the relevant environment came to be constituted by their peers. (This led to the result that fitness may be a matter of certain equilibria rather than simply of an optimization of features). Moreover, when the communities started to function as what can be called societies (i.e., when rules started to play a crucial role), the tangible barriers of nature that channel evolution became increasingly replaced by artificial ones. We, twenty-first-century Westerners, evolve due to pressures that are often not directly a matter of the availability of natural resources or of fighting for survival with our own hands; the pressures that shape us now have to do with social standards and our abilities to live up to the needs of our society.

And what I want to stress is that it is rules that have led us to the establishment of 'virtual worlds': the 'inner spaces' we discussed above, especially the space of meaningfulness aka the space of reasons. They are virtual not in the sense of being unreal, but in the sense of owing their existence to the attitudes of people, namely to our normative attitudes that sustain the integrative rules necessary to underpin such virtual edifices. In this way, rules provide for a basic alteration of the human niche and consequently of its evolution-fueling features. And it is in this way, too, that rules provide for an acceleration of evolution, for they rob genetic replication of its exclusive right to promulgate behavioral patterns. Now we see the mechanism behind it in full plasticity: rules provide for evolution's self-adjusting of the barriers against which the selection that fuels it takes place.

Consider the development of computers. At first the development ('evolution') was a matter of the improvements of hardware. But once there appeared the idea of a multipurpose hardware – a hardware that is not devoted to one preconceived task, but is rather versatile and can be adapted, via software, to cope with various kinds of tasks – the situation changed radically. It is not that the evolution of hardware has stopped, but that it is no longer guided directly by the tasks the computers are to cope with (the 'environment'); rather it is guided by the task to support, as efficiently as possible, the kind of software that is able to cope with the more specific tasks. And the 'front-end' layer of evolution is that of software; it is software that, though not able to exist without the hardware, faces the environment directly.

The metaphor of hardware and software is well known from the philosophy of mind; there it is usually the brain that is compared to the hardware and mind is thought of as the software (see, e.g., Block, 1995). But here I am employing it in a different way (of course not claiming originality even for this metaphor): cultural evolution as software running on the hardware of the natural one. I think that this metaphor is much more realistic than that of Dawkins memes born by the stream of proceedings driven by genes.

What is the key idea, then, is that we humans tend to move increasingly into the 'virtual' spaces from the 'natural' one. It is not that we would be free to devise the 'virtual' spaces deliberately. One thing that prevents us from doing so is that the 'virtual' worlds cannot escape some embodiment in the sense of 'supervening' on the natural, physical space and having to fully respect all its possibilities and limitations. Another thing is that even the constitution of the 'virtual' worlds within these limits is not a matter of human will, but rather is 'led by an invisible hand'.

6.6   Evolution and language

What have evolutionary theorists to say about the development of discursive practices? An interesting hypothesis was put forward by Krebs and Dawkins (1984), who conjectured that language, as we know it, came into being as 'conspirational whispering'. Signals, which, according to Dawkins and Krebs, originally evolved from the tendencies of organisms to predict other organisms' behavior and from the countertendencies of organisms to exploit the fact that they are being predicted for the purposes of manipulation of other organisms, may further develop in two opposing directions. In cases where such manipulation harms the manipulated organism, the signals tend to require an increasing energetic investment till they become so costly that they fade away, whereas in cases when they are useful even for the manipulated, the energy invested may continually decrease and the manipulative behavior reduces to mere 'symbols'. What makes the whole difference is the distinction between the 'competitive' and the 'cooperative' environment.

Hence cooperation, again. However, now the relation between a rule and cooperation is not so straightforward as in the cases we talked about in connection with the Prisoner's Dilemma cases. Now we do not see following a rule as directly one side of the coin the other side of which is cooperation; we rather see them as establishing a 'virtual world' which provides for 'virtual' – or symbolic – signaling. As Knight (2008) puts it, whereas 'each animal can make a difference only physically, only with its body – with signals inseparable from the body', 'a human linguistic utterance – a "speech act" – is an intervention in a different kind of reality. … A speech act, like a move in a game of "let's pretend", is internal to reality of this kind'.[3]

On the face of it, the resulting claim merely repeats the conclusion we reached earlier in the book, a conclusion that might sound almost trivial: just as the rules of chess allow us to make pieces of wood into *bishops*, *rooks*, and *queens* and play chess, so the rules of language allow us to make various kinds of shrieks into contentful expressions and play our language games. But by now we have already assumed a vantage point from which we can clearly see that under this seeming triviality there looms the fantastically complex work of rules: they are erected as barriers we bounce off as we bounce off the limits of our physical worlds (spelled out by our laws of nature); they interlock in multifaceted ways to open up virtual spaces where we can wield our freedom; they let us pass the rules and hence the spaces from generation to generation, so that they become not merely frail and transient, but rather solid and enduring.

Consider a sound that members of a (proto-) human community tend to emit in a situation of danger. It is clear that this does not yet mean that the sound *means danger* in a similar sense in which our current English word does. And we know what, from the inferentialist viewpoint, makes the difference. Our word *danger* is embedded in a hugely complex web of inferential relationships. (We know that *Danger!* is inferable from *A furious tiger is approaching* but not from *A snail is crossing our path*, that *We can safely rest* is not compatible with it, that whoever claims it should be able to put forward something from which it is inferable and which can be considered as a reason for the claim, etc.) Moreover, we know that the tendency or disposition to emit a sound in a situation is not enough to contribute to the meaningfulness of the sound in our sense; there must be a *rule*. How can such a rule of 'inference', and indeed the rules of inference in general, come into being?

Once there is a tendency to associate a sound with a situation and the association serves some useful purpose (and, of course, crying *Danger!* in dangerous situations *is* useful), the association may come to be taken, by members of the community in question, as *proper*, as something that *ought to be*. This is to say that the members may start trying to avert one another from emitting the sound in inappropriate situations (and at least in some cases from not emitting it in appropriate ones). Thereby the link ceases to be a matter of a mere association, of tendencies or dispositions, and starts to be that of a *propriety*; it acquires a normative character.

The existence of a propriety of this kind may also be addressed in terms of the concept of *incompatibility*: a sound is treated as *incompatible* with a situation iff it is not correct to emit it in the situation. Now once the number of sounds entering such normative relationships with situations multiplies, there appear also incompatibilities between individual sounds (i.e., between the acts of emitting them). Imagine, for example, that there is also a sound tied to the absence of a danger; emitting it, then, would be clearly incompatible with emitting the danger-indicating one, because the respective situations to which they are tied cannot co-occur. Moreover, some sounds may be appropriate whenever some other sounds are, without this being also vice versa, laying the foundations of inferential articulation. (Imagine, for example, the relationship between a sound related to an occurrence of a tiger and that related to danger.)

But here it is crucial to distinguish between possible senses of *incompatibility*. We can perhaps say that two situations are incompatible, in the sense that they cannot co-occur. Thus we can say that if it is day, it cannot be (at the same time and the same place) night, or we can say that a box being empty is incompatible with the box containing a beetle. These are claims about the causal order of the world; they are constituents of Sellars's *scientific image* of the world.

The sense of *incompatibility* that is more important for us is the normative one: the claim that carrying out an action renders carrying another one incorrect or improper. Claiming that it is day is, in this sense, incompatible with claiming, at the same time, that it is night; claiming that a box is empty is incompatible with claiming that the box contains a beetle. This is not a matter of causal impossibility: I *can* carry out both the incompatible actions; the point is not that this would be impossible, but rather that it is improper – that I *should not* do it. Hence *causal* incompatibility (which amounts simply to the physical impossibility of co-occurrence) may induce normative incompatibility (which amounts to two actions contradicting each other, where we may further distinguish linguistic and extralinguistic actions).[4]

There are many proposals with respect to what makes us, humans, special: *soul*, *mind*, *language*, *culture*, *reason*, and so on. I have indicated that we may characterize man as a normative being. Not that this proposal by itself would be original; I have, however, tried to show that if we accept the analyses of the concept of *rule* put forward by Sellars, we can embed this characterization into the evolutionary stories of how we humans have become what we are. I have tried to indicate that the crucial break which enabled man to live not only within the realm of nature, conforming to its laws, but also to enter the realm of freedom, where one can obey rules (while being free to *dis*obey them), has to do with the emergence of a behavioral 'meta-pattern', amounting to what

Sellars calls an *ought-to-be* and making people comprehend and endorse patterns that they are taught.

Thus the story about language I have been putting forward throughout this first part of this book finally becomes integrated into a more general story about the role of rules within human life. As Sellars (1949, p. 298) put it: 'When God created Adam, he whispered in his ear "In all contexts of action you will recognize rules, if only the rule to grope for rules to recognize. When you cease to recognize rules, you will walk on four feet."' It is rules that make for a great deal of the environment in which we humans live our lives; they made it possible for us to develop our languages, to become rational in that we formed the languages into the vehicles of giving and asking for reasons, and to become social. Man is indeed a normative being.

6.7 Summary of Chapter 6

In this chapter we have considered the phenomenon of rules in the context of evolution. We conjectured that the emergence of rules is closely connected with the emergence of cooperation, and that rule-based cooperation is the form of cooperation that minimizes vulnerability to free-riding, thus contributing to its being a relatively stable evolutionary strategy. Moreover, we conjectured that rules introduce an unprecedented evolutionary mechanism, namely that they provide for the possibility of a cultural (non-genetic) spreading of behavioral patterns, thus essentially restructuring the dynamics of evolutionary trajectories.

We also conjectured that from this viewpoint it is the emergence of the very ability to follow rules that marks an essential break within human history. This, we argued, is connected to what we have earlier envisaged as the ability of certain systems of rules to open new 'virtual spaces', social arenas where brand-new kinds of actions become possible. We argued that the emergence of language can be seen as the opening up of a 'space of meaningfulness', which is inaugurated when we converge upon the rules that lay the foundations of our natural languages.

Part II
Logic, Inference, and Reasoning

7
Inference in logic

7.1 A disambiguation and first steps to explication

One of the crucial disputes accompanying the development of modern logic is the dispute regarding the relationship between inference and consequence, and consequently between proof theory and model theory. This is something that usually does not permeate into philosophy of language, and that makes the agenda of inferentialism in the context of logic relatively different from the kind of inferentialism exposed so far. The point is that the revolution in logic effected in the 1930s by Gödel, Tarski, and others apparently taught us an important lesson: choose our rules of inference how we might, you will never manage to make inference coincide with consequence (in particular, you will never make all truths, e.g., of arithmetic, inferable from an empty set of premises). This might seem to condemn inference as an always imperfect approximation of consequence, and to orient logic upon model-theoretic tools that give us a direct grip on consequence. And this might also seem to compromise any inferentialist construal of logic at its very outset. Therefore, it is important to clarify the concepts of inference and consequence and to elucidate the kind of gap that separates them.

We have already seen that the term *inference* is ambiguous: it may refer to the acts of inferring carried out by concrete people in concrete circumstances, or alternatively it may refer to the relationship of *correct inferability* since we often hold the acts of inferring (reasoning) that people undertake to be either right or wrong. In logic there is, additionally, a third sense: *inference* can be used to refer to an arbitrarily defined abstract relation, usually generated by a system of inferential rules related to an artificial language. Such a relation may be used as an explication of inference in the *correct inferability* sense, but it might also be brought into being by purely mathematical interests. The discipline primarily focused on inference in this third sense is (universal) algebra.

Let us call the three senses *inference$_1$*, *inference$_2$*, and *inference$_3$*. Confusing these three senses of 'inference' can lead to fatal perplexities within philosophy of logic, and, unfortunately, such confusions are not uncommon.[1] Hence it is crucial to distinguish between them. As in the first part of the book, we will continue to sidestep inference$_1$, keeping our interest focused on inference$_2$ as explicated in terms of inference$_3$; this will be the default sense in which we will use the term *inference*. From this viewpoint, inference is a kind of relationship between finite sequences of sentences and sentences of a language. For the sake of perspicuity, let us start from a simplified definition which we will generalize later:

A *protoinferential structure* is an ordered pair $<S, \vdash_S>$, where S is a set whose elements are called *sentences* and $\vdash_S$ is a relation between finite sequences of elements of S and elements of S. (The prefix *proto-* is used because by far not every such structure can be reasonably seen as an explication of what we would intuitively see as a relation of inference.) Let us denote the set of all sequences of elements of S as Seq(S) and the set of all *finite* sequences as FSeq(S). Let us call elements of FSeq(S)×S *inferons over S*. (An inferon $<<A_1, ..., A_n>, A>$ will be said to be *n-ary*.) Hence an inferon is an ordered pair whose first constituent is a finite sequence of elements of S and whose second constituent is an element of S; and $\vdash_S$ is a set of inferons. An inferon $<<A_1, ..., A_n>, A>$ will also be written in the more traditional way as:

$$A_1, ..., A_n \vdash A$$

If it belongs to a particular relation, such as $\vdash_S$, we will also write:

$$A_1, ..., A_n \vdash_S A$$

and we will say that it is *in force* in the structure $<S, \vdash_S>$. We will use the letters A, A_1, A_2, ..., B, C to stand for unspecified sentences; these letters will also be called *parameters*. The letters X, Y, Z will stand for unspecific finite sequences of sentences.

It is clear that not just any relation of this kind can be meaningfully taken as explicating inference$_2$ for a real language, for inference$_2$ is, essentially, a matter of *rules*. Hence we should restrict our attention to protoinferential structures whose relation of inference is that of *inferability by means of a finite collection of inferential rules*. What is an inferential rule?

It is clearly a relation between *n*-tuples of sentences and sentences, but not every such relation can be meaningfully considered an inferential rule, for an inferential rule is supposed to be *formal*,[2] i.e., to be defined exclusively with recourse to the *form* of the sentences involved. Let us account for this fact as follows:

Letters A, A_1, A_2, ..., B, C and X, Y, Z, as introduced above, allow us to express schemata, inferential templates that can be instantiated by many concrete instances of inference. Thus, the schema

$$A \vdash A$$

has as many instances as there are elements of the underlying set of sentences. Now we will use schemata to represent *inferential rules*, and as the set of inferons that are instances of such a schema can be seen as a relation between *n*-tuples of sentences and sentences, we can see rules as relations of this kind. We will say that a rule is in force within a structure iff all its instances are in force. A finite collection of inferential rules will sometimes be called an *inferential pattern*.

The above inferential rule is clearly trivial, and nontrivial inferential rules emerge only when we assume that the set of sentences is somehow structured. If, for example, for every two sentences A and B there is a sentence denoted as $A{\wedge}B$, we can have, e.g., the pattern:

($\wedge$E1)	$A{\wedge}B \vdash A$
($\wedge$E2)	$A{\wedge}B \vdash B$
($\wedge$I)	$A, B \vdash A{\wedge}B$

A *language* will be a set of lexical items, possibly divided into categories, plus a set of grammatical rules producing complex expressions and especially sentences out of simpler expressions. A *propositional* language is constituted by a finite stock of elementary sentences plus a finite stock of operator symbols, each of which has a fixed arity *n* and is used to join *n* sentences into a complex sentence (and hence can be identified with an *n*-ary function from sentences to sentences). In a similar way we can define a predicate language and so forth.

An example of a propositional language is the language:

$$L_* = < \{s\}, \{R_*\} >,$$

where R_* is the rule that maps two sentences on the sentence that results from writing '***' in between them. A more realistic language is that of the classical propositional calculus (hereafter CPC):

$L_{CPC} = < \{a,b,c, ...\}, \{R_\wedge, R_\vee, R_\rightarrow, R_\neg\} >,$

where $R_\wedge$, $R_\vee$, $R_\rightarrow$, $R_\neg$ are the usual grammatical rules of propositional logic. Examples of forms of sentences of L* are $A*A$ or $A*(A*A)$; examples of those of L_{CPC} are $A \wedge B$ or $(A \rightarrow B) \rightarrow (\neg B \rightarrow \neg A)$.

Hence if the set S underlying a protoinferential structure is a set of sentences of a language, it may be possible to pick up various, even infinite sets of inferons over S by means of schemata; we may, for example, use the rule ($\wedge$E1) to refer to the set of all the inferons over S that are its instances. And if all the inferons valid in the structure are instances of a set of rules over the language, we may take the structure as the explication of inference$_2$ over the language. However, if we put forward a set of rules, then it is not plausible to say that the relation of inference specified by the rules is constituted by merely the instances of the rules; the relation of inference appears to involve *more* inferons. It would seem, for example, that by stipulating ($\wedge$E1) we put in force not only all instances of $A \wedge B \vdash A$, but also all instances of $A \wedge B, C \vdash A$ for every C.

Let us consider the following two rules over the language L*:

(*1) $A, A*B \vdash B$

(*2) $\vdash A*(A*A)$.

What kind of relation of inference over L* do these inferential rules i.e., the inferons that are their instances, give rise to?

In general, having a collection of inferential rules over a language, how do they 'induce' an inference relation? The usual answer is that A is inferable (or provable) from X by means of the collection $\mathbb{R}$ of inferential rules if there is a *proof* of A from X: a sequence of sentences such that A is its last element and each of its elements is either an element of X or is the result of the application of a rule from $\mathbb{R}$ to sentences that occur earlier in the sequence. We will say that such an A is $\mathbb{R}$-inferable from X.

If, for example, $\mathbb{R}$ consists of (*1) and (*2), then the sentence $(s*(s*s))*(s*(s*s))$ is $\mathbb{R}$-inferable from the empty sequence. The proof is as follows:

1. $s*(s*s)$ derived from nothing by means of (*2)
2. $(s*(s*s))*((s*(s*s))*(s*(s*s)))$ derived from nothing by means of (*2)
3. $(s*(s*s))*(s*(s*s))$ derived from 1. and 2. by means of (*1)

Consider the language L_{CPC} of propositional logic and a set of rules containing (∧E1), (∧E2), (∧I) and some others. In this system $a∧(b∧c)$ is inferable from $(a∧b)∧c$ as follows:

1. $(a∧b)∧c$ assumption
2. $a∧b$ from 1. by (∧E1)
3. c from 1. by (∧E2)
4. a from 2. by (∧E1)
5. b from 2. by (∧E2)
6. $b∧c$ from 5. and 3. by (∧I)
7. $a∧(b∧c)$ from 4. and 6. by (∧I)

Hence our first approximation of the explication of the concept of inference (construed in the way clarified above) would be a protoinference 'induced' by a finite collection of rules via the concept of proof. But as we will now indicate, this definition may be too narrow, so the task of the next section will be to generalize it.

7.2 Going substructural

There seems nothing particularly controversial about the definition of inference offered at the end of the previous section. However, there are logicians who are busy inquiring into its modifications. To see what kind of modifications may come naturally, let us characterize ℝ-inferability in an alternative way. ℝ-inferability is, just like R itself, obviously a relation between finite sequences of sentences and sentences; let us denote it as ℝ*. It is obvious that ℝ⊆ℝ*. To characterize the relationship between ℝ and ℝ* more explicitly, let us call a protoinferential structure <S, $⊢_S$> *standard* iff it complies with the following conditions:

for every A, $A ⊢_S A$
for every A, B, X, Y,   if $X, Y ⊢_S A$, then $X, B, Y ⊢_S A$
for every A, B, X, Y,   if $X, A, A, Y ⊢_S B$, then $X, A, Y ⊢_S B$
for every A, B, C, X, Y,   if $X, A, B, Y ⊢_S C$, then $X, B, A, Y ⊢_S C$
for every A, B, X, Y,   if $X, A, Y ⊢_S B$ and $Z ⊢_S A$, then $X, Z, Y ⊢_S B$

These five conditions are, in effect, due to Gentzen (1934). The properties of the relation of inference spelled out by them may be called *reflexivity*, *extendability*, *contractibility*, *permutability*, and *transitivity*. We will use the summary name *structural properties* to refer to all of them.

If we grasp these conditions as rules for deriving rules from rules (hence, in effect, as 'metarules', separating the consequent from the antecedents by the sign '/' and individual rules in the antecedent by ';'), we have

(REF) $/ A \vdash A$
(EXT) $X, Y \vdash A / X, B, Y \vdash A$
(CON) $X, A, A, Y \vdash B / X, A, Y \vdash B$
(PERM) $X, A, B, Y \vdash C / X, B, A, Y \vdash C$
(CUT) $X, A, Y \vdash B; Z \vdash A / X, Z, Y \vdash B$

These metarules are then sometimes also called *identity*, *thinning*, *contraction*, *permutation*, and *cut*. We will call them *structural rules*.

Now the following holds: if $\mathbb{R}$ is a set of inferential rules over a language L, then a sentence A of L is $\mathbb{R}$-inferable from the sequence X of sentences of L iff $X \vdash_S A$ in every standard structure $<S, \vdash_S>$ in which all elements of $\mathbb{R}$ are in force. In other words, A is $\mathbb{R}$-inferable from X iff it belongs to the smallest subset of $FSeq(S) \times S$ that contains all instances of all elements of $\mathbb{R}$ and is closed under the structural rules. (For the proof of this claim see Appendix, Theorem 1.)

Returning to the system constituted by L_* plus the rules (*1) and (*2), we can transform the proof of $(s*(s*s))*(s*(s*s))$ from the void sequence of sentences into the proof of the inferon $\vdash (s*(s*s))*(s*(s*s))$ from the void sequence of inferons as follows:

1. $\vdash s*(s*s)$ (*2)
2. $\vdash s*(s*s))*((s*(s*s))*(s*(s*s)))$ (*2)
3. $s*(s*s), (s*(s*s))*((s*(s*s))*(s*(s*s))) \vdash (s*(s*s))*(s*(s*s))$ (*1)
4. $(s*(s*s))*((s*(s*s))*(s*(s*s))) \vdash (s*(s*s))*(s*(s*s))$ from 1. and 3. by (CUT)
5. $\vdash (s*(s*s))*(s*(s*s))$ from 2. and 4. by (CUT)

Similarly, we can transform the proof of $a \wedge (b \wedge c)$ from $(a \wedge b) \wedge c$ within the system of CPC (the language L_{CPC} plus an axiomatic system of CPC) into the proof of the inferon $(a \wedge b) \wedge c \vdash a \wedge (b \wedge c)$ from the void sequence of inferons:

1. $(a \wedge b) \wedge c \vdash a \wedge b$ ($\wedge$E1)
2. $(a \wedge b) \wedge c \vdash c$ ($\wedge$E2)
3. $a \wedge b \vdash a$ ($\wedge$E1)

4. $a \wedge b \vdash b$	($\wedge$E2)
5. $(a \wedge b) \wedge c \vdash a$	from 1. and 3. by (CUT)
6. $(a \wedge b) \wedge c \vdash b$	from 1. and 4. by (CUT)
7. $b, c \vdash b \wedge c$	($\wedge$I)
8. $(a \wedge b) \wedge c, c \vdash b \wedge c$	from 6. and 7. by (CUT)
9. $(a \wedge b) \wedge c, (a \wedge b) \wedge c \vdash b \wedge c$	from 2. and 8. by (CUT)
10. $(a \wedge b) \wedge c \vdash b \wedge c$	from 9. by (CON)
11. $a, b \wedge c \vdash a \wedge (b \wedge c)$	($\wedge$I)
12. $(a \wedge b) \wedge c, b \wedge c \vdash a \wedge (b \wedge c)$	from 5. and 11. by (CUT)
13. $(a \wedge b) \wedge c, (a \wedge b) \wedge c \vdash a \wedge (b \wedge c)$	from 10. and 12. by (CUT)
14. $(a \wedge b) \wedge c \vdash a \wedge (b \wedge c)$	from 13. by (CON)

The fact spelled above indicates that the protoinferential structures we should be interested in are those that are closed with respect to the structural rules. Considering a language L, we should be interested in the structure constituted by the set S of sentences of L plus the smallest subset of FSeq(S)×S containing all instances of inferential rules of L and closed to the structural rules. And this invites the following generalization: as the structural rules can also be construed as metarules, as rules for producing rules from rules, let us introduce the concept of *metainferon over S*, which is an ordered pair whose first constituent is a finite sequence of inferons over S and whose second constituent is an inferon over S. A *metainferential rule over S* will be the result of replacing some of the sentences occurring in a metainferon over S by parameters.

An *inferential basis*, then, is an ordered triple <S, R, M>, where S is a set (of sentences; typically the set of sentences of a language); R is a finite set of inferential rules over S; and M is a finite set of metainferential rules over S. (Let us assume that all metarules in M have a non-empty antecedent, for metarules with the empty antecedent can be treated simply as rules and put into R.) The *inferential structure generated by* <S, R, M> is the protoinferential structure whose inferential relation is the smallest class that contains all instances of the elements of R and is closed to all elements of M. We will call an inferential basis *standard* iff R contains REF and M consists of CON, EXT, PERM, and CUT. An inferential basis whose M is a proper subset of CON, EXT, PERM, and CUT will be called *substandard*. An inferential structure will be called (sub)standard if it is generated by a (sub)standard inferential basis.

Substandard relations of inference, i.e., relations intermediary between $\mathbb{R}$ and $\mathbb{R}^*$, constitute the subject matter of the theory of substructural logics.[3] This theory clearly makes mathematical sense, but does it also make extramathematical sense? The relation of provability in terms of a set of rules $\mathbb{R}$, which gets explicated as $\mathbb{R}^*$, seems to represent the intuitive concept of *inferability* (or *provability*) *by means of $\mathbb{R}$* very naturally; do also some of its substructural variants correspond to something natural?

One way to make sense of substructural inferability relations is to claim that the standard explication overgenerates – i.e., that it provides for 'proofs' that are not proofs in the intuitive sense. Assume that we have the rule taking us from A and B to $A \wedge B$. Using (EXT), we also have a proof of $A \wedge B$ from A, B, and C. Is this a proof in the intuitive sense? This may be disputable. If I tell somebody that I can prove $A \wedge B$ from A, B, and C using the $\wedge$-introduction rule, the answer might well be 'but it is the proof of $A \wedge B$ from A and B only; C plays no role'. Hence canceling (EXT), as the proponents of relevant logic[4] would do, may perhaps be seen as a way of making the explicandum closer to (a certain understanding of) the explicatum.

Can we make a similar sense of canceling (CON)? Hardly. A proof is an abstract matter and there are no grounds to dispute the reusability of premises. But there might be a different way of vindicating the kind of substructural notion of proof arising from canceling (CON). Perhaps this notion will not be useful for explicating the intuitive notion of proof, but it might be useful for explicating something else. Thus, canceling (CON), as the exponents of linear logic would do, may lead us to a notion of inferability that does not correspond to proving, but it may lead us to an explication of some other relation, perhaps one from computer science.[5]

All in all, aside from the purely mathematical point of the theory of substructural logic, there may be at least two other reasons to engage in it:

(a) our conviction that an alternative kind of relation may provide for a better explication of the intuitive concept of proof; and

(b) our conviction that though the alternative relation may not provide for a better explication of the intuitive concept of proof, it may provide for an explication of something else.

7.3 Inference vs. consequence

Current orthodoxy appears to be that inference is merely the logicians' tool for approximating consequence.[6] Whereas consequence is the very way in which the truth of some of our sentences depends on that of other sentences, inference is merely the result of the logicians' attempt to account for consequence in handy terms, an attempt that has been shown, by Tarski and Gödel, to be doomed to failure.

At the outset of modern formal logic it seemed that the *only* way to get a hold on the relation of consequence was to reconstruct it as a relation of inference within a formal system built upon explicit inferential rules. Indeed, it seems nobody even thought of any kind of consequence other than one 'induced' by some rules. Even Alfred Tarski in 1930 seemed to foresee no kind of consequence other than one induced by a set of inference rules:

> Let *A* be an arbitrary set of sentences of a particular discipline. With the help of certain operations, the so-called *rules of inference*, new sentences are derived from the set *A*, called the *consequences of the set A*. To establish these rules of inference, and with their help to define exactly the concept of consequence, is again a task of special metadisciplines; in the usual terminology of set theory the schema of such definition can be formulated as follows: The set of all *consequences of the set A* is the intersection of all sets which contain the set *A* and are closed under the given rules of inference. (p. 63)

Thereby also the concept of truth came to be reconstructed as inferability from the empty set of premises. (More precisely, this holds only for nonempirical, necessary truth; but, of course, logic never set itself the task of studying empirical truth.) From this viewpoint, a principal task of logic was then thought to be the enterprise of the *explication of consequence in terms of inference*, or searching out the rules that gave rise (or at least might have given rise) to the particular relation of consequence.

However, this view was soon shattered by the incompleteness proof of Kurt Gödel and by the arguments of Tarski himself, which appeared to indicate that inference can never provide for a fully satisfactory explication of consequence, and that hence we must find a more direct way of dealing with consequence. In a nutshell, Tarski (1936) presents what he takes to be an obvious case of consequence, which, however, cannot be seen as a case of inference, namely the sentence *All natural numbers have the given property P* being the consequence of the infinite set of sentences $\{n \text{ has the property } P\}_{n=1,\dots,\infty}$. The reason it cannot be seen as a case of inference is that an inference, by its nature, can only have a finite number of premises, and the case in question clearly is not one where the conclusion follows from just a finite subset of its set of premises.[7]

Can we say that this argument shows that inference and consequence never coincide? Well, there is a rather shallow sense in which this is obvious: while it is not clear to make sense to talk about inference with an infinite number of premises (insofar as the inference relation amounts to the correctness of human inferrings and no human could actually handle an infinite number of sentences), there seems to be no reason not to consider consequences with infinite numbers of premises (this follows from the fact that it seems reasonable to agree that if something follows from some premises, then it also follows from the same plus *additional* premises).

However, extending the concept of inference to cover cases with an infinite number of premises does not seem particularly problematic: just as in the case of consequence, we can simply admit that if something is inferable from some premises, then it is also inferable from more premises.[8] This erases the trivial difference, but it would render the concept inference thus extended trivially *compact*: something can be inferable from an infinite set of premises *only if* it is inferable already from a finite subset of the infinite set. The question now is whether the same must hold for consequence. Hence a *nontrivial* difference between consequence and inference would obtain only if there were a sentence that was to follow from an infinite set of premises without following from any of its finite subsets – if consequence were *not* compact. And we have seen that Tarski's example claims to show that precisely this is the case.

A parallel case against the identifiability of consequence with inference is entailed by Gödel's incompleteness proof. What is usually taken to be one of the direct consequences of the proof is that for any axiomatic system of arithmetic there is an arithmetical sentence that is true, but not provable within the system (intuitively, it is the sentence that 'codifies' the claim that it itself is unprovable). Moreover, as the truth of mathematical sentences does not depend on states of the world, this sentence must be true necessarily, i.e., must be entailed, given the axioms of arithmetic, by the empty set, or be logically entailed by the axioms. However, it is not *inferable* from the empty set (nor, for that matter, from the axioms of arithmetic), hence, again, inference would seem to lag behind consequence.

Both Tarski's and Gödel's cases concern, at least prima facie, arithmetical, hence not directly *logical*, consequence. However, while in the former case this seems to be essential (though Edwards, 2003, argues that what Tarski had in mind *was* a specific, disguised case of *logical* consequence), the latter is easily convertible to the domain of pure logic. It would imply that the undecidable sentence is a logical consequence of the axioms of arithmetic (and within second-order logic, where arithmetic is *finitely* axiomatizable, it thus follows logically from a *finite* number of sentences) without being inferable from them.[9]

Tarski (1936) not only pointed out this problem, but also proposed a solution: to explicate consequence not in terms of inferential rules, but in terms of *interpretations* of forms of sentences. This proposal was later elaborated, by Tarski as well as by others, to yield what is now called *model theory*: a mathematical theory of the relationship between linguistic forms and extralinguistic structures whose elements are potentially denoted by linguistic items. In this way consequence started being seen as something *categorically different* from inference.

7.4 What is consequence?

Let us inspect the concept of consequence in some more detail. As we have already noted, consequence is generally understood as truth-preservation: A is a consequence of $A_1, ..., A_n$ iff A is true whenever $A_1, ..., A_n$ are true. However, what does the *whenever* amount to here? It appears to be a matter of a universal quantification over some universe of cases – so what are these cases supposed to be?

At first sight, it seems that the *whenever* has to mean simply *in all possible circumstances*. This construal may be plausible for empirical sentences, but it is important to realize that for nonempirical, especially mathematical sentences it would identify consequence with material implication: thus, any true mathematical sentence would be a consequence of any mathematical sentences whatsoever and any mathematical sentence whatsoever would be a consequence of every false mathematical sentence. This sounds quite implausible, and hence it is worth paying attention to other explications of the relevant *whenever*.[10]

An alternative idea can be traced back to Bernard Bolzano (1837),[11] who proposed, in effect, that the *whenever* should be construed as *under every interchange of certain parts of the expressions in question*. (Bolzano's direct target was *analyticity*, which, however, is interdefinable with consequence, at least within 'usual' languages[12] and for instances of consequence with a finite antecedent: A is a consequence of $A_1, ..., A_n$ iff the sentence *if $A_1, ..., A_n$, then A* is analytic.) Hence the generality alluded to here is not factual, consisting in considering possible states of affairs, but rather linguistic, consisting in considering possible substitutions of expressions for other expressions (and hence substitutional variants of the relevant sentences).

Note that this latter generality partly emulates the former one. Consider the sentence:

Dumbo is an elephant.

This sentence is true with respect to some circumstances (those in which Dumbo is an elephant) and is false with respect to others (those in which Dumbo is not an elephant). But these kinds of circumstances can be seen as 'emulated' by kinds of interpretations, namely the first by interpretations interpreting *Dumbo* as the name of an (actual) elephant and the second by interpretations interpreting *Dumbo* as the name of something else.

The problem is how to draw a line between that part of vocabulary we should hold fixed and that which we are to vary. Take the following obvious instance of consequence:

Dumbo is an elephant
Every elephant is gray
There is something that is gray

Intuitively, this is an instance of consequence for it is inconceivable that Dumbo is an elephant, that every elephant is gray, and yet there exists nothing gray. To this there corresponds the fact that, substituting names of other entities for *Dumbo* and names of other sets of entities for *elephant* and *gray*, we cannot make the sentences in the antecedent be true without making, at the same time, also that in the consequent be true. Hence it might seem that what we should vary is simply empirical vocabulary; we have, however, already noted that this would make it impossible to make any nontrivial sense of consequence within mathematics.

Moreover, take the following similar case of consequence:

Dumbo is an elephant
Every elephant is an animal
There is something that is an animal

Could there be a situation in which an elephant is not an animal? Hardly – if something were not an animal, we could not reasonably call it an elephant. (Note that it would be wrong to reason: 'if *elephant* represented not elephanthood, but, say trainhood, then elephants would *not* be animals'; as Abraham Lincoln already observed, a dog would still have four legs even if we decided to call his tail a leg.) Hence, as the second premise does not seem to exclude any conceivable situation, it seems that this instance of consequence can be reduced to:

<u>Dumbo is an elephant</u>
There is something that is an animal

And it is clear that the only part that can be safely varied here is the name *Dumbo*; the identity of the predicates *elephant* and *animal* becomes substantial. So, precisely *which* kinds of expressions should we require to be varied?

Bolzano seemed to imply that analyticity emerges wherever there is a *salva veritate* variation of *any* part of a sentence. However, this cannot be correct. Take the sentence:

Dumbo is sleeping and nothing that George Bush thinks of it can change it.

It would seem that if it is indeed the case that Dumbo is sleeping, then the truth of the sentence cannot be affected by replacing the name *George Bush* by any other name – but should we see the sentence therefore as analytic?

One way to avoid this problem is to narrow our focus and concentrate on merely *logical* consequence: consequence 'in force of' logical vocabulary alone. This settles the boundary between the fixed and the varied parts of the vocabulary as that between logical and extralogical words. (And in a sense it does *not* narrow down the scope of instances we can consider, for, as Frege (1879) already noticed, if B is a consequence of A, then it can also be understood as B being a *logical* consequence of A and *if A, then B*.[13]) This boundary is, admittedly, not *sharp*, for there is no strict criterion for distinguishing between logical and extralogical words; however, loose criteria, such as topic-neutrality, are at hand.

But there is also a more serious shortcoming of the Bolzanian method, noted already by Bolzano himself: it makes consequence depend on the contingent fact of the richness of the language in question (something might cease to be an instance of consequence by the introduction of a new expression enabling us to articulate a counterexample). We can call this the problem of the (possible) *poverty of language*. Bolzano avoided it by basing his definition on an 'ideal' language, language per se, which as such cannot lack anything.

Bolzano's modern successors, in particular Tarski (1936), avoided this recourse to an ideal language by offering an alternative solution. The point of interchanging expressions within Bolzano's approach is to gain other sentences with the same structure as the original, and clearly the same could be effected by varying the meanings of the original expressions. (Replacing the meaning of *Dumbo* by that of *Batman* has clearly the same effect as replacing the word *Dumbo* itself by the word *Batman*.) Hence we could replace Bolzanian substitutions by *interpretations*: assignments of appropriate kinds of objects to expressions as their denotations. This has the advantage that we solve the problem of the *poverty of language* without having to presuppose some such entity as an ideal language per se.[14]

How, given this explanation, should we *explicate* consequence? We have seen that consequence is, in essence, truth preservation, hence it must be based on some space of acceptable truth valuations of sentences. Hence the following definition: the pair $<S,V>$, where S is a set (the elements of which are called *sentences*) and V is a subset of $\{0,1\}^S$ (i.e., a set of mappings of S on $\{0,1\}$, also representable simply as a set of subsets of S[15], its elements being called the *admissible truth-valuations*) will be called a *semantic system*.[16] The relation of consequence based on this system is the relation $\vDash$ defined as follows:

$X \vDash A$ iff $v(A) = 1$ for every $v \in V$ such that $v(B) = 1$ for every element B of X

In the case of $\vDash$, unlike that of $\vdash$, there seems no reason to restrict ourselves to a *finite* number of premises, so we will take $\vDash$ to be a relation between arbitrary sequences of elements of S and elements of S.

Returning to our disambiguation of the concept of *inference*, what can we now say about the relation between consequence and inference? Consequence has very little to do with inference₁. Consequence is an objective matter (what follows from what does not depend on whether I or you believe it to follow[17]), whereas inference₁ is purely individual. The fact that somebody announces that he will soon cease seeing me, from which I infer that he is about to kill me, has very little to do with consequence, and the fact that somebody is disposed to infer *This is a fish* from *This is a cat* does not undermine the fact that (in English) *This is a fish* is *not* a consequence of *This is a cat*.

On the other hand, consequence and inference₂ can be seen as simply two sides of the same coin (at least when we restrict ourselves to cases with a finite number of premises). The reason is that *to be correctly inferable from* is nothing other than *to be a consequence of*: on the one hand we can correctly infer B from A if the truth of A guarantees the truth of B; on the other hand, we can do so only if there is such a guarantee. Hence insofar as inference$_3$ is a suitable tool for the explication of inference$_2$, it is a suitable tool for the explication of consequence.

Elsewhere (Peregrin, 1995) I talked about this kind of explication as *criterial reconstruction*. What is going on here is that a concept whose extension is originally not delimited by an explicit rule (but rather only in terms of practical know-how) is being associated with a *criterion*. The explicit criterion cannot exactly replicate the boundaries of the implicitly delimited extension, for the extension has no exact boundaries; it is more or less fuzzy, but this is simply what *explication* amounts to.

However, it is important to note that criteriality can be seen as coming in degrees. In general, a criterion for deciding which X's are Y's may be of several kinds:

(i) It may be a direct algorithm for reaching the verdict, given an X, whether it is Y.

(ii) It may be an algorithm for potentially generating all Y's. Such an algorithm does not give us the power to always decide whether a given X is Y, or not; if we are given an X, we can start generating the Y's and, if we are lucky, we reach the X and thus find out that it is Y, but if we do not reach it, we can never know whether we have not reached it only so far, or whether we are not going to reach it at all. Despite this, it seems to be appropriate to talk about a *criterion* even in this case: the algorithm does, it would seem, uniquely determine which X's are Y's and which not.

(iii) There may be a yet looser kind of determination of which X's are Y's, one that would make it possible neither to decide in each individual case, nor to *generate* all of the cases. We can, for example, say that an X is Y if all of an infinite number of some objects (perhaps some variants of the X in question) have some property. As we are unable to check an infinite number of objects for having a property, we may be unable to use this for any practical identifications of the X's that are Y's. But we may still feel that there is a sense in which the X's that are Y's are delimited. Of course, it is here that the usage of the term *criterion* is most problematic.

In the case of consequence, we have its explication in terms of inference, which is of kind (ii), the adequacy of which was put into jeopardy, and the subsequent Tarskian, more direct explication, which is considered adequate, but falls into category (iii). More generally, the most basic distinction between proof theory and model theory is that proof theory restricts itself to the means of category (ii), whereas there is no such restriction for model theory, so that model-theoretic delimitations often fall into category (iii). From this vantage point, we can see the completeness proofs as proofs of the fact that some 'loosely-criterial' delimitations of truth or consequence can be turned into more 'strictly criterial' ones.

7.5 Bridging the gap

The cleft that Tarski and Gödel opened between consequence and inference, and consequently between model theory and proof theory, paved the way into vast new realms of interesting mathematics; should we truly read it, however, as has become rather common, as showing that consequence is wholly independent of inference, being only – in a better or worse way – mimicked by inference? The inferentialist is committed to a more substantial role for inference. In particular, as for him it is inference that determines meaning, and as it seems obvious that meaning determines consequence,[18] there must be a sense in which consequence itself is determined by inference.

Let us inspect this argument in greater detail. The fact that a sentence, say, *There is something that is gray*, can be a consequence of other sentences, say, *Every elephant is gray* and *Dumbo is an elephant* only in virtue of the *meanings* of all the sentences involved does not seem controversial. (We have seen, in the first part of this book, that there is no sharp boundary of meaning, and hence of what holds in virtue of meaning, therefore consequence construed thus is not something to be found, in a pure form, in natural language; it is an abstraction embodied into the artificial languages of logic. Thus we should keep in mind that speaking about consequence in natural language is a similar kind of approximation as speaking about meaning.) But, of course, controversies may begin with the question of why sentences have the meanings they have. It is clear that this must be a matter of the way we, as members of the relevant community, treat them (sounds and inscriptions do not mean anything without our endeavor; see Section 3.1). Hence, what have we done to the sentences to make them mean what they do?

The opposite of the inferentialist answer, which maintains that we have made the sentences into vehicles of a complicated system of rules, is the representationalist one: our sentences mean something because we have let them stand for this something. Let us first consider the ultimate version of representationalism, according to which there is *no other* source of meaning than the relation of representation. It follows that any semantic relation between expressions, such as that of consequence between sentences, cannot but be a mimic of a relationship between the entities stood for by them. One may, for example, want to claim that sentences entail other sentences because they stand for facts and some facts contain other facts, hence that the relation of consequence is a linguistic reflection of the nonlinguistic relation of containment.

Is this answer viable? Hardly. It would mean that *Dumbo is an elephant* entailing *Dumbo is an elephant or is a rhino* is the result of the following three facts:

(i)   that we have introduced the former sentence as a name of a fact;
(ii) that we have introduced the latter as a name of *another* fact (*entirely independently* of the first naming); and
(iii) that the first of these facts happens to contain the second.

Needless to say, even if we disregard all problems connected to the concept of fact and admit that a sentence like *Dumbo is an elephant* can be reasonably seen as a name of a fact, it is hard to lend any credibility to a theory that assumes that the fact named by *Dumbo is an elephant* is only discoverable empirically to be part of the fact named by *Dumbo is an elephant or is a rhino*.

It seems more plausible to assume that whatever the meaning of *Dumbo is an elephant* is, if it gets combined with another sentence by means of *or*, the meaning of the result derives from the meanings of the parts in a way determined by *or*, and the determination consists especially in (though it is perhaps not reducible to) the consequential links between the complex sentence and the parts. Is this still compatible with representationalism? Well, it may be compatible with a version of representationalism according to which it is only some part of the vocabulary of language (perhaps the empirical part?) that acquire their meanings via representing, and that there is another part, including *or* and the like (i.e., logical vocabulary) that does not. And as in this part of the book we are concentrating on the latter vocabulary, this brings us to the inferentialist paradigm of meaning: logical (and perhaps some other) words are governed exclusively by inferential rules.

If we agree with this, then conferring a meaning on a logical word is accepting a basic inferential pattern governing the usage of some sentences containing the word. Conferring the usual meaning on *and* is accepting that it is correct to infer *A and B* from *A* and *B,* and that it is correct to infer both *A* and *B* from *A and B*. Now, however, it seems that consequence must be entirely brought into being by inference, for consequence is a product of meaning and meaning is a product of inferential rules. Hence we have two claims:

(i) consequence cannot be reconstructed as inference (some 'loosely criterial' delimitations cannot be transformed into 'strictly criterial' ones); and

(ii) consequence is uniquely determined by inference.

As inference is a matter of a set of rules, the crucial point is obviously the relationship between this set and the relation of consequence. The rules determine (in the standard way brought out in Section 7.1) inference, and there are relations of consequence that cannot be determined by any finite sets of rules in this way. Hence, is there some extended sense of *determining* – some, as we would expect, 'loosely criterial' sense – in which the rules do determine consequence? We will deal with these questions in the next section.

In order to apply our formal explication of inferential structures to the structures emerging when we see semantic systems through the prism of their relations of consequence, a generalization of our concept of protoinferential structure is called for. Let us call elements of Seq(S)×S *semiinferons over S*, hence a semiinferon is an ordered pair consisting of a sequence of sentences (that is not necessarily finite) and a sentence. (An inferon, then, is a semiinferon whose first constituent is finite). A *protosemiinferential structure* is an ordered pair <S, $\vdash_S$> where $\vdash_S$ is a set of semiinferons over S, i.e., $\vdash_S$ is a relation between sequences of elements of S and elements of S. Given this terminology, it is evident that where <S, V> is a semantic system and $\vDash$ its consequence relation, <S, $\vDash$> constitutes a protosemiinferential structure.

7.6   Omega rule

In his *Logical Syntax of Language*, Carnap (1934) distinguished – just like Tarski (1936) – between inference and consequence, but unlike Tarski he struggled to reconstruct both of them in terms of his 'logical syntax', that is, inferentially. In a sense he investigated which (meta)rules must be added to the standard rules to reach consequence rather than inference.

Now let us return to our motivations for considering substructural logics, namely to point (a) (that a substructural relation may provide for a better explication of the intuitive concept of proof). It is based on the fact that the standard explication of the concept of proof may be seen as *overgenerating*. But could it not be seen as *undergenerating* – is there a case of something that would intuitively count as a proof, but which does not come out as such in a standard explication?

Well, in the previous section we did encounter such a case. We saw that there is a sense in which the truth of Gödel's undecidable sentence G is established by the axioms of Peano arithmetic. Moreover, the line of reasoning that Gödel displayed, and which is easily reproduced in any advanced logical textbook, can make us *see* that G is true. But a line of reasoning that leads us to seeing that G is true is what we would intuitively call a *proof* of G. So could it not be that we have a kind of a proof of G, but a proof that cannot be accommodated into our standard framework of articulating proofs?

This brings us back to Carnap. His book contains two languages, called Language I and Language II. In the case of the former it is quite straightforward what we must add to move from inference to consequence: namely the *omega rule*, claiming that whatever holds for *every* number holds for *all* numbers:

$$(\omega)\ P(1), P(2), \ldots \vdash \forall x\, P(x)$$

This rule, obviously, may replace the usual $\forall$-introduction rule, according to which we can prove $\forall x P(x)$ once we can prove $P(x)$ without presupposing anything about x. But there appear to be two problems connected with this replacement.

The first trouble is that this rule is valid only in the specific case of arithmetic – only in the case where we know (or better, stipulate) that the natural numbers exhaust the whole universe of discourse. If this were not the case, (ω) would have to be reformulated as:

$$(\omega')\ P(1), P(2), \ldots \vdash \forall x\, (\mathbf{N}(x) \rightarrow P(x)),$$

where $\mathbf{N}$ is the predicate true of all and only natural numbers. But then we would need a theory conferring just this meaning on $\mathbf{N}$.

We might also consider (ω) as a special case of a 'generalized omega rule' of the form:

$$(\omega^*)\ \{P(n)\}_{n \in N} \vdash \forall x\, P(x),$$

where N is the set of all individual terms – or some 'canonical' individual terms – of the language in question. Such a rule may be seen as fixing the universe of the corresponding theory (of course, for some theories it may not be reasonable to accept any instance of the rule; refraining from accepting one might be seen as an inferential counterpart of acknowledging the presence of nameless individuals in the universe). It is, however, clear that such kind of rule would be *extralogical*, for logic itself does not care for the nature or cardinality of the universe.

The second problem is that (ω) is not really a rule, for a rule (or, for that matter, metarule) should be humanly applicable, and no human can check an infinite number of premises. This, of course, is a serious problem. On the other hand, remarkably this rule is able to close the gap between inference and consequence; if we add it to Peano arithmetic, it becomes complete (though at the cost that its relation of provability is not finitary and hence no longer expressible within the system). This means that (ω) seems to be the best proof theory can do to compete with model theory.

Moreover, it is noteworthy that we can *see* that this rule does close the gap – we can see this quite directly in Tarski's case, and with some-what more effort in Gödel's case. (In the latter, we must go through Gödel's proof and realize that having (ω) allows us to take a step that we cannot take without it and the unavailability of which makes G unprov-able.) Hence, though we cannot strictly speaking *apply* (ω), we can find out what the result of applying it would be. Hence, aside from actually applying rules, we can also reason about applying them potentially. And in the case of rules like (ω), this is the *only* way to exploit them. So there is a sense in which we *can* adopt a rule like (ω), though it is not really a humanly usable rule we can 'as-if' use it – use it in the potential modus, i.e., consider what would be the result if we were, *per impossibilium*, able to apply it.

That (ω) is not a rule of proof in the strong sense, but that it still deserves to be considered as such a rule in a relaxed sense, is clearly seen from the interest paid to it by a number of proof-theoreticians, starting with Hilbert (1931). Particularly the German mathematical logi-cians (Schütte, Lorenzen, etc.) realized that if we want to make inference into the very basis of logic and mathematics, we cannot shun a relaxing of the concept, and the ω-rule, of course, suggests itself. Thus, Schütte (1960, p. 168) writes

> The rule UJ of infinite induction [our rule (ω) – J.P.] does not belong, like the syntactic rules of proof, which we have dealt with so far, to the strongly formal rules of proof. The point is that the employment of the rule requires a metalogical investigation. It is required, that infinitely many formulas $F(z_1, ..., z_n)$ are shown, on the basis of a

general investigation, to be deducible, before we can conclude the deducibility of $F(a_1, ..., a_n)$. [Here $a_1, ..., a_n$ are variables, whereas $z_1, ..., z_n$ are metavariables standing for numerals. – J.P.] Therefore a system that contains this kind of rule as one of its basic rules cannot be seen as a strongly formal system. We call a system of this kind and also the rule UJ 'semiformal'.

From this vantage point, the gap between inference and consequence might appear as the gap between restricting ourselves to the actual usage of ('normal') rules and allowing ourselves also the reasoning about potential usage (of 'generalized' rules).[19] Now, what is the difference between the latter and doing the usual, Tarskian semantics?

We have stated that we can use rules like (ω) in the *as-if* modus: we can try to find out what would result if we were able to apply them. In this way we have the resulting theorems only *potentially*. On the other hand, if we start to treat them as our *actual* possessions, we are in the Tarskian semantics. In fact, we make what is implicit in the potentiality explicit by making it actual.

Therefore, consequence can be seen as 'loose' inference: what inference becomes when we allow for rules that we cannot apply actually, but only potentially, and hence are forced to move from directly applying rules to reasoning about what would happen if the rules were applied. Viewed in this way, the gap between consequence and inference may be seen as a gap more of degree than of kind. Thus, although the facts pointed out by Tarski and Gödel undoubtedly point to *a* gap, the nature of the gap is not quite nonnegotiable. In particular, I do not think it can be seen as undermining inferentialism.

7.7   What makes inferences reliable?

In previous sections we have been arguing that if we relax the concept of inference, it can catch up with consequence, construed model-theoretically (or 'truth-theoretically'). The relaxation means that inferability is not able to provide for a truly criterial reconstruction, so there is a trade-off between 'criteriality' and 'completeness'. Hence inference and consequence might seem to be in a certain equilibrium. But there is an additional aspect that, to my mind, makes inference prevail. To see it, I must ask myself what makes me believe that I can safely infer A from X: that if the premises are true, there is no danger that the conclusion will be false.

A possible answer would be that I know that A is a consequence of X, where consequence is construed along the above lines. What does it take, on this construal, for A to be a consequence of X? In general, it means that a certain class of truth-valuations, *including the actual one*, does not contain a valuation that would map all elements of X on 1 while mapping A on 0.

Can it be that the class in question is a singleton? Not in the case of *empirical* sentences (we would not say that A is a consequence of X if the truth of the premises did not guarantee that of A come what may) and not in the case of *logical* consequence (logical consequence holds in force of the logical vocabulary alone, so the truth of the premises must guarantee that of the conclusion independently of any interchange of extralogical vocabulary). But consider the degenerate case first: someone might perhaps want to say that $2+2=4$ is a consequence of $1\times1=2$ on the sole basis of the fact that the latter is materially implied by the former (i.e., that it is not the case that the former is true and the latter false).[20]

In this case the circularity of the truth-theoretical explanation is obvious: the question was why I know that the step from X to A will not take us from truth to falsity; the answer was that this is because A is the consequence of X, where A being a consequence of X turned out to consist in the fact that it is not the case that all of X are true and A is false. Hence the answer to the question why I know that the step from the premises to the conclusion will not bring us from truth to falsity turns out to be: because I know that it is not the case that the premises are true and the conclusion is false.

What about the less trivial situations, where the class of truth-valuations that are relevant for the fact that A is a consequence of X has more than one element? Here the situation seems no better. On the contrary, just as in the previous case, to know that the step from the premises to the conclusion will not bring us from truth to falsity I need to know that it is not the case that the premises are true and the conclusion is false (the difference being that in this case I need to know also some other things). Prawitz (2005, p. 675) characterizes the situation as follows:[21]

> But if the validity of an inference is equated with (1) (or its variants) [where (1) is the claim that inference is truth-preserving merely because of the logical form of the sentences involved, which, according to Prawitz, leads directly to the Tarskian account – J.P.], then in order to know that the inference is valid, we must already know, it seems, that the conclusion is true in case the premises are true. After all, according to this analysis, the validity of the inference just means that the conclusion is true in case the premisses are, and

that the same relation holds for all inferences of the same logical form as the given one. Hence, on this view, we cannot really say that we infer the truth of the conclusion by the use of a valid inference. It is, rather, the other way around: we can conclude that the inference is valid after having established for all inferences of the same form that the conclusion is true in all cases where the premisses are.

How can we break out of this vicious circle? In the case of empirical sentences it seems that we must take an inductive leap into the darkness: to conclude that though we do not know that it is not the case that the premises are true and the conclusion is false, we know this for plenty of similar cases. Much ink has been spilled over the question whether such induction is warranted, but this is not something we will investigate here.

But there is another possible breakthrough: I may have a *proof* of *A* being inferable from *X*. In this case, the concept of truth does not occur at the start of our considerations at all; it occurs only at the end, where we conclude that the truth of *A* is guaranteed by the truth of *X*. How can we know? Because truth is simply *construed* as that which is preserved by valid inferences and the proof shows that the inference is valid (see Section 5.6). Prawitz (2005, p. 692) concludes:

> [T]he necessity of logical consequence is expressed by the condition that for A to be a logical consequence of G, there must exist a proof or valid argument for A from G, and second, that the awareness of such a proof or valid argument compels or commits us to hold A true, given that we hold the sentences of G true.

An objection might be that I may prove that an inference is valid by decomposing it into a chain of elementary valid inferences, but what about the elementary ones? They have no proof. However, in their case I know they are valid because for such inferences to be valid is simply for the terms occurring in the premises and/or conclusions to mean what they do. This is where the point of inferentialism comes into the open: meaning and basic inferences are one and the same thing.

The crucial point is that *rules of inference are more basic than truth*. If this were not the case, then having a proof would again have to be underlain by knowing that the conclusion must be true if all the premises are true, hence the proof would not be able to *show* us that the conclusion is true.

7.8   Summary of Chapter 7

In this chapter we have investigated the nature of the relation of inference and the gap between this relation and the relation of consequence, as scrutinized by Gödel and Tarski. This gap is often seen as rendering inference notoriously incapable of serving as the basis of logic – as a tool, that is, to probe the ultimate subject matter of logic, consequence, and the laws of truth. We have tried to point out that though this gap is important, its construal as the divide between the 'inferentialistically accessible' and 'inferentialistically inaccessible' is disputable. True, the inferentialist can get to the other side of the gap only if she sacrifices a part of her true self – if she agrees to abandon the strict notion of inference as something that can be carried out by a human being. This is to say, we have concluded that the gap can be construed as a gap between the 'strictly criterial' and the 'loosely criterial': between that which can be shown by directly applying rules, and that which can be shown only indirectly, by considering 'generalized' rules and speculating about their outcomes on the metalevel.

8
Logical Constants

8.1 Tonk

In the previous chapter we considered how far we can use inference as the very basis of logic: in particular, how far we can make sense of consequence (in the Tarskian use of the word) in terms of inference. Now we turn to a more specific tenet of logical inferentialism, namely its ambition to explicate the meanings of logical constants in terms of inferential rules (thus having the ambition to produce a *theory of meaning* in the specific sense entertained by Dummett, 1991).

Challenges to this ambition are often based on an argument that inferential patterns alone are not able to provide us with the 'right' or the 'needed' kinds of logical operators. Let us call this the *Constitution Objection*:

Inferential patterns cannot constitute some indispensable logical constants.

The obvious question, then, is what, if not inference, is able to constitute them, and the usual answer is that it is some kind of 'semantics' or 'model theory'. Thus research into the foundations of logic over the last few decades has been marked by an ongoing controversy over whether one should disclose the nature of logical constants (and consequently also the nature of logic) in terms of proof theory or in terms of model theory. Our starting point here will be the discussion between Prior and Belnap on the possibility of conferring meaning on a constant by means of an inferential pattern, as mentioned in Chapter 1; subsequent to this, two influential attempts at characterizing logical constants have appeared, one couched in model theoretic terms (Tarski, 1986), the other in terms of proof theory (Hacking, 1979).[1] Both have inspired healthy followings.

One way to see this is as a dispute over the viability of inferentialism on a strictly gerrymandered playground of logical expressions. (From the viewpoint of the general tenets of inferentialism we can see it as a test of viability in extremely favorable laboratory conditions, for clearly if anything in language is to be susceptible for inferential treatment at all, then it will be logical expressions.) On the other hand, inferentialism with respect to logical constants is a project detachable from the project of general inferentialism (it is Brandom's *weak inferentialism*); and indeed some logicians have started to use the term *inferentialism* to refer only to this narrower project.[2]

Let us start from the most extreme version of the *Constitution Objection*, namely from the claim that inferential patterns cannot yield us any constants whatsoever, for they are simply not the right kind of device to make a sign meaningful. The classical example of this argument is given in Prior's (1964) follow-up to his earlier paper in which he introduced the ill-famed *tonk*.

Let us, however, first briefly return to Prior's (1960/1961) original challenge concerning *tonk*:

$S_1 \vdash S_1 \ tonk \ S_2$

$S_1 \ tonk \ S_2 \vdash S_2$

In a language containing this operator, any sentence is inferable from any other (for we can go from S_1 to $S_1 \ tonk \ S_2$ and then to S_2); in particular, any sentence that has a negation is inferentially equivalent to it. Hence any language containing *tonk* is eo ipso contradictory, and it would seem that we should block the very possibility of introducing such an operator. The moral often drawn from this exercise is that it is pernicious to let inferential patterns institute meanings (though whether this is exactly the moral Prior himself wanted to draw from it is not stated quite clearly in his paper).

In fact, it is not clear why anyone should think that this example compromises the very possibility of inferential patterns' conferring meaning. Of course, it does show that *not every* inferential pattern can be seen as capable of establishing a meaning of a word (a meaning, that is, worth the name), but why should this be impossible in general? Indeed, we saw that in the case of conjunction, the inferential pattern confers meaning if anything does. The only substantial problem the inferentialist can see in this is to account for the difference between those inferential patterns that are 'meaning-constitutive', and those that are not.

We encountered the concept of conservativity earlier (Section 2.7), and concluded that *in general* it is not a reasonable demand: to require that the inferential role of *every* expression be conservative with respect to the rest of language would deprive language of its important function. But in the context of logic the situation is different: the role of logical vocabulary, as we will argue later (Section 9.1), is merely to make material inferential rules explicit, so its conservativity *can* be generally required. Hence we can accept Belnap's solution for separating benign from malign patterns: he showed that it is conservativity that can be seen as the marker that distinguishes benign, meaning-conferring inferential patterns from malign, language-vitiating ones.

In the previous chapter we based the explication of inference on the concept of a protoinferential structure $\langle S, \vdash_S \rangle$, such that

$$\vdash_S \subseteq \mathrm{FSeq}(S) \times S.$$

Assume that S is the set of sentences of a language L and that we extend the language by adding some new sentences (typically by adding a logical connective enabling us to combine the old sentences into new logically complex ones); hence we have a new language with the set S^* of sentences such that $S \subset S^*$. Assume that we also stipulate an inferential pattern extending $\vdash_S$ to $\vdash_{S^*}$:

$$\vdash_{S^*} \subseteq \mathrm{FSeq}(S^*) \times S^*.$$

The stipulation is called *conservative* iff it does not affect the inferability of the original sentences, i.e., if it does not make any of the original sentences become inferable from other original sentences. Formally,

$$\vdash_{S^*} \cap (\mathrm{FSeq}(S) \times S) = \vdash_S.$$

In his follow-up paper, therefore, Prior produces a more severe challenge. He appears to object that only an expression which already *has* a content (like conjunction) can meaningfully occur in an inferential rule (Prior claims that 'each of the above definitions implies that the sentence formed by placing a conjunction-forming sign between two other sentences already *has* a meaning', 1964, p. 191), and that the trouble with *tonk* is that it has none. Hence, according to him, either the constant figuring in the inferential pattern already had a meaning in advance, and then the pattern is well defined but not conferring any meaning, or it had none, and then there is no real inferential pattern at all. Prior (ibid.) writes:

> It is one thing to define 'conjunction-forming sign', and quite another to define 'and'. We may say, for example, that a conjunction-forming sign is any sign which, when placed between any pair of sentences P and Q, forms a sentence which may be inferred from P and Q together, and from which we may infer P and infer Q. Or we may say that it is a sign which, when placed between any pair of sentences P and Q, forms a sentence which is true when both P and Q are true, and otherwise false. Each of these tells us something that could be meant by saying that 'and', for instance, or '&', is a conjunction forming sign. But neither of them tells us what is meant by 'and' or by '&' itself.

Hence the objection is that there is no conferring meaning, and hence no constitution of a logical constant, in terms of inferential patterns; they are simply not the proper kind of item that can accomplish this. But Prior tells us nothing about the proper kind, and as a result his argument seems to have a ring of 'logical mysticism': we cannot construct meaning inferentially simply because meaning is something essentially different from any inferential role. This is a negative semantics (analogous to negative theology): it tells us what meaning is not, but never what it is. And, what is worse, it does not tell us *why* this is the case.

In contrast to this, the inferentialist has a forthright answer: the meaning of a constant like $\wedge$ is its inferential role; it is created by stipulating an inferential pattern governing the constant. (The conviction of the inferentialist is precisely that being *and* – more precisely, meaning what *and* means in English – *is* nothing over and above being a 'conjunction-forming sign'.[3]) What, then, about *tonk* and *its* inferential pattern? Does it give *tonk* a meaning? No, but rather than because of any mystical reasons, it is because what the inferentialist calls meanings are nodes of inferential structures that have a certain kind of complexity, whereas *tonk* cannot be a part of such a structure (for its very presence causes the complexity of any structure to collapse).[4]

Also, the conclusion, reached in the previous chapter, that inference is not inevitably explicable in terms of *standard* inferential structures (i.e., structures generated by all and only the structural rules), may offer us new and interesting perspectives on *tonk*. Such a perspective was elaborated by Cook (2005) and Wansing (2006). These authors pointed out that the standard view of *tonk* results from taking for granted the standardness of the underlying inference relation. Cook gives an example of a reasonable logic for which cut fails, and shows that *tonk* can be added conservatively to it. Wansing investigates adding *tonk* to a substructural language more generally. That means that once we realize that it makes sense to think about inferential relations that do not comply with all the structural rules, our view of *tonk* gains in plasticity.

8.2 'Reasonable' and 'unreasonable' inferential patterns

Before moving to weaker versions of the *Constitution Objection*, let us stay with *tonk* a little longer, for although Prior's argument cannot be taken as contravening the possibility of an inferential delimitation of logical constants, it does give an important message. It points out that there exist inferential patterns that are not 'reasonable' in that they could be seen as conferring a meaning (worth its name) on constants. We have already seen that Belnap (1962) provided for their delimitation: he claimed, in effect, that a pattern is reasonable (in the present sense) iff the addition of the constant governed by it to any language is *conservative*, – i.e., does not tamper with the inferences within the underlying language. There are other, though related ways of approaching this, and these we will sketch in this section. To get a grip on them, we must realize that, historically, inference and inferential patterns were originally studied not so much for the purpose of explicating meaning, as for the purpose of clarifying the concept of proof and thereby gaining firmer foundations for the sciences, especially mathematics.

What is a proof? In the previous chapter we gave the standard definition of a proof of the sentence A from from the sentences X, as a sequence of sentences such that its last element is A and each of its elements is an element of X or the result of the application of a rule to sentences occurring earlier in the sequence. This presupposes the context of an inferential structure. Given such a structure, the crucial task is to find out whether a given sentence is provable, i.e., inferable from the empty set of premises.

Hence imagine that we have a system, each of the rules of which being such that all the sentences in its antecedent have 'less syntactic complexity' than its consequent sentence (whatever 'syntactic complexity' may precisely involve here). In this case we would always know that if a syntactically complex sentence is provable, then this cannot but be a consequence of some less syntactically complex sentences being provable. In other words, moving from consequence to premises would be bound to reduce the syntactical complexity and therefore would be bound to terminate. So, facing the task of finding out whether a sentence is provable, we can, in a finite number of steps, either show that it is, by reducing it to the provability of the empty set of premises, or show that it is not, by reducing it to some premises that are not provable (cannot be further reduced).

From this viewpoint, an inferential system with the above property would be highly desirable. However, we can immediately see that it is hardly attainable. Take conjunction. We have the rule:

($\land$I) $A, B \vdash A \land B$

which does have the desired property of going from less to more complex sentences, but, aside from this, it seems that we would also need the rules:

($\land$E1) $A \land B \vdash A$

($\land$E2) $A \land B \vdash B$

which go the other way around. And the situation is no simpler for other connectives.

However, Gentzen, who was the first to study logical constants from this viewpoint, realized that if the undesired rules are in a certain sense well behaved, they need not spoil the overall picture. Let us call, as is usual, ($\land$I) the *introduction* rule for conjunction and ($\land$E1) plus ($\land$E2) the *elimination* rules. In a sense, Gentzen claimed, the elimination rules are already 'contained' in the introduction one, and hence they are harmless.

What is the sense in which the elimination rules are 'contained' in the introduction rule? Well, of course they are not literally contained in the rule, but they are 'entailed' by the rule plus the assumption that the rules give something like the *canonical grounds* for conjunction. This is to say that not only does $A \land B$ follow from A plus B, but that whatever else it might follow from must entail both A and B.

In fact we can replace the elimination rules by the following minimality condition (cf. Koslow, 1992):

if $X \vdash A \land B$, then $X \vdash A$ and $X \vdash B$.

And this seems to only reinforce the reducibility requirement, for it says that anything that is grounds for the conjunction cannot but also be grounds for each of the conjuncts; in other words, it says that in considering the provability of conjunction, we can restrict ourselves to the introduction rule. (Imagine that we had another inferential rule for obtaining conjunction, e.g., C, $C \rightarrow (A \wedge B) \vdash A \wedge B$. Then we can simply disregard it, for we know that any proof containing this step can be replaced by a proof in which $A \wedge B$ would, in the final step, be introduced on the grounds of A and B, for we have the guarantee that both A and B are provable from C and $C \rightarrow (A \wedge B)$.)

Hence, aside from complexity-expanding introduction rules, we can have complexity-reducing elimination rules, *if these hook up with the introduction rules in the right way*. Now what exactly is this 'right way'? One kind of answer leads via the concept of the normal form of proofs: a proof based on a system of natural deduction is said to be in *normal form* if it contains no formula that would be introduced and subsequently eliminated (see Prawitz, 1965, for details). A system of natural deduction is called *normal* iff everything that can be proved in the system has a proof that is in normal form (or, expressed differently, if any proof within the system can be brought to a normal form). And we can say that a system is normal iff its introduction and elimination rules fit together in the way deemed 'right' above.

Dummett (1991) attempted a more general answer, introducing the concept of *harmony* (which we mentioned in Section 2.7):

> The two complementary features of any such practice [establishing verification and drawing consequences] ought to be in harmony with each other: and there is no automatic mechanism to ensure that they will be. The notion of harmony is difficult to make precise but intuitively compelling: it is obviously not possible for the two features of the use of any expression to be determined quite independently. Given what is conventionally accepted as serving to establish the truth of a given statement, the consequences of accepting it as true cannot be fixed arbitrarily; conversely, given what accepting a statement as true is taken to involve, it cannot be arbitrarily determined what is to count as establishing it as true. The supposition that the two features could be determined independently was the error of the theory, now long discarded, of descriptive and emotive meaning. The 'descriptive' meaning represented the criterion for applying the term, and the miscalled 'emotive' meaning what one committed oneself to by applying it; the theory assumed that the glue holding them together was nothing more than impermanent convention. On the contrary, the requirement that each be in full harmony with the

other is far more stringent than that there be some degree of natural congruence between them. The failure to observe this was the fallacy in the notorious 'paradigm case' argument.

Unfortunately, Dummett did not specify his concept of harmony with full explicitness. At some places in his book, it seems that harmony amounts to nothing more than the kind of conservativity tabled by Belnap; elsewhere he seems as if to equate it with normalizability.[5] But Dummett's basic idea seems to be more general, as documented by the following passage:

> There can be no a priori ground, however, for denying that a natural language can be defective in the sense of operating imperfectly and thereby failing fully to realise the ends it is intended to serve. The ends of language are internal: there is no form of description of what a language is required to do – to communicate thoughts, for example – that would represent it as something in principle achievable without the use of language. But this is not to say that a language does not have ends, which one who has language can apprehend, and which it may attain more successfully or less successfully. The possibility of failure arises primarily because of the multiplicity of principles governing our linguistic practice. For the language to function as intended, these principles must be in harmony with one another; but the mere fact that certain principles are observed in no way guarantees that the necessary harmony will obtain. Inconsistency is the grossest type of malfunction to which a language, considered as governed by a complex of accepted practices in using it, may be subject.

The basic idea, therefore, is that as meaning is a matter of a set of principles (especially inferential rules), the elements of the set may get into conflict and bear contradictions or some weaker kind of 'disharmony'. In particular, the principles that determine what counts as grounds for establishing a sentence may be in 'disharmony' with those determining what counts as a consequence of the sentence. Concerning a logical constant, its introduction rules may not be in harmony with its elimination ones. However, apart from generalizing the morals to be drawn from the Priorian *tonk*, Dummett did not manage to specify the distinction between harmony and disharmony in this regard much beyond Belnap's requirement of conservativity.

Anyway, it does seem feasible to distinguish inferential patterns that are reasonable, in that they can be seen as meaning-conferring, from those that are not reasonable in this sense, without abandoning the framework of proof theory. Hence Prior's criticism loses its bite: the claim that meanings are creatures of inferential patterns does not involve the claim that any inferential pattern is as good at creating meaning as any other.

8.3 Inference and truth-valuations

Let us return to more general versions of the *Constitution Objection*. In order to evaluate this objection, we need to get some grip on the constants that, allegedly, are beyond the reach of inferential patterns. We have already indicated that for this purpose we need some 'semantic' tools. If, to begin with, we stay on the level of propositional logic and adopt classical logic as the standard, then what we need seems to be truth tables.

Let us, therefore, for the sake of argument, adopt the framework of the opponent and assume that it is truth tables that yield 'standard' logical constants, and let us look at which of such constants can be constituted in terms of inferences. Let us consider a language consisting of three sentences: A, B, and C. Let us assume that C is the conjunction of A and B, that is to say that C is true just in the case that both A and B are. This means that if we list, in the following table, all possible assignments of truth values to the three sentences, some of them get excluded:

	A	B	C
1.	1	1	1
2.	1	1	0
3.	1	0	1
4.	1	0	0
5.	0	1	1
6.	0	1	0
7.	0	0	1
8.	0	0	0

Now it is clear that the standard introduction and elimination rules for conjunction (together with those that follow from them via Gentzenian structural metarules) have the effect of excluding the very same rows of this table: (∧E1) excludes 5 and 7, (∧E2) excludes 3 and 7, whereas (∧I) excludes 2; hence altogether the excluded rows are precisely the rows 2, 3, 5, and 7.

The situation is different with disjunction. Here the table is

	A	B	C
1.	1	1	1
~~2.~~	~~1~~	~~1~~	~~0~~
3.	1	0	1
~~4.~~	~~1~~	~~0~~	~~0~~
5.	0	1	1
~~6.~~	~~0~~	~~1~~	~~0~~
~~7.~~	~~0~~	~~0~~	~~1~~
8.	0	0	0

In this case, however, the situation is different in that we cannot find an inferential pattern that would have the effect of striking out precisely the same rows. We have the obvious introduction rules

($\vee$I1) $A \vdash A \vee B$

($\vee$I1) $B \vdash A \vee B$

where the former excludes 2 and 4, while the latter excludes 2 and 6, and there is no way of excluding row 7 without excluding some of the rows that should not be excluded. This indicates that there seems to be no straightforward 'translation' of truth-tables into inferential patterns; thus we do not have an inferential capturing of the meaning of even the most basic, classical logical constants.

To gain a deeper insight into this problem, let us consider it in a yet more general framework to find out which of the operators definable in some semantic or model-theoretic framework are accessible to inferential patterns. But ways of defining semantics or model theories for various languages are numerous; what we would need is a framework neutral to the differences between the idiosyncrasies of individual articulations: a framework that would be, as it were, their common denominator.

So how can we delimit a general concept of semantics independent of inferences? In fact we can use the one we have already introduced, in Section 7.4. Semantic interpretation seems obviously to go hand in hand with a truth-valuation of sentences: sentences, by being semantically interpreted, become true or false. Of course, when considering an *empirical* language, semantic interpretation will not fix the truth values of all sentences: a sentence such as *The sun is shining* does not become true or false by being made to mean what it does. The same holds of a logical language with uninterpreted parameters or extralogical constants. What semantic interpretation generally will do is impose *limits* on possible truth-valuations: e.g., it determines that if *The sun is shining* is true, then *The sun is not shining* must be false; hence that the sentence *The sun is shining and the sun is not shining* is bound to be always false and so forth. This means that semantic interpretation should put some *constraints* on the possible truth-valuations of sentences.[6]

Truth tables can be looked at as the most straightforward means of determining which valuations of the language under consideration are acceptable. (For example, the truth table for conjunction tells us that a valuation is acceptable only if it assigns 1 to a conjunction just in the case it assigns 1 to both its conjuncts.) The trouble is that a truth table cannot be associated with every expression: nonlogical expressions appear to need more substantial semantics and even many logical expressions are not truth-functional. What is often suggested as a cure is to move from truth *values* to truth *conditions*. Now let us think about the ways truth conditions can be articulated. We must say something of the form:

  X is true iff *Y*,

where *X* is replaced by the name of a sentence and *Y* by a description of the conditions, i.e., a sentence. Hence we need a language in which the truth conditions are expressed: a *metalanguage*. However, then our theory will work only so long as we take the semantics of the metalanguage at face value; in fact we will merely have reduced the truth conditions of the considered sentence, *X*, to a sentence of the metalanguage, namely the one replacing *Y*. And to require that the semantics of the latter be explicated equally rigorously as that of *X* would obviously set an infinite regress in motion.

This indicates that it might be desirable to refrain from having recourse to a metalanguage and instead to make do with the resources of the object language, the language under investigation. Hence, suppose that we would like to use a sentence of this very language in place of *Y*. Which sentence should it be? The truth conditions of *X* are clearly best captured by *X* itself, but using *X* in place of *Y* would clearly result in an uninteresting truism. But, at least in some cases, there is the possibility of using a *different* sentence of the same language. So let us assume that we use a sentence *Z* in place of *Y*. Saying *X is true if…* or *X is true only if* ... with Z in place of the ... amounts to claiming that X is entailed by Z and that X entails Z, respectively. (Claiming *'Fido is a mammal' is true if Fido is a dog* is claiming that *Fido is a mammal* is entailed by *Fido is a dog*.) And claiming that X is entailed by Z in turn amounts to claiming that every truth-valuation which verifies Z verifies also X, or that any truth-valuation not doing so is not acceptable. Hence the specification of the range of acceptable truth-valuations represents the part of the specification of truth-conditions that can be accounted for without mobilizing the resources of another language.[7]

Hence we have a general question: given that the semantics of a language determines which truth-valuations of sentences are admissible, which kinds of such spaces of admissible truth-valuations can be determined inferentially? In the conceptual setting established in the previous chapter, this amounts to asking which semantic systems are determined by proto(semi)inferential structures. But what does it take for a proto(semi)inferential structure to *determine* a semantic system?

Inference can be looked at as a means of excluding certain truth-valuations of the underlying language: stipulating $X \vdash A$ can be seen as excluding all truth-valuations that map all elements of X on 1 while mapping A on 0. In this sense, every inferential structure determines a certain semantic system. And hence the question which kinds of meanings are conferrable inferentially is intimately connected with the question which semantic systems can be determined by inferential structures. This leads to the following definition: the protosemiinferential structure $<S, \vdash_S>$ *determines* the semantic system $<S,V>$, where V is the set of all v fulfilling the condition that if $v(B) = 1$ for every constituent B of X and $X \vdash_S A$, then $v(A) = 1$.

8.4   Inference structures and semantic systems

Why there are semantic systems that are not determined by any inferential structure? In fact, that there are such systems might seem, prima facie, strange: after all we have seen that every semantic system together with its consequence relation forms a protosemiinferential structure, and does this structure not determine this very system? An important thing to realize is that the answer to this question is *negative*: a structure of a semantic system might determine a *different* semantic system (though, of course, a system having the same structure).

Consider, as an example even simpler than the above ones, the system <$\{A,B\},V$> with only two sentences. Let V consist of the two 'truth-value-swapping' valuations, i.e., the valuations $\{A\}$ and $\{B\}$:

	A	B
~~1.~~	~~1~~	~~1~~
2.	1	0
~~3.~~	~~0~~	~~0~~
4.	0	1

What is the proto(semi)inferential structure of the system? It is clear that all instances of consequence within this system such that their antecedent contains their consequent (i.e., (semi)inferons of the form ..., A, ... $\vdash A$ or of the form ..., B, ... $\vdash B$) are valid. On the other hand, instances that are not of this form (i.e., instances with the antecedent consisting of zero or more A's and with the consequent B and instances with the antecedent consisting of zero or more B's and with the consequent A) are *not* valid (the former kind is excluded by the valuation 2, whereas the latter is excluded by 4).

Hence the structure of the system is the protosemiinferential structure <$S, \vdash_S$> whose inference relation consists of all the inferons of the shape $X \vdash_S A$, where A is a component of X, plus those of the shape $Y \vdash_S B$, where B is a component of Y. It can be checked that this is the inferential structure 'induced' by the empty set of rules, and it is readily seen that none of these inferons excludes *any* valuation. In other words, this inferential structure does not determine the original semantic system <$S, \{\{A\}, \{B\}\}$>, but rather the 'full' system <$S, \{\varnothing, \{A\}, \{B\}, \{A, B\}\}$> in which every sentence is a consequence of any others.

It is also readily seen that no extending of $\vdash_S$ would help. What we could add would be either a (semi)inferon with the antecedent consisting of zero or more A's and with the consequent B, or a (semi)inferon with the antecedent consisting of zero or more B's and with the consequent A. The former kind of inferon would exclude the valuation $\{A\}$, the latter one the valuation $\{B\}$; the inferons $\vdash B$ (of the former kind) and $\vdash A$ (of the latter kind) would, in addition to this, exclude the valuation $\varnothing$. This implies that no combination of the inferons is capable of excluding the valuation $\{A, B\}$, and also no combination is capable of excluding $\varnothing$ without excluding either $\{A\}$ or $\{B\}$. In other words, no protoinferential structure determines the system <$\{A, B\}, \{\{A\}, \{B\}\}$>.

This indicates that the relation between proto(semi)inferential structures and semantic systems that results from associating a structure with the system it determines is many-one: there may be many structures determining the same system. (There is, obviously, only one structure that is the structure *of* the system: it is the structure whose relation of inference coincides, for a finite number of premises, with the relation of consequence of the system.) The fact that there are more structures *determining* the same system, then, is due to the fact that some (semi)inferons do not exclude any valuation that has not already been excluded, and hence adding them to a structure determining a semantic system produces *a different structure* determining *the same system*. Only when we add all such (semi)inferons does the structure become 'saturated' , thereby becoming the structure of the system.

Similarly, the relation that results from associating a system with its structure is many-one (whereas there is only one system that is determined by the structure). Again, addition of some valuations to a system causes no change to the relation of consequence of the system (and hence to the structure of the system) and it is only when all such valuations are present that we gain a system that is 'saturated' and hence is determined by its own structure. Hence the systems that share the same structure may differ in the richness of the valuations they admit, and it is only the one admitting their 'maximum' that is determined by the structure.

What is the nature of such 'idle' valuations and when is a semantic system determined by its own structure? An answer to this question was given by Hardegree (2005): the 'idle' valuations are what he calls *supervaluations*; a supervaluation of a set of valuations is a valuation that maps a sentence on 1 just when all the elements of the set do. And, as Hardegree (ibid.) showed, $<S,V>$ is determined by its own structure iff V contains the supervaluations of each of its subsets.

Hardegree also answered the previous, dual question: namely, when is a protoinferential structure the structure of the semantic system it determines? His answer is that a necessary and a sufficient condition for the inference relation is constituted by the following two constraints:

$X \vdash A$ if A is an element of X

$X \vdash A$ if $X \vdash B$ for every element B of Y and $Y \vdash A$

Unlike us, however, Hardegree considers inference as a relation between sets (rather than sequences) of sentences and sentences; hence to align our framework to his requires us to add the principles that the order of the elements of our sequences is insignificant and that a repeated occurrence of the same symbol within a sequence does not count. Moreover, Hardegree's first principle can be replaced by two more elementary ones: one stating that every sentence is inferable from itself and the other stating that a sentence is inferable from any superset of a set from which it is inferable. This yields us nothing other than Gentzen's structural metarules articulated in the previous chapter. We can prove a claim more general than Hardegree's, namely that $<S, \vdash_S>$ is a structure of a semantic system over S just in the case that $\vdash_S$ complies with all the structural rules. (Hardegree's own claim then follows via the obvious fact that if an inferential structure is a structure of a semantic system, there is a system that it determines.) See Appendix, Theorem 2 for the proof.

It follows that a valuation is 'idle' in the above sense iff it is a supervaluation of a set of admissible valuations and that a (semi)inferon is idle if it follows from already valid (semi)inferons by means of the structural metarules. (In this case, let us call the former (semi)inferon the *structural consequence* of the latter.) Hence the following picture:

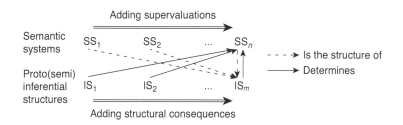

8.5   Inferentialism and classical logic

We have concluded that inferential rules do not allow us to precisely carve out the space of those truth valuations admissible by truth tables for classical logical operators. However, we do know that we have sound and complete axiomatizations of CPC, and what is an axiomatic system, from our viewpoint, other than an inferential pattern? So how is it possible that we both cannot have an inferential pattern that determines the semantics of CPC, and yet at the same time we do seem to have one doing precisely this?

The key to this quandary is to realize that the space of valuations admissible from the viewpoint of an axiomatic system of CPC is *not* the same as that which is determined by truth-table semantics. Hence, from the semantic viewpoint we have *two versions* of CPC. (Carnap, 1943, was probably the first to notice this, and the two versions are occasionally discussed in the literature.)[8] In view of this, the situation with CPC may resemble, at least at first sight, the situation of second-order predicate calculus, where we also have two versions of the logic according to whether we take it to be equipped with standard, or with Henkin, semantics.[9] Belnap and Massey (1990) call the two kinds of semantics for CPC *classical* and *inferential*. However, whereas in the second-order logic case the different semantic systems yield different sets of tautologies (giving us two logics in a strong sense), here the difference is more subtle (making it more appropriate to talk about two variants of a single logic).

As the only valuations excluded by the truth tables, but admitted by the axiomatic systems, are those that are 'inferentially idle' (in the sense of our previous section), the two versions of CPC share the same relation of consequence (and a fortiori the same set of tautologies). Hence the difference between the two versions remains so delicate that it is often reasonable to ignore it. The situation is such that, for example, it is compatible with the axioms of CPC that an $A \lor B$ is true despite both A and B being false; this, however, does not surface in the shape of the fact that $A \lor B$ would be compatible with $\neg A$ and $\neg B$. If this is the case, then either $\neg A$ or $\neg B$ must be false (despite the fact that A and B are false – just as the disjunction of two falsehoods can be true, a negation of a falsehood may be false).

What follows from this? Classical logic is 'inferentializable' in a weak sense, but not in a strong one. In particular, we cannot say that inferences are able to directly furnish logical constants with the very meanings they have in classical logic. The axiomatics of classical logic does not render the disjunction of A and B as true iff either A is true or B is true – it admits the disjunction being true even when both A and B are false. If we stipulatively exclude the possibility of operators denoting anything other than truth-functions, then the axioms would be able to pin down the denotation of disjunction to the correct truth table, for no other truth function is compatible with the axioms. However, by themselves, they are *not* able to exclude all non-truth-functional alternatives.

What is the response the inferentialist should give to this? There are several options. One is to bite the bullet and say that classical logic is simply not a 'natural logic', that it is a late-coming product of logicians' engineering, streamlining logic into an 'unnatural shape' to make it extremely simple. This answer has something to it, for, as we will see in greater detail in Chapter 9, it is intuitionist logic that can be seen as most organically flowing from the inferentialist viewpoint. But this is not the only way the inferentialist can react.

Another option is to deny that it is only single-conclusion inference that we should take as our point of departure. Once we admit a multiple-conclusion variant on board, problems with classical logic vanish immediately. For example, the missing elimination rule for disjunction will be simply (where we assume that $X \vdash Y$ excludes all valuations that map all elements of X on 1 and all those of Y on 0):

$A \lor B \vdash A, B$.

Negation will be characterizable in terms of the rules:

$A, \neg A \vdash$

and

$\vdash A, \neg A$.

This will be studied, in greater detail, in the next chapter. However, multiple-conclusion inference might be much less natural than the single-conclusion one from the viewpoint of the inferentialist theory of language.[10]

And, last but not least, there is the option of refusing to put any value on the distinction between classical and inferential valuations of classical logic. After all, *inferential rules* are the only thing that matter to an inferentialist. If criticized for *ignoring* something vital – namely that inferentialism is not able to render the *truly* logical constants – the inferentialist can reply that such criticism is on a par with criticizing an atheist for ignoring the secrets of the Holy Trinity.

In any case, the problems with the inferentialization of classical logical constants are not something at which the inferentialist should despair. True, inferentialism and classical logic do not form an ideal couple, but this does not undermine inferentialism as such.

8.6   Varieties of inference

We have already noticed that inferentialism (similarly to *finitism* or other similar *isms*) may be seen as coming in degrees. Apart from the strict version, according to which an inferential rule is a matter of a passage from a finite set or sequence of premises to a conclusion, we might consider, for example, rules with an infinite number of premises. Let us consider further ways of weakening the inferentialist paradigm until it virtually coincides with our semantic framework.

In the previous chapter we generalized our concept of a protoinferential structure to the concept of protosemiinferential structure (where the relation of semiinference differs from that of inference in that it allows for infinite antecedents). Now let us consider another generalization: allowing for multiple conclusions. Let us call elements of Seq(S) × Seq(S) *semiquasiinferons over* S; hence a semiquasiinferon is an ordered pair consisting of two sequences of sentences (not necessarily finite). A semiinferon is a semiquasiinferon whose second component is of length 1; it is a quasiinferon iff both its constituents are finite, and it is an inferon iff its first constituent is finite and its second constituent is of length 1. A *protosemiquasiinferential structure* is an ordered pair <S, $\vdash_S$> where $\vdash_S$ is a set of semiquasiinferons over S, i.e., $\vdash_S$ is a relation between sequences of elements of S. In this way we have two dimensions of generalization of inference, and consequently four different kinds of systems of generalized inference: inferential, semiinferential, quasiinferential and semiquasiinferential.

To make our terminology more readable, let us abbreviate 'proto' to 'P', 'semi' to 'S', 'quasi' to 'Q' and 'infer(ential)' to 'I'. Moreover, as in this chapter we will restrict our attention to inferential structures that are standard (i.e., are closed to the Gentzenian structural (meta)rules), from now on we will assume that (semi)(quasi)inferons are relations not between *sequences* of sentences, but rather *sets* of sentences (thus incorporating two of the Gentzenian rules, namely contraction and permutation, into the very definition of inference). (We have seen that structural consequences are 'idle' as regards excluding valuations; hence we can always assume their presence. In other words, we can assume that the structures we are dealing with are standard.)

Hence, from now on, the symbols X, Y, Z will be considered to represent sets of sentences. Thus, a semiquasiinferon, or SQI-on for short, is an element <X,Y> of Pow(S) × Pow(S). Striking 'S' means going finite, i.e., an SQI-on is a QI-on iff it is an element of FPow(S) × FPow(S). Striking 'Q' means restricting the second component to a sequence of length 1, i.e., an SQI-on is an SI-on iff it is an element of Pow(S) × S, and a QI-on is a I-on iff it is an element of FPow(S) × S. A P(S)(Q)I-structure is a set of sentences and a set of (S)(Q)I-ons. A semantic system is a P(S)(Q)I-system iff it is determined by a P(S)(Q)I-structure.

To illuminate the conceptual apparatus, let us summarize the definitions of these concepts in the following table:

<S, ⊢> is a ...	iff ⊢ is a ...	⊢ thus being a subset of ...
PI-structure	a set of I-ons	$\mathrm{FPow}(S) \times S$
PQI-structure	a set of QI-ons	$\mathrm{FPow}(S) \times \mathrm{FPow}(S)$
PSI-structure	a set of SI-ons	$\mathrm{Pow}(S) \times S$
PSQI-structure	a set of SQI-ons	$\mathrm{Pow}(S) \times \mathrm{Pow}(S)$

It can be shown that the generalization we have reached, namely the concept of PSQI-structure, is ultimate – that there are no semantic systems that would not be PSQI-systems.

All the concepts we have introduced so far give us the following hierarchy:

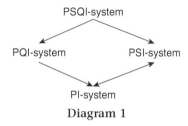

Diagram 1

The arrows indicate containment in the sense that an arrow leads from one concept to another if whatever falls under the latter falls also under the former. It can be shown that the arrows capture *all* inclusions among the types of semantic systems listed on the diagram, and that all the inclusions are *proper*. (For a proof, see Appendix, Theorem 6.)

8.7   Structured systems of sentences

As we have already stressed, we are interested in those protoinferential structures whose relation of inference can be seen as explicating inferability by means of a finite collection of inferential rules (and for such structures we can drop the prefix *proto-* and consider them simply as *inferential* structures). And though concentrating on structures with only a finite number of (S)(Q)I-ons would be too restrictive, we have already seen (in Section 7.1), how we can use parametric letters to build sentential schemata and use them to articulate rules. Now we will concentrate on those structures that can be delimited in this finitary way; this means, however, that we must modify the definition of the proto(quasi)(semi) inferential structure to include some information about the language underlying the set *S*.

Let us generalize the concept of language in such a way that a language would be individuated not only by its sets of sentences, but also by a set of its schemata. We can introduce the concept of a *parametric (S) (Q)I-on (p(S)(Q)I-on)* over such a language so that it is an (S)(Q)I-on in which some sentences are replaced by parameters. (Each such p(S)(Q) I-on then has a number of (S)(Q)I-ons as its instances.) Now a P(S)(Q) I-system is called an (S)(Q)I-system iff it is delimited by a finite number of p(S)(Q)I-ons.

Consider, for example, the structure $<S^*, \vdash_{S^*}>$ such that S^* is the set of sentences of the language $L_* = <\{s\}, \{_*\}>$ introduced in Chapter 7. Now we will see it as the generalized structure $<<S^*, F^*>, \vdash_{S^*}>$, where F^* is the set of all those subsets of S^* that are the sets of instances of schemata of L_*. The sentences of L_* are s, s^*s, $s^*(s^*s)$ etc., hence $<\{s\},s>$, $<\{s,s^*s\},s>$ are I-ons, $<\{s\},\{s\}>$, $<\{s^*s\},\{s^*(s^*s),(s^*s)^*s\}>$ are QI-ons etc. Now using parameters we can have, for instance, the pI-on

$$<\{A,B\}, \{A^*B\}>$$

or the pQI-on:

$$<\{A^*s\}, \{A^*(s^*s), (s^*s)^*A\}>.$$

The instances of the former are:

$$<\{s,s\}, \{s^*s\}>, <\{s,s^*s\}, \{s^*(s^*s)\}> \text{ etc.;}$$

those of the latter are:

$$<\{s^*s\}, \{s^*(s^*s), (s^*s)^*s\}>, <\{(s^*s)^*s\}, \{(s^*s)^*(s^*s), (s^*s)^*(s^*s)\}> \text{ etc.}$$

Considering generalized semantic systems and entering the concepts of (S)(Q)-systems provides for a substantial refinement of Diagram 1, doubling the number of categories. As it is clear that every (S)(Q)I-system is a P(S)(Q)I-system (for a valuation is excluded by a pSQI-on iff it is excluded by one of its instances), we have the following hierarchy:

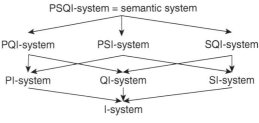

Diagram 2

Now we will concentrate especially on inferential, not protoinferential systems. This leaves the following four highlighted categories in the focus of our attention:

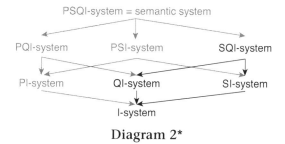

Diagram 2*

Let us consider some nontrivial examples of systems which fall into these categories. (For the rigorous proofs of the following claims see Appendix, Theorem 7.) The semantic system consisting of the formulas of propositional logic and valuations that do justice to all the truth tables of the classical connectives is a QI-system, but not an I-system. (The reason is that, as we saw, to exclude all the valuations that do not comply with the truth tables we need QI-ons.) If we replace this set of valuations with the more inclusive set of all those valuations that map all axioms of a system of classical propositional logic on 1 and map a b on 1 whenever there is an a so that a and $a{\rightarrow}b$ are mapped on 1, we get an I-system. If we replace this set of valuations by the set of all those valuations that map all axioms of a system of intuitionist logic on 1 and map a b on 1 whenever there is an a so that a and $a{\rightarrow}b$ are mapped on 1, we again have an I-system.

Now let us consider the language of predicate logic and the set of all its valuations that do justice to all the truth tables of the classical connectives and that map formulas of the shape $\forall x p(x)$ (or $\exists x p(x)$) on 1 iff all instances (or at least one instance) of $p(x)$ is mapped on 1. (It can be seen as a version of predicate logic not allowing for nameless individuals.) It can be shown that it is a SQI-system, but neither an SI-system, nor a QI-system. (This system is perspicuous in the sense that we can assimilate universal quantification to infinite conjunction and, in the same way, existential quantification to infinite disjunction.) In the case of general predicate logic, however, there may be cases of $\forall x p(x)$ being mapped on 0 despite the fact that all instances of $p(n)$ are mapped on 1. Hence, while the pI-on $<\{\forall x p(x)\}, p(n)>$ is unproblematic, the pSI-on $<\{p(n)\}_{n \in N}, \{\forall x p(x)\}>$ is not – at least, not if what we want is standard classical predicate logic. Can we simply abandon the pSI-on for good? Well, it is clear that not *every* valuation mapping $\forall xp(x)$ on 0 should be admissible (which would be the result of simply striking out the pSI-on). In some cases $\forall xp(x)$ cannot be mapped on 0 at all (if $p(x)$ is a tautology); in some other cases it cannot be mapped on 0 unless some $\forall xq(x)$ is also mapped on 0 (if $p(x)$ is entailed by $q(x)$). The usual axiomatization of the classical predicate calculus solves this by replacing the generalized omega rule with certain axioms plus the rule of generalization, which is, in fact, a metarule: it says that if A is inferable from the empty set of premises, then so is $\forall xA$.

The employment of metarules opens up a further way of generalizing the concept of (S)(Q)I-system. Remember that an (S)(Q)I-structure is a 'finitely determined' P(S)(Q)I-structure. Explicating the 'finitely determined', we rejected 'with a finite number of (S)(Q)I-ons' and embraced 'with a set of (S)(Q)I-ons determined by a finite number of schemata'. Now we might want to further replace it by 'with a set of (S)(Q)I-ons determined by a finite number of schemata and a finite number of rules generating schemata from schemata'. This creates the possibility of rendering more semantic systems as (S)(Q)I-system (e.g., the classical predicate logic), but we are not going to follow this further generalization here.

8.8   Summary of Chapter 8

In this chapter we considered how to find the inferential patterns that would constitute logical constants defined truth-theoretically, with special emphasis on the constants of classical logic. We started from what we dubbed the *Constitution Objection*, namely the objection that inferential patterns cannot yield us certain indispensable logical constants. We dismissed the extreme version of the objection (which claims that an inferential pattern is not able to yield any logical constant, for meaning is an entity that cannot be brought into being by such a pattern for some mysterious reasons), and we set out to investigate which kinds of constants might be difficult to be produced by such patterns.

We saw that there is no straightforward way to transform truth tables into inferential patterns, and hence no straightforward inferential way to classical logic. However, the fact that classical logic is axiomatizable shows that it is not beyond the reach of inferential treatment. In general, although classical logic is not 'natural' from the inferentialist viewpoint, there are various ways of getting an inferentialist grip on it.

We defined a very general framework to delimit the semantics of a language (namely a framework in which *semantics* equates to the delimitation of the space of admissible truth-valuations) and we investigated some general features of those semantics (in this sense of the word) that can be delimited in terms of inferential patterns. We have considered two possible generalizations of standard, single-conclusion inference, namely quasiinference, which allows for multiple conclusions (turning inferential rules, in effect, into Gentzenian sequents), and semiinference, which allows for infinite sets of premises (and, in the case of sequents, also infinite sets of conclusions). We have shown that relaxing inference in both these ways, i.e., moving from inferons to semiquasiinferons, is an ultimate generalization in the sense that it is effectively equivalent to semantics; in other words it is able to delimit any set of truth valuations whatsoever. We have also indicated what kinds of sets of truth-valuations can be delimited by means of semiinferons, quasiinferons, and inferons.

9
Logic as Making Inference Explicit

9.1 Inferentially native operators

In the preceding two chapters we used 'truth-theoretic' means to delimit the landscape of logical operators on which we then attempted to map the regions accessible to various versions of inferentialism. This, however, was not to admit that inferential patterns are mere means of approximating 'real' semantics which is directly accessible by the truth-theoretic (or other model-theoretic) methods. According to inferentialism, the meaning of a logical constant is its inferential role; hence there is no access to this meaning more direct than via explicitating the inferential pattern that confers the role on it. The strategy of our last two chapters was adopted simply in order to show that however you define a logical operator, there should be some kind of inferential way to it (albeit, in some cases the way may be somewhat arduous).

Thus we were taking a 'defensive' attitude to inferentialism. Now we will switch to a more 'offensive' strategy and challenge the assumption that the 'real' semantics of logical constants must, by its nature, be noninferential. The truth-theoretic approach assumes that truth allows us to furnish logical constants with meanings without any recourse to inference. But, according to inferentialism, inference is the *sole* basis of meaning, so, as inferentialists, we require that truth, too, must be based upon it (of course, to the extent to which truth is determined by semantics), and indeed in the first part of the book (Section 5.6) we sketched the outline of an inferentialist theory of truth. Thus the truth-theoretical standpoint cannot be an Archimedean point independent of inference, and it cannot serve as an absolute measure of the success of inferentialism's achievements.

The kind of inferentialism defended in this book involves a theory of the *point* of logic, and hence of logical constants. As Brandom (2000) suggested, logical vocabulary is a means of making explicit our inferential practices and the rules, especially material inferential rules, implicit to them. What does this mean? As long as an inferential rule is merely implicit to our practices (in the sense that we treat some inferences as correct, and others as incorrect), our only option is to either obey or disobey the rule. We cannot, for example, argue for or against its reasonableness. We cannot say that an alternative version of such a rule (e.g., that the premise of the inference from *There is a striped animal over there* to *We should run away* should be amended to *There is a tiger over there*) would be more useful.

Our thesis, then, is that logical vocabulary renders it possible to bring the rules, articulated as sentences, into the public space and thereby legitimize them as potential subject matter for argumentation. They become a regular part of the game of giving and asking for reasons. Once we have the connective *if...then...*, we can form the claim *If there is a striped animal over there, we should run away* and we can ask for and give reasons for this claim.

This thesis is special in that it states that a logical vocabulary has a clear purpose; moreover, it allows us to assess various kinds of logical words from this viewpoint: we might find reasons to say that some logical words are *better* than others. We might even be able to argue to the effect that one kind of logic (say, intuitionist) is better, or at least more faithful to the task assigned to logic, than another (say, classical). (Of course, we cannot expect the verdict that there is only one true logic, for the task is delimited with great leeway; 'making inferences explicit' may be helped in different ways by various means and different logics may contribute to it in their different ways.)

Suppose now that we have an inferential structure, in the sense of the previous chapters, in which B is inferable from A, i.e., that

$$A \vdash B.$$

What would it mean to make this fact *explicit* within the underlying structure? We need a sentence which *expresses* the fact that B is inferable from A. But what does it take for a sentence of such a structure to *express* this? Presumably to be true iff B is inferable from A. But the relation $\vdash$ is unchanging and hence the explicitating claim would be true necessarily, and the counterpart of necessary truth within the structure is clearly theoremhood (i.e., inferability from a void sequence).

Hence to make the inferability of a sentence from another sentence explicit is to have, for every pair of sentences A and B, a sentence that is a theorem iff $A \vdash B$. Let us form the name of such an 'explicitating' sentence by means of the sign $\triangleright$, hence let, for every A and B,

(*) $A \vdash B$ iff $\vdash A \triangleright B$,

and, more generally,

(**) $X, A \vdash B$ iff $X \vdash A \triangleright B$.

We will call the operator $\triangleright$ defined in this way a *deductor* (for the inferential structure). (Note the indefinite article; (*) can obviously be satisfied by rather different operators.) Given this, to claim $A \triangleright B$ (as a necessary truth, i.e., $\vdash A \triangleright B$) *is* to claim that B is inferable from A.

It is clear that (**) is valid for every A and B iff the following two metarules are in force:

(DED) $\dfrac{X, A \vdash B}{X \vdash A \triangleright B}$ (CODED) $\dfrac{X \vdash A \triangleright B}{X, A \vdash B}$

This yields us also the answer to the question of how to *build* a structure with a deductor: it is clearly enough to have the binary operator $\triangleright$ and to include (DED) + (CODED) into its basis.

It is also easily seen that if we restrict ourselves to standard structures, (CODED) becomes equivalent to the *modus ponens* inferential rule:

(MP) $A \triangleright B, A \vdash B$.

For suppose that (CODED) is in force. As $A \triangleright B \vdash A \triangleright B$ (according to (REF)), (CODED) yields us $A \triangleright B, A \vdash B$, hence (MP) is in force. Suppose, conversely, that (MP) is in force, and assume that $X \vdash A \triangleright B$. From this and from (MP) we get, using (CUT), $X, A \vdash B$. Hence (CODED) is in force. Thus, within a standard inferential structure, (CODED) is in force iff (MP) is.

If we now look at $\triangleright$, we can see that it is the standard implication of intuitionist or classical logic (the two implications do not differ until they come to interact with their respective negations). Hence what we have is implication as delimited within the so called *positive logic*:[1] it constitutes the purely implicative part of the intuitionist as well as classical propositional calculus (if 'implicative part' is interpreted as referring to what is provable from purely implicative axioms).[2]

Does $\rhd$ defined in this way allow us to express not only that a sentence is inferable from another sentence, but that it is inferable from a *sequence* of sentences? Of course it does, for

$A_1, ..., A_n \vdash B$

becomes equivalent to

$\vdash A_1 \rhd (...(A_n \rhd B)...).$

But this is a slightly oblique way of expressing this; a straightforward way would lead via introducing, for every pair of sentences A and B, another new sentence, say $A \otimes B$, such that

$X, A, B, Y \vdash C$ iff $X, A \otimes B, Y \vdash C.$

Let us call the new operator $\otimes$ the *amalgamator*. The definition of amalgamator can again be given in terms of a pair of metarules:

(AMLG) $\quad \dfrac{X, A, B, Y \vdash C}{X, A \otimes B, Y \vdash C}$ $\qquad$ (DEAMLG) $\quad \dfrac{X, A \otimes B, Y \vdash C}{X, A, B, Y \vdash C}$

If X is the sequence $A_1, A_2, ..., A_{n-1}, A_n$, then we will write $\otimes X$ as the shorthand for $(A_1 \otimes (A_2 \otimes (...(A_{n-1} \otimes A_n))))$. Now it is obviously the case that

$X \vdash A$ iff $\vdash (\otimes X) \rhd A$

It is not difficult to show that within a standard inferential structure, (AMLG) and (DEAMLG) become equivalent to (ICN), (ECN1), and (ECN2):

(ICN) $\qquad A, B \vdash A \otimes B$
(ECN1) $\qquad A \otimes B \vdash A$
(ECN2) $\qquad A \otimes B \vdash B$

Suppose that (AMLG) and (DEAMLG) are in force. We get (ICN) from $A \otimes B \vdash A \otimes B$ by (DEAMLG), and we get (ECN1) or (ECN2), from $A, B \vdash A$, or $A, B \vdash B$ (which we get from (REF) by (EXT)) by (AMLG). Suppose, conversely, that (ICN), (ECN1), and (ECN2) are in force. We get from the premise X, $A{\otimes}B$, $Y \vdash C$ of (DEAMLG) to its conclusion using (ICN) and (CUT); and we get from the premise X, A, B, $Y \vdash C$ of (AMLG) to its conclusion using (ECN1), (ECN2), (CON) and (CUT). Hence within a standard inferential structure (AMLG) and (DEAMLG) are in force iff (ICN), (ECN1), and (ECN2) are.

Both the deductor and the amalgamator are operators which emerge as natural tools once we set out to make the relation of inference explicit.[3] Are there some other similarly 'inferentially native' operators?

9.2   Anti-deductor?

The operators we have introduced so far have enabled us to explicitate claims to the effect that a sentence is inferable from other sentences. But we might also want to claim the contrary: namely that a sentence is *not* inferable from other sentences. If we write $X \nvdash A$ for 'A is not inferable from X', then we might want to have an 'anti-deductor' $\rhd$ such that

X, $A \nvdash B$ iff $X \vdash A \rhd B$.

However, in contrast to the previous cases, it is wholly unclear how this could be turned into inferential (meta)rules which could be integrated into a basis for an inferential system. Moreover, such an operator would not be feasible at all. It is clear that nondeducibility does not admit weakening, in the sense that a conclusion's not being deducible from premises surely does not entail its not being deducible from *more* premises. But the presence of the anti-deductor would force just this: if X, $A \nvdash B$ yields $X \vdash A \rhd B$, then it yields also X, $C \vdash A \rhd B$, and hence X, A, $C \nvdash B$. (In particular, if $A \nvdash B$, then A, $B \nvdash B$, which is hardly what we could accept.)[4]

It follows that the fact that a sentence is not inferable from other sentences should not be a premise of the introduction rule of a logical operator (at least until (EXT) is in force). But what might still be possible is to consider a weakened version of the project of an anti-deductor, which would not feature non-inferability in this problematic way. We can consider the possibility that what we will make explicit in terms of $A \rhd B$ would not be that B is not inferable from A, but that B *cannot* become inferable from A.

But could this happen at all? Are we in certain cases warranted in requiring that an inferential link between A and B cannot be forged as a matter of principle? Well, a situation that we should surely want to avoid is a breakdown of the whole inferential structure. Therefore, if an extension of an inferential relation could bring about such a breakdown, we had better block it. Can this happen? Can an inferential structure 'break down'?

It would surely be such a breakdown if it turned out to be *trivial*. A structure with an empty inference relation is, from this viewpoint, clearly anomalous. And the same holds for a structure in which everything is inferable from everything. Structures like these are clearly worthless, and we should avoid turning ours into one such. (This is precisely what results from the introduction of a connective like *tonk*.) Hence, the situation in which making A inferable from X would result in making everything inferable from everything (it is clear that it cannot result in making nothing inferable from nothing!) should make us block the inference. Therefore, writing '$X \vdash \bot$' for *everything is inferable from X* (or X *is inconsistent*), we might, coming back to our vague notion of an anti-deductor, want at least:

$$\frac{B \vdash \bot \quad \vdash A}{\vdash A \not\vartriangleright B}$$

and, more generally,

$$\frac{X, B \vdash \bot \quad X \vdash A}{X \vdash A \not\vartriangleright B}$$

(As for the latter, it is important to realize that the intuitive sense of $X \vdash A \not\vartriangleright B$ is *not* 'B should not be inferable from X and A', but rather 'B should not be inferable from A in the case that all elements of X are theorems).'

Moreover, it seems that if $B \vdash \bot$, we should also have to block the very possibility of $\vdash B$, for which we would need not an anti-deductor, but a unary operator $\varnothing$ such that

$$\frac{B \vdash \bot}{\vdash \varnothing B}$$

and, more generally,

$$\frac{X, B \vdash \bot}{X \vdash \varnothing B}$$

(Again, it is important to realize that $X \vdash \varnothing B$ should not be read as 'B should not be inferable from X', but rather 'B should not be a theorem in the case that elements of X are theorems.')

Let us call an operator marking potential inferences that would lead to the fatal explosion of the inference relation an *explosion-detector*. Hence an explosion-detector $\varnothing$ is governed not only by:

(ED) $$\frac{X, B \vdash \perp}{X \vdash \varnothing B}$$

but also by the converse:

(COED) $$\frac{X \vdash \varnothing B}{X, B \vdash \perp}$$

It is easy to see that once we have an explosion-detector $\varnothing$ and a deductor $\triangleright$, we can define a (sort of) anti-deductor in their terms: $A \not\triangleright B$ can be a shorthand for $\varnothing(A \triangleright B)$.

However, let us stress we are still only halfway to the definition of the explosion-detector:

$$X \vdash \perp$$

does not denote an inferential rule, it is merely our shortcut for

$X \vdash A$ for every A.

In some contexts it would be possible to replace $X \vdash \perp$ simply by $X \vdash A$ (where A is not a constituent of X), but this would clearly not work in the position of the antecedent of a metarule:

$$\frac{X, B \vdash A}{X \vdash \varnothing B}$$

does *not* state that if everything is inferable from X and B, then $\varnothing B$ is inferable from X, but rather that this is the case if *anything* (i.e., at least one sentence) is inferable from X and B. Also, it is not possible to replace $X \vdash \perp$ by all inferences of the form $X \vdash A$, for these are infinite in number (unless our language is finite, which is clearly not an interesting case).

There is the well-known easy way out of this: namely to adopt '$\perp$' as a new logical constant ('nullary operator') characterized by the rule:

(EXPL) $\quad \perp \vdash A$

Given this, we can construe (ED) and (COED) as fully fledged metarules.[5] (It is clear that once we do this, (ED) and (COED) become the respective instances of (DED) and (CODED) so that the whole 'work of explosion-detecting' becomes loaded on $\bot$.)

Within the framework of a standard inferential structure, we can reduce (COED) to

(COED*) $\varnothing A, A \vdash B.$

For suppose (COED*) is in force. We get from the premise $X \vdash \varnothing A$ of (COED) to its conclusion using (COED*) and (CUT). Suppose, conversely, that (COED) is in force. We get (COED*) from $\varnothing A \vdash \varnothing A$ by (COED). Hence within a standard inferential structure, (COED) is in force iff (COED*) is.

Similarly, we can reduce (ED) to (ED*):

$$(ED^*) \quad \frac{X, A \vdash B \qquad X, A \vdash \varnothing B}{X \vdash \varnothing A}$$

Suppose (ED*) is in force. The premise of (ED) yields us $X, A \vdash B$ and $X, A \vdash \varnothing B$, from which we can get the conclusion of (ED) by (ED*). Suppose, conversely, that (ED) is in force. We have $B, \varnothing B \vdash \bot$ by (COED*), and this, together with the premises of (ED*), yields us, via (CUT), (PERM) and (CON), $X, A \vdash \bot$. Then we get the conclusion of (ED*) by (ED). Hence, within a standard inferential structure in which (COED*) is in force, (ED) is in force iff (ED*) is.

So now we have the following set of rules:

(DED)	$\dfrac{A \vdash B}{\vdash A \triangleright B}$
(MP)	$A \triangleright B, A \vdash B.$
(ICN)	$A, B \vdash A \otimes B$
(ECN1)	$A \otimes B \vdash A$
(ECN2)	$A \otimes B \vdash B$
(ED*)	$\dfrac{X, A \vdash B \qquad X, A \vdash \varnothing B}{X \vdash \varnothing A}$
(COED*)	$\varnothing A, A \vdash B$

It is easy to see that what we have reached in this way is the intuitionist propositional calculus, with $\triangleright$ acting as implication, $\otimes$ as conjunction, and $\varnothing$ as negation.[6] Hence, what we have shown is that the native inferential operators coincide (within the 'normal' environment, i.e., within standard inferential structures) with the intuitionist ones. Therefore we can say that it is intuitionist logic that appears as 'natural' from the inferentialist viewpoint.

9.3   Multi-conclusion inference?

So far we have restricted our attention to standard inferential structures. What if we alleviate this restriction?

First, let us consider allowing for multi-conclusion inference, i.e., for what we have termed quasiinference. What immediately springs to mind is that, in analogy to the amalgamator, the multi-conclusion inference would invite us to introduce its analogue on the right; namely the operator $\oplus$ such that:

$$X \vdash Y, A, B, Z \text{ iff } X \vdash Y, A \oplus B, Z$$

Of greater interest is that it opens new ways to define the deductor: besides our (DED) and (CODED), we can now consider the more general:

$$(\text{DED}^+) \quad \frac{X, A \vdash B, Y}{X \vdash A \rhd B, Y} \qquad (\text{CODED}^+) \quad \frac{X \vdash A \rhd B, Y}{X, A \vdash B, Y}$$

And it is well known (see, e.g., Došen, 1994) that this makes a difference: for example, if $\rhd$ is introduced by means of $(\text{DED}^+) + (\text{CODED}^+)$, though not if it is introduced by means of (DED) + (CODED), it holds that:

$$(\text{PL}) \quad (A \rhd B) \rhd A \vdash A$$

That this does not hold for a deductor introduced by (DED) + (CODED) follows from the fact that this deductor, as we have seen, yields the intuitionist implication, whereas PL amounts to Peirce's Law, notorious for being valid classically, but not intuitionistically. We will prove that it does hold for $\rhd$ introduced in terms of $(\text{DED}^+) + (\text{CODED}^+)$, but first we must generalize our concept of standardness (as defined in Section 7.2) from inference to quasiinference. The structural rules with which the quasiinference must comply in order to be standard are obvious:

$$(\text{REF}) \quad \frac{}{X \vdash X}$$

(EXT)
$$\frac{X,\,Y \vdash Z}{X,\,A,\,Y \vdash Z} \qquad\qquad \frac{X \vdash Y,\,Z}{X \vdash Y,\,A,\,Z}$$

(CON)
$$\frac{X,\,A,\,A,\,Y \vdash Z}{X,\,A,\,Y \vdash Z} \qquad\qquad \frac{X \vdash Y,\,A,\,A,\,Z}{X \vdash Y,\,A,\,Z}$$

(PERM)
$$\frac{X,\,A,\,B,\,Y \vdash Z}{X,\,B,\,A,\,Y \vdash Z} \qquad\qquad \frac{X \vdash Y,\,A,\,B,\,Z}{X \vdash Y,\,B,\,A,\,Z}$$

(CUT)
$$\frac{X,\,A,\,Y \vdash Z \quad U \vdash V,\,A,\,W}{X,\,Y,\,U \vdash Z,\,V,\,W}$$

Now we can see that if (DED⁺) and (CODED⁺) are in force in a quasiinferential structure, then so is (PL). The reason is that we can get $\vdash A \triangleright B$, A from $A \vdash B$, A by (DED⁺), and from it plus $(A \triangleright B) \triangleright A$, $A \triangleright B \vdash A$, which is an instance of (MP), we get $(A \triangleright B) \triangleright A \vdash A$ by means of (CUT) and (CON).

The fact that (DED⁺) + (CODED⁺) validate Peirce's Law indicates that they, in contrast to (DED) + (CODED), would lead us to *classical* implication. And this is indeed the case. Hence we have two kinds of deductors, depending on whether or not we restrict ourselves to (single-conclusion) inference.

The situation is similar with respect to the explosion-detector ('negation'). We have at least three possibilities for capturing the intuitive idea underlying it:

(ED⁻)
$$\frac{B \vdash}{\vdash \varnothing B}$$
(COED⁻)
$$\frac{\vdash \varnothing B}{B \vdash}$$

(ED)
$$\frac{X,\,B \vdash}{X \vdash \varnothing B}$$
(COED)
$$\frac{X \vdash \varnothing B}{X,\,B \vdash}$$

(ED⁺)
$$\frac{X,\,B \vdash Y}{X \vdash \varnothing B,\,Y}$$
(COED⁺)
$$\frac{X \vdash \varnothing B,\,Y}{X,\,B \vdash Y}$$

It is again clear that it is only the last version of the definition that allows us to prove the law of double negation, and hence that it introduces the *classical* negation: if (ED⁺) and (COED⁺) are in force in a quasiinferential structure, then so is $\varnothing\varnothing A \vdash A$. The reason is that we get $\vdash \varnothing A$, A from $A \vdash A$ by (ED⁺), and we get $\varnothing\varnothing A$, $\varnothing A \vdash$ from $\varnothing\varnothing A \vdash \varnothing\varnothing A$ by (COED⁺), while we get $\varnothing\varnothing A \vdash A$ from them using (CUT). This indicates that for multi-conclusion inference, classical logic is as natural as the intuitionist one for the single-conclusion inference.[7]

Note that to say that classical logic is *natural* for multi-conclusion inference is to say that multi-conclusion inference leads us to classical logic in the strong sense, in which the semantics of classical logic is *classical* in the sense of Belnap and Massey (1990) (see Section 8.5), i.e., it admits only truth-valuations compatible with the classical truth-tables. Of course we can move from intuitionist to classical logic also more directly, by adding some rule of inference – such as the rule of double negation – but in this way we do not exclude all the non-classical valuations, hence we reach that semantics of classical logic that Belnap and Massey (ibid.) call *inferential*.

9.4 Necessity

The fact that the functioning of the operators $\rhd$, $\otimes$, and $\varnothing$ is governed by the standard set of axioms of either classical or intuitionist logic may be understood, in the spirit of the previous chapter, in terms of carving out a space of acceptable truth valuations. In the case of the axioms of classical logic, the description of this space is quite straightforward: it contains all valuations that respect the classical truth-tables for implication, conjunction, and negation (and, possibly, as we pointed out in Section 8.5, also some other, 'devious but idle' valuations which we can disregard for now). That is, it does not prevent a sentence like $A \rhd B$ from changing its truth value. Indeed, if it is the axioms of classical logic which do the separation of the admissible from the inadmissible valuations, '$\rhd$' will behave like material implication. But if we accept this view, the sentence '$A \rhd B$' can hardly be said to express – hence, nor to make explicit – the *inferability* of B from A. It would seem that what it expresses is merely that (right now) A is 0 or B is 1. In short, if '$A \rhd B$' is to be understood as saying that B is correctly inferable from A, should it not be true or false *necessarily*?

Of course, what we actually did when introducing the deductor was to state the equivalence of $A \vdash B$ not with $A \rhd B$, but rather with $\vdash A \rhd B$. Hence it is the latter as a whole that is expressive of the inference. But this only says that it is not $\rhd$ alone that does the expressive work, and the question is whether we can have a connective that would do better in this respect. What would we have to request, in proof-theoretic terms, to achieve the intended, 'strong' version of the deductor?

It would seem that what we need to stipulate over and above the equivalence of $A \vdash B$ and $\vdash A \rhd B$ is that if not $A \vdash B$, then $A \rhd B$ not only is not a theorem, but is *false*, and cannot be true at all. We have already stressed that the inferentialist need not pay too much attention to such truth-theoretic considerations; what she is after is not capturing constants the semantics of which is 'really' given in terms of truth or truth conditions, but rather capturing and explicating the inferential patterns that are constitutive of the constants. But the problem we have just hinted at in truth-theoretic terms can be stated even in proof-theoretic ones. In these terms, the fact that the inferability of B from A, i.e., the fact that $A \vdash B$ yields $\vdash A \triangleright B$ does not seem to be sufficient, for it seems it should be complemented by the fact that if B is *not* inferable from A, $A \nvdash B$, then $\vdash \varnothing(A \triangleright B)$. If this is the case, then for any A and B either $\vdash A \triangleright B$, or $\vdash \varnothing(A \triangleright B)$, and $A \triangleright B$ becomes rigid in the required way (corresponding to being, in truth-theoretic terms, constantly true or constantly false).

Hence it seems that what we might need is:

(NDED)
$$\frac{A \nvdash B}{\vdash \varnothing(A \triangleright B)}$$

But, needless to say, this is not a (meta)rule, hence to make $\triangleright$ into a 'strong' deductor, we would need to transform it into one. As we know that $A \vdash B$ iff $\vdash A \triangleright B$, and hence that $A \nvdash B$ iff $\nvdash A \triangleright B$, we may rewrite (NDED) into the form of:

(NDED*)
$$\frac{\nvdash (A \triangleright B)}{\vdash \varnothing(A \triangleright B)}$$

We may want to approach the problem from a more general vantage point, and think about introducing a specific 'necessity' operator $\boxdot$ that would turn a given sentence into a 'rigid' sentence $\boxdot A$ such that $\vdash \boxdot A$ iff $\vdash A$ and $\nvdash A$ iff $\vdash \varnothing \boxdot A$. (The 'strong' version of the deductor could then be built from the 'weak' one as $\boxdot(A \triangleright B)$.)

Hence we have the following desiderata on $\boxdot A$:

(NEC)	$\dfrac{\vdash A}{\vdash \boxdot A}$	(CONEC)	$\dfrac{\vdash \boxdot A}{\vdash A}$
(NNEC)	$\dfrac{\nvdash A}{\vdash \varnothing \boxdot A}$	(CONNEC)	$\dfrac{\vdash \varnothing \boxdot A}{\nvdash A}$

Of course, while (NEC) and (CONEC) are directly inferential rules, (NNEC) and (CONNEC) are not, and it is questionable how far they can be approximated by ones. Assuming that $\vdash \varnothing \boxdot A$ excludes $\vdash \boxdot A$ ('consistency'), (NEC) entails (CONNEC). However, there is still the task of converting (NNEC) into an inferential rule, or at least approximating it by one.

In fact, what we are aiming at, in this way, is the modal logic of Carnap (1947), which is sometimes called C. As Thomason (1973) showed, this logic is characterized precisely by the fact that its class of theorems contains ¬□A whenever it does not contain A. Thomason presents an (infinitary) axiomatization and shows that there is a close connection between C and the strongest Kripkean logic, S5; indeed, the set of theorems of S5 constitute the greatest 'well-behaved' part of C. (A theorem of C is a theorem of S5 iff all its substitutional variants are also theorems of C.) Hence we can think about settling for the S5-kind necessity operator, which has the well-known neat axiomatization. Another possibility is to base the logic on incompatibility which, as we will discuss in the next section, secures us direct access to C-kind necessity.

9.5   Incompatibility

Brandom and Aker (2008) developed a version of inferentialist semantics based on the concept of incompatibility, rather than on the concept of inference. And, surprisingly, what they thus reached was classical, rather that intuitionist logic. Is it so that it is essential to inference and incompatibility that they lead to such different systems?

Brandom and Aker's logic is based on the operators ∧ and ¬, the definitions of which, in terms of the relation of incompatibility, is as follows:

$X \cup \{A \wedge B\} \in \text{Inc}$ iff $X \cup \{A, B\} \in \text{Inc}$,

$X \cup \{\neg A\} \in \text{Inc}$ iff $X \vdash A$;

where Inc is defined as follows:

(Inc1) if $X \in \text{Inc}$ and $X \subset Y$, then $Y \in \text{Inc}$; and

(Inc2) $X \vdash A$ iff for every Y such that $Y \cup \{A\} \in \text{Inc}$ it is the case that $X \cup Y \in \text{Inc}$;

and it represents the set of all incompatible sets of formulas.

Admitting inconsistency as a primitive notion may be accommodated, within our framework, as a partial relaxation of the single-conclusion framework in the direction of a multiple-conclusion one, in that we allow sequences of the lengths 0 or 1 on the right side of ⊢; hence we

can write $X \vdash$ instead of $X \in$ Inc; which turns Brandom and Aker's definitions into:

(BA∧) $X, A \wedge B \vdash$ iff $X, A, B \vdash$
(BA¬) $X, \neg A \vdash$ iff $X \vdash A$;
(Inc1) if $X \vdash$, then $X, A \vdash$
(Inc2) $X \vdash A$ iff for every Y such that $Y, A \vdash$ it is the case that $X, Y \vdash$.

(Inc1) is then just the structural rule (EXT) ((PERM) and (CON) being
implicit to the fact that Brandom and Aker work with *sets* of sentences
rather than sequences). The direct implication of (Inc2) further follows
from (CUT). Note that for the multiple-conclusion inference (and also
already for our restricted version of it, with the right-hand side possibly
empty), we would need a generalization of (Inc2):

(Inc2*) $X \vdash Y$ iff for every Z such that $Z, A \vdash$ for every A from Y it is
the case that $Z, X \vdash$

Dividing (BA∧) into the two implications we have:

(ECN*) $\dfrac{X, A \wedge B \vdash}{X, A, B \vdash}$ (ICN*) $\dfrac{X, A, B \vdash}{X, A \wedge B \vdash}$

which turn out to be equivalent to our definition of conjunction, i.e.,
to:

(ICN) $A, B \vdash A \wedge B$ (ECN1) $A \wedge B \vdash A$ (ECN2) $A \wedge B \vdash B$

This can be shown in the following way: $X, A, B \vdash$ can be obtained from
$X, A \wedge B \vdash$ by means of (ICN), and we can, vice versa, obtain $X, A \wedge B \vdash$ from
$X, A, B \vdash$ by means of (ECN1) and (ECN2). To see, conversely, that (ICN),
(ECN1), and (ECN2) are in force given (ECN*) and (ICN*), we must see
that $X, A \vdash$ (or $X, B \vdash$) entails $X, A \wedge B \vdash$ (using (Inc1) and (ICN*)), which,
in turn, yields (ECN1) (or (ECN2)), and that $X, A \wedge B \vdash$ entails $X, A, B \vdash$,
which is nothing other than (ICN).

The situation is less trivial with respect to negation. Note also that
our definition of $\varnothing$ within the single-conclusion framework, (ED) and
(COED), amounts to making the $\varnothing B$ into the *minimal incompatible* of
B. We saw that (COED) is equivalent to (COED*), stating that $\varnothing B$ is
incompatible with B, and (ED) can be read as stating that $\varnothing B$ is minimal

among the sentences incompatible with B: if X is incompatible with B, then $\varnothing B$ is inferable from it.

This appears to be the most natural way of introducing negation within the inferentialist framework. However, if we base the framework on the concept of incompatibility and need to find the necessary and sufficient condition for X being incompatible with $\neg B$, then it is the inclusion also of the converse to (ED)+(COED) that comes naturally. The point is that the simplest condition of the required sort, as used by Brandom and Aker, amounts to:

$$(\text{ED}^{BA}) \qquad \frac{X \vdash B}{X, \neg B \vdash} \qquad\qquad (\text{COED}^{BA}) \qquad \frac{X, \neg B \vdash}{X \vdash B}$$

Now, it is easy to see that (ED^{BA}) + (COED^{BA}), unlike (ED) plus (COED), yield the law of double negation, the hallmark of intuitionist logic:

$$(\neg\neg) \qquad \neg\neg A \vdash A$$

As $\neg A \vdash \neg A$, we have, according to (ED^{BA}), $\neg\neg A, \neg A \vdash$, and we then get $(\neg\neg)$ directly according to (COED^{BA}).

This indicates that the fact that Brandom and Aker reach classical, rather than intuitionist logic is not a matter of an inherent difference between incompatibility and inference, but rather of what appears as 'natural' from the viewpoints forced on us when we accept the respective basic notions. Keep in mind what we mentioned at the end of the previous section: an inferentialist way to classical logic need not lead via fully fledged quasiinference (i.e., multi-conclusion inference); if we do not strictly require that 'classical' semantics of classical logic, fiddling with axioms is all that is needed.

Let us now turn our attention to the way Brandom and Aker (ibid.) introduced the necessity operator into their logic:

($\square$) $X \cup \{\square A\} \in$ Inc iff $X \in$ Inc or there is a Y such that $X, Y \notin$ Inc and not $Y \vdash A$.

Rewritten into our notation this reads:

($\square$) $X, \square A \vdash$ iff $X \vdash$ or there is a Y such that $X, Y \nvdash$ and $Y \nvdash A$.

Brandom and Aker showed that these two theorems follow:

(□1) □*A* ⊢ iff there is no *Y* such that *Y* ⊬ or there is a *Y* such that *Y* ⊬ and *Y*, *A* ⊢

(□2) *X*, □*A* ⊢ iff (*X* ⊢ or □*A* ⊢)

This enables us to show that (□) can be considerably simplified. For if we substitute the right hand side of (□1) for its left-hand side in (□2), we get

X,□*A* ⊢ iff (*X* ⊢ or there is no *Y* such that *Y* ⊬ or there is a *Y* such that *Y* ⊬ and *Y*, *A* ⊢).

Hence, provided not every set is inconsistent, Brandom and Aker's prima facie complex definition reduces to something rather simple: a consistent set is incompatible with □*A* iff there is a consistent set incompatible with *A*; in other words, if there is a consistent set incompatible with *A*, then every set is incompatible with □*A*, whereas if there is no such set, no set is incompatible with □*A*.

Notice that this definition of necessity leads to the straightforward fulfillment of the problematic condition (NNEC) discussed in the previous section. For ⊬ *A* iff there is a *Z* such that *Z* ⊬ and *Z*, *A* ⊢, and this, according to (□), is the case iff *X*, □*A* ⊢ for every *X*, which, in turn, is the case iff *X* ⊢ ¬□*A* (according to the definition of ¬). Hence ⊬ *A* entails ⊢ ¬□A.

This shows that this definition of incompatibility leads to the logic C; or, if we take 'structurality' (i.e., the constraint that nothing is a theorem of logic unless all its substitutional variants are also such theorems) as a *conditio sine qua non* of logic, to S5. (Remember that the theorems of S5 are all those theorems of C all the structural variants of which are also theorems.) Here it is, then, where basing logic on incompatibility may make a difference.[8]

9.6   Logical operators as structural markers and substructural logics

Došen (1994) suggested seeing logical operators as 'punctuation marks'.[9] This is a view close to the one entertained here, only I think that it overemphasizes the syntactical function of the operators. Rather than seeing logical operators as merely syntactic devices, I prefer to see them as marking certain structural features of inferential structure(s). This is very much of a piece with the view of the nature of logic put forward here:

we tend to shape the frameworks of our linguistic utterances (i.e., our languages) into certain kinds of structures and we use logical vocabulary to refer to certain distinguished vertices of the structures. For example, we can say that classical as well as intuitionist conjunction refers to an *inferential supremum* of two sentences: the conjunction of A and B is a sentence from which both A and B are inferable and which is, moreover, the minimal sentence with this property; if any other sentence entails both A and B, then it must entail also their conjunction.

From this viewpoint, each operator maps sentences on a minimum/maximum[10] of a propositional function. Thus the conjunction of A and B is the minimal sentence C such that:

$C \vdash A$,
$C \vdash B$

The minimality is understood in such a way that if there is a D satisfying the same pattern, then:

$D \vdash C$

Hence, from this vantage point, logical constants are devices that serve to refer to the extremal points of inferential structures.

What is important is that the whole of this structure need not be explicitly articulated in the language in question, i.e., not for every vertex of the structure must there correspond a sentence. The 'making it explicit' that is effected by the logical operators then amounts to revealing the whole of the structure, which is partly represented by the language in question. Let us indicate, in greater detail, what this amounts to in the case of a standard inferential structure.

In the previous chapter we saw that an inferential structure $<S, \vdash>$ is the structure of a semantic system iff it is standard, i.e., iff it complies with the structural metarules. This is to say that if $<S, \vdash>$ is standard, then it is embeddable into a Boolean algebra. Let us, conversely, assume that $<S, \vdash>$ is embeddable into a Boolean algebra in the sense that there is a function i such that $A_1, ..., A_n \vdash A$ iff $i(A_1) \cap ... \cap i(A_n) \subseteq i(A)$. It is easy to see that this can be the case only when $<S, \vdash>$ is standard: hence *an inferential structure is standard iff it is embeddable into a Boolean algebra*.

This indicates that there is a sense in which elements of a standard inferential structure do *implicitly* have their conjunctions, disjunctions, and so forth, although they do not have them explicitly: if there are no expressions within the language that would express them. They do have them implicitly in the sense that they form a (proto-)structure that can naturally be extended to a structure in which these elements are present. The 'naturally' can also be read as 'conservatively', thus achieving the characteristic of logical operators we discussed in Section 8.1; the addition of logical operators adds nothing substantial to the stratum of language to which it is added, it only institutes a new stratum.

Now, the view of the nature of logic put forward above is that the point of such a new stratum is in making explicit what is implicit within the old one. And natural languages appear to have the peculiar tendency to be explicitated in this way: what is first implicit in the behavior (making inferences) tends to find an explicit expression (in the form of a sentence stating that the inference holds). This is important, for only what is explicit can be assessed, discussed and possibly also modified or rejected.

9.7   Summary of Chapter 9

In this chapter we started from the hypothesis that logical vocabulary plays a role that is essentially expressivist; that this vocabulary makes it possible for us not only to follow the material rules of our discourse, but also to formulate these rules in the form of claims that may enter the game of giving and asking for reasons. We indicated what kinds of words, in general, we would need for this task, and we arrived at some basic, generic logical operators which we dubbed *native*. We found that the kind of logic to which these considerations lead most directly is the intuitionist one.

We have also shown that it is not the case that there is no room for classical logic within this inferentialist-expressivist framework. First, we indicated that classical logic comes as the most natural, if we embrace the multiple-conclusion variety of inference (quasiinference). Second, we showed that the gap between it and intuitionist logic diminishes if we take incompatibility rather than inference as the basis of logic. Finally, we indicated that the 'making it explicit' effected by logic can, from the algebraic viewpoint, also be construed as revealing all the vertices of a logical structure which appears to us to be only imperfectly embodied in our language.

10
Rules of Logic

10.1 Substantiation of logical rules

Our inferentialist stance has led us to an attitude to the nature of logic that can be called *expressivist*. (However, we have to keep in mind that this sense of the term *expressivism*, which is due to Brandom, 2000, is different from some more usual senses).[1] In order to explore the consequences of taking this attitude, we must distinguish carefully two possible senses of *logic*: one being related to natural language, the other to the languages of formal logic. In the former sense, we use the term to refer to the loosely delimited 'logical' (i.e., 'topic-neutral', 'argumentative', etc.) words of natural language and the rules governing them, whereas in the latter sense it refers to the explicitly defined logical constants of the formal languages with their governing rules.

Let us first consider *logic* in the former sense. From our viewpoint, the logical vocabulary of natural language has materialized as a result of the tendency 'of the language' (i.e., of those who speak it) to make the implicit inferential rules governing the employment of its utterances explicit. Once the utterances come to be governed by (material) inferential rules, these rules tend to become explicit by being articulated as sentences formulated with the help of the 'logical' words. Thus the nature of logical vocabulary derives from the explicitating drift, and we have the particular logical words and rules governing them that we do because these are the ones that have served us well at making our material inferences explicit.

As for the logical vocabulary of the languages of formal logic, there is more than one way to understand it. One of these ways is to see it as an attempt to improve on the 'logical' vocabulary of our natural language: of providing more appropriate means to make the inferences of natural language explicit than are provided by 'natural' logic. Though I think this was the preferred construal of the role of logic at the dawn of modern logical theory and I am afraid it may still hold significant sway, I am extremely skeptical about its viability. I feel suspicious about endeavors to really 'improve' on natural language; as already noted (see Section 5.4), I am convinced that language, having been formed by millennia of natural selection, is more perfect than we can make it via our engineering. (Of course, it is perfect *with respect to the ends it serves*, not if we assign it some *other*, deliberately chosen ends.)

Another way to see the logical vocabulary of the languages of logic, and indeed the whole logical languages, is as simplified and idealized models of natural language. Such models disregard many features of natural language and thus reach an idealized form that is, though not more functional, more perspicuous. The situation is perhaps similar to building a wooden model of a spaceship: the point is clearly not that the model would be better in terms of functioning as a ship, but rather that it disregards many features of the actual ship and thus gives us a perspicuous view of some of its most salient features.[2]

What logic studies, from this viewpoint, are inferential patterns governing logical words (usually not directly the 'logical' words of natural language, but the logical constants of the languages of formal logic as their regimentations). This seems to be neither too controversial, nor too unusual. However, if we explore this through to its consequences, it will give us a picture of the nature of logic very different from the usual one. To see this, let us consider the traditional problem of the nature of logical laws.

What guarantees that the rules of our logic are the 'right' ones, the ones that make us *rational* in the way we are convinced we *are* rational? Well, it was this very kind of rules, and the ensuing structure, which were responsible for powerfully upgrading our cognition, for equipping us with the ability to reason.[3] But of course no kind of necessity other than the pragmatic necessity of evolutionary advantage is in play here. The rules of our languages are not 'correct' or 'substantiated' in any sense beyond this pragmatic one: without them, we would not be reasoning (hence rational), concept-mongering creatures.

Boghossian (2012, pp. 222–223), writes:

> It seems obvious, then, that even the most sophisticated and powerful philosopher will face the following dilemma: with regard to her most basic logical rules, either she has no entitlement to them, or she has an entitlement that is not grounded in her ability to provide an explicit

argument for them. The skeptical alternative is dire. For if she has no entitlement to her most basic rules, then she has no entitlement to anything that is based upon them; and that means that she will have no entitlement to any of the rules of logic that she is inclined to use and therefore no entitlement to any of the beliefs that she will have based on them. This seems to me too fantastic to believe. It also seems to me to tee up an extreme form of relativism about rationality, one that I find worrisome, both philosophically and socially. For if none of us is entitled to the particular set of logical rules that we operate with, then if others among us were to find it natural to operate with a different and incompatible set of logical rules, then they would have to be deemed as rational as we are, in so far as their use of logical rules is concerned. We could not say that such people were irrational, for they are surely no worse off in their entitlements to their logical rules than we are with respect to ours.

Hence the question is: why is it that we have *reasonable* rules of inference? How is it possible to substantiate them, and how is it possible to substantiate the claim that they are the correct rules as compared with alternative possibilities?

What we are claiming is that we cannot expect a justification in terms of reasons (for these rules establish the very framework in which we can give reasons in the first place),[4] but only a pragmatic kind of justification: they have turned out to work. But this substantiation seems radically insufficient. Is there not more to treating implication in accordance with modus ponens (rather than, e.g., *affirming the consequent*[5]) than usefulness? Should we not be able to say that the first (but not the second) *is correct* and those who follow it (and not the second) are *rational*?

We have already observed that the distinction that inferentialism provides between what people really do and what they take for correct allows us to talk about correctness in one straightforward sense: it is correct to accord with the rules that are in force and it is incorrect to violate them (this is simply what it takes to be a rule!). To use implication (i.e., to use something generally taken to be correctly treated as governed by modus ponens) not in accordance with this rule is incorrect.

But does *being implication* really involve *being governed by modus ponens*? It is important to see that this is part and parcel of inferentialism. (In fact, this is a slight oversimplification: *being implication* must consist in being governed by *some* specific rule or rules, and as modus ponens appears to be the hottest candidate for this role, we disregard alternatives.) Remember that the sentences came to express propositions – and their constituents came to express concepts – as a result of the inferential rules they came to be governed by. And, in fact, the only alternative to this view seems to be the view that implication is in essence a mental token that is such just essentially, independently of what we do with it – a view which I find not only hard to substantiate, but already hard to make sense of.

Can a whole community be incorrect? Can we say that if a given community is employing *affirming the consequent* in place of modus ponens, then it is doing something incorrect or irrational? From what we have just said it follows that, if inferentialism is right, an incorrect employment like this simply *cannot happen*.[6] Suppose that a community does take it for correct to argue from *If it rains, then the streets are wet* and *The streets are wet* to *It rains*: in these circumstances it would then follow that the *If...then...* in the corresponding dialect simply cannot express implication (perhaps *If A then B* expresses what is expressed by *If B then A* in ordinary English?).[7]

Hence, as I have argued elsewhere (see Peregrin, 2010b), it is not possible to have an implication not obeying modus ponens, for modus ponens is (one of the things that is) constitutive for implication.[8] Of course, it is possible not to have implication at all. Languageless brutes do not have it.[9] Are they therefore irrational? Well, this is largely a question of terminology, but we usually do not call them *rational*, at least not in the sense we call ourselves thus.

Can there be creatures that have words (or similar tokens) governed by rules that are comparable to our logical rules, but different? Well, surely there may be various kinds of rather harmless differences. Perhaps they do not have implication, but they have conjunction and negation. Perhaps they have an implication that is more intuitionist than classical; perhaps they have some probabilistic connectives the alignment of which with standard logical operator is not straightforward. (In fact, the logical connectives of our common logical systems are idealizations that we should not expect to find in a pure form in natural languages.) But every language we know does contain a logical skeleton which can be understood as incorporating some basic logic. And the difference from our way of implementing logic does not make us call users of other languages irrational.

Could users of another language have logical constants/rules unlike anything we know? Well, the question then would be why call them *logical* words or *logical* rules and take them as relevant for judging rationality. Perhaps some creature emits sounds chained in a way that is governed by incredibly complex rules which have to do with how the sounds relate to one another in terms of similarity, difference, rhyming and so forth. Why call this logic? What we call logic has to do with implications, conjunctions, negations and so on, with a relatively large, but certainly not unrestricted, spectrum of variation.

Rationality, viewed from this vantage point, is a matter of mastering certain ('cognitive') tools. Just as a creature is called *carnivorous* if it has been equipped, by evolution, with tools to digest meat and with the skills needed to kill and eat other animals, so we can call an animal *rational* if it has been equipped, by evolution, with the tools and skills needed to reason. And it is the contention of inferentialism that such tools are not available to a solitary individual; an individual can come to have them only if there is a community of peers through which it can sieve its protobeliefs to become real beliefs.

10.2   How do we know that the rules of logic hold?

Consider modus ponens as a paradigmatic example of the law of logic. Boghossian (2000) poses the following question:

> To keep matters as simple as possible, let us restrict ourselves to propositional logic and let us suppose that we are working within a system in which modus ponens (MPP) is the only underived rule of inference. My question is this: is it so much as *possible* for us to be justified in supposing that MPP is a valid rule of inference, necessarily truth-preserving in all its applications?

The author classifies the possible answers to this into the following schema:

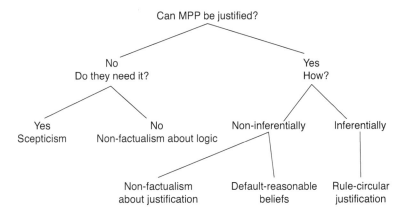

From the viewpoint of expressivism, as exposed in the previous chapter, this schema appears somewhat misleading. What is quite clear, to begin with, is that the rules of logic cannot be justified *in the same way in which we justify sentences within the framework of the rules*; as the rules are what make justification possible, we cannot also hope to have justification for them. Nevertheless, this does not mean that the rules are arbitrary in the sense that there would be no kind of substantiation for them whatsoever – no saying why we should stick to them and not to some alternatives.

The rules *are* arbitrary in the sense that to play the 'game' they let us play, namely the game of giving and asking for reasons, is not *inevitable* for us to play. However, it has turned out that this game is extremely useful; it equips us with the ability to argue and reason. Hence the game, and its rules, are substantiated on grounds that could perhaps be called pragmatic.

Boghossian speaks about expressivism in his exposition of two of the answers in his schema: he talks about 'non-factualist expressivism about logical truth' (p. 238) falling into the category *non-factualism about logic* and also about 'expressivism about justification' (p. 242) that falls into the category *non-factualism about justification*. The difference between the two positions is not quite clear. Therefore we will approach the matter from a slightly different angle, moving from the basic question:

(*) Are we justified in accepting MP?[10]

to a 'meta-question' that, I think, may come to preempt (*):

(**) Can (*) (and especially the term 'MP' it contains) be interpreted so that the question is both (i) meaningful and (ii) nontrivial, i.e., not self-answering?

To understand the fundamental shift in perspective prompted by inferentialism, we must consider (**) thoroughly. The point is that we have come to see logical laws as rules constitutive of the semantics of logical constants, and hence MP is part and parcel of the inferential pattern that governs (classical) implication (and most, if not all, of its nonclassical variants too). So to ask whether MP holds *for implication* does not seem to make much sense, for implication is, by definition, what is governed (besides other) by MP. And to ask whether MP holds for a connective other than implication does not make much sense either, for usually we do not want the other connective to obey MP.[11]

No doubt this short argument may seem shaky, glossing over many important details. Therefore we will now explain these consequences of the inferentialist standpoint in greater detail. Our starting point will be the examination of the meaning of 'MP' in (*).

10.3   What is MP?

What exactly is MP? As Boghossian speaks about 'a system of propositional logic' (hereafter PL), what he could have in mind is, prima facie, something like:

(1) For every pair of sentences A and B of the language of PL it is correct (truth-preserving) to infer B from A and $\overline{A \to B}$ (where $\overline{A \to B}$ is a name of the sentence which arises out of the combination of A and B by means of the implication sign '$\to$').

However, on reappraisal, it seems pretty obvious that this interpretation of 'MP' would not fulfill the second criterion, (ii), of (**), for on this interpretation, there would be no reason to contemplate a positive answer to (*). (1) is a stipulation that we may decide to accept or not to accept for various practical reasons, but how can a stipulation be *justified*? If we do not accept it, then '$\to$' will probably not be an implication, or not an implication of classical logic, but so what? (Note that rejecting (1) would not even preclude our way to classical logic; we could simply use another sign for the classical implication.) The language of PL, of which (1) is a standard part, is our artificial construct and so are the rules we have let govern its symbols, especially '$\to$'. Hence there is no reasonable sense in which we could be *justified*, let alone a priori, in letting '$\to$' be governed by MP in the sense of (1), and (*) would be straightforwardly answered in the negative.

It might be objected that what is in question is not the bare possibility of rejecting (1), but the possibility of rejecting (1) *without depriving $\to$ of the status of implication*. Does this help? I am afraid not, for what grants '$\to$' the status of implication? There would appear to be two possibilities: either it is inferential rules by which it is governed, or the truth table which fixes its semantics. In the first case, MP would be one of the rules constitutive of its being implication, so to say that we cannot reject (1) without depriving $\to$ of the status of implication would boil down to the truism that we cannot reject MP without rejecting MP. And the second case is only slightly less trivial: if '$\to$' is associated with the truth table, then we cannot reject (1) simply because it describes one line of the table (namely the one saying that if A is 1 and B is 0, then $A{\to}B$ is bound to be 0), and the impossibility of canceling our stipulation without canceling our stipulation does not have anything to do with the a priori/a posteriori status of any of our beliefs.

A similarly unhelpful move would be to say that what is in question is the possibility of rejecting (1) *without abandoning classical logic* (with the implication $\to$). Again, (*) interpreted in *this* way would be straightforwardly self-answering. It is simply (co-)constitutive of classical PL that '$\to$' behaves the way it does, in particular that it obeys MP; hence rejecting MP simply *is* abandoning classical logic. In short, if we consider Boghossian's 'MP' as a matter of a formal language, then its acceptance/rejection is simply a matter of our decision (which, in some senses, might be relatively 'reasonable', or relatively useful, but surely not justified in a nonnegotiable manner). Hence this could hardly be the right sense of 'MP' in Boghossian's question.

All of this seems to indicate that if (*) is to be nontrivial, then 'MP' cannot be conceived of as a matter of a formal, artificial language. The rules of languages of this sort are *our* creatures: we are free to set them up as we like, and it makes little sense to ask whether we are *justified* (let alone a priori) in accepting this or that rule. Of course we can say that we are justified in the sense that by adopting some rules we reach something *useful* or *interesting*, but this pragmatic sense is clearly not the sense of *justification* relevant for (*).

This may make us try to interpret 'MP' in a wholly different way: not as a matter of a formal language, but rather as a matter of a natural one. So let us try:

(2) For every pair of sentences A and B of English it is correct (truth-preserving) to infer B from A and $\ulcorner$If A, then $B\urcorner$.

However, whether this is valid appears to be an empirical question concerning English, hence to believe it would be reasonable only if we had some empirical knowledge about English, and hence it can hardly be a candidate for a priori knowledge. Hence also this can hardly be the right sense of Boghossian's 'MP'.

What about, then,

(3) For every pair of sentences A and B of English it is correct (truth-preserving) to infer the proposition expressed by B from that expressed by A and that expressed by $\ulcorner$If A, then $B\urcorner$.

There are two ways to read the phrase *the proposition expressed by ...* in this claim: rigidly and non-rigidly. In the latter case, *the proposition expressed by A* would be just any proposition that happens to be expressed by *A* at the moment of its utterance, and consequently (3) would come out as equivalent with (2), so we are left with the rigid reading. On this reading, (3) talks about definite propositions: the ones that are now (in the moment when I am writing this, and hence presumably, but not necessarily, also when you read it) expressed by the English sentences that become the instances of *B*, *A*, and ⌐If *A*, then *B*⌐. Hence, if we assume that propositions are some kind of Platonist entities, MP is, on this reading, no longer an empirical thesis.

However, is it, on this reading, *true*? I am afraid we have no guarantee (and in fact I am afraid it is *not* true). For take *A* to be *Fido is hungry* and *B* to be *He is nervous* – then it would seem that *B* is simply, as such, neither true, nor false, even in cases in which both *A* and ⌐If *A*, then *B*⌐ are. Moreover, an English sentence of the form *If A, then B* is usually taken as true also in many cases when the truth of *A* and the falsity of *B* is improbable, but conceivable (*If there is lightning, thunder will follow shortly*).[12] Such apparent fallacies are usually ascribed to 'logical imperfections' of natural language, in particular to the fact that the English *if ... then ...* is not a true implication, but only something fairly close to it. Therefore, to avoid them and to make (3) valid, we would have to replace *if ... then ...* by its better, 'regimented' version. Perhaps '→' governed by the rules of the classical PL, especially by MP? But then, it would seem, we have gone full circle and are back at (1).

The moral seems to be that if we interpret Boghossian's 'MP' as a matter of natural language, then his question will again come out as self-answering, in the negative. The validity of MP thus interpreted is either an empirical matter, or otherwise it is essentially dubious.[13] Therefore interpreting 'MP' in this way also fails to render (*) as meaningful and nontrivial.

It seems that the only way to render Boghossian's question both meaningful and nontrivial would be to relate MP to a language that is neither natural (in the sense of being an empirical entity), nor formal (in the sense of being the product of our definitions). Is there such a language? What about, for instance, a Fodorian language of thought?[14] (This is, to be sure, a language that is supposed to be empirical in the sense that it is wired in empirical, human beings, but seen from the viewpoint of such an individual being, it might seem to be a suitable medium of the a priori.)

(4) For every pair of sentences *A* and *B* of our language of thought it is correct (truth-preserving) to infer *B* from *A* and ⌜If *A*, then *B*⌝.

I leave aside any possible reservations about the very concept of a language of thought the reader might have. The basic problem is again the identification of the sentence ⌜If *A*, then *B*⌝ of our language of thought. How do we recognize it? Do we see it before our mind's eye, with a sign like '→' in its middle? How can we avoid the regress diagnosed in the case of English and not be obliged to *identify* the sentence in terms of MP in the first place?

Analogous problems emerge when we try to interpret MP as an immediate matter of propositions of a Platonist breed, i.e., not mediated by sentences of any language. Again, bracket any possible reservations and suppose that there is a Platonist world: it contains propositions and for every two propositions *A* and *B* it contains a proposition, call it ⌜If *A*, then *B*⌝, which obeys MP. Suppose, moreover, in the spirit of medieval metaphysicians, that our 'intellect' has some direct access to this realm. How does it recognize the proposition ⌜If *A*, then *B*⌝? Does this proposition contain a sign like '→'? As signs of this kind are our, conventional matters, this can hardly be the case. So, is it the case that the owner of the 'intellect' in question simply, in some indescribable way, 'noninferentially knows' that this very proposition is ⌜If *A*, then *B*⌝? But what does this knowledge amount to? It seems that the only available senses in which we can say that a proposition is an *implication* is a 'syntactic' one or a 'semantic' one. The former amounts to the proposition's consisting of such-and-such parts, one of which is the implication operator; the latter, as it clearly cannot amount to the proposition *denoting* something (which would obviously start an infinite regress), cannot but amount to the *behavior* of the proposition (i.e., that it inter alia obeys MP).

This seems to indicate that the only way to make MP nontrivial in the way required by Boghossian's considerations would be to assume that there exists (within a Platonist heaven? within (transindividual?) realms of mind(s)) something which is *essentially* implication, independently of whether it fulfills MP. Only then does it make sense to take MP as a principle that might be a reasonable candidate for a priori knowledge. I do not think this idea is any more meaningful than the idea of somebody being 'essentially bald', independently of the actual density of his hair.

10.4 The dilemma of triviality and contingency

Summarizing the considerations of the previous section, it seems that we face a dilemma: either we can see (MP) as a trivial consequence of a definition (which is not an attractive option, for it threatens to render (MP), and, by way of generalization, the whole of logic, trivial), or we can see it as a contingent claim that may be refutable on an empirical basis (again, unattractive). However, as our considerations have not thrown up any other options, it would seem that here we have a real *tertium non datur*. What we are facing is the *dilemma of triviality or contingency*.

Let us recapitulate these considerations on a more general level. Given (MP) as we formulated it above, we must specify what exactly it is that is to be substituted for '→' or what this sign is to refer to (call such an item *implication*). Obviously, there are two possibilities: either we may take (MP) as taking part in this specification, which results into the triviality of (MP), or we assume that the specification is independent of (MP). Only in the latter case can (MP) be taken as a nontrivial, substantial claim.

How can we specify implication without making use of (MP)? Perhaps there is something, within the world around us, that has already been called *implication* (and can thus – literally or metaphorically – be pointed at), and has been so-called not directly with the help of (MP). The only thing of this kind I can see is the English connective *if...then...* and its counterparts in other languages. In this case the validity of (MP) is obviously a contingent matter, to be verified by empirical means.

But maybe, although we cannot *point at* an implication, we are in possession of a criterion that enables us to single it out from among other things? Here there are, again, two possibilities: either the criterion is a matter of how it *looks* (its *form*), or it is a matter of something else (its *content*, what it *stands for*, how it *behaves*, or *how it is used*). Can implication, in general, have a specific *look*? Surely not, if it is to be seen as a linguistic item, we know all too well that any kind of look would do, and that candidates for implication in actual formal and natural languages have very distinct appearances. But, even if we see it as a nonlinguistic item (an ideal object of a Platonist heaven or a mental content), the idea that it has a specific *look* seems far-fetched (putting *implicationhood* side by side with *redness* or *circularity* appears to be an exercise too mind-boggling to take seriously).

Hence it would seem that implication must be identified by means of something other than its form. But by means of what? Its meaning? (Let us note that this would make straightforward sense only if we construe implication as a linguistic item; it is less clear that it would make sense if we construe it as a mental or ideal entity, for such an object may be more prone to *be* a meaning than to *have* a meaning. But this is not worth dwelling on now.) So what must an item mean in order to be an implication?

One answer is that it must *stand for* something or *represent* something. What could an implication represent? Perhaps the well-known truth table for material implication? (This would yield equating implication with its material variety, which would prevent us from talking about, e.g., intuitionist implication; but let us waive this.) But if this were the case, the triviality of (MP) would be forthcoming again. Another answer might be that it must *function* in a certain way. And here it is hard to imagine the specification of the functioning of implication that would not involve – directly or indirectly – (MP). All in all, *contingency* or *triviality* of (MP) appear to be the only two options.

I suspect that many of the discussions about the nature of logical laws are fuelled by the implicit assumption that there *is*, somewhere in some Platonist heaven or in the structures constitutive of the human mind, an item that is *essentially* implication, but for which we must establish (albeit not empirically) whether it obeys (MP). I hope that the above considerations help render such an assumption illusory: *implication* is a *functional* concept, and hence it makes no sense to say that something falls under it *essentially*, irrespective of what function it has. The view underlying such an approach to (MP) is the view that not only can we empirically investigate empirical objects (that we can identify ostensively, as we do within natural science) and compute with ideal objects (that we must identify by means of definitions, as we do in abstract mathematics), but, moreover, we can also investigate an intermediary realm that is accessible somehow 'quasiempirically': we can put its denizens somehow 'in front of our mind's eye', point at them, and check them for their properties.[15]

We may summarize the above considerations into the following diagram:

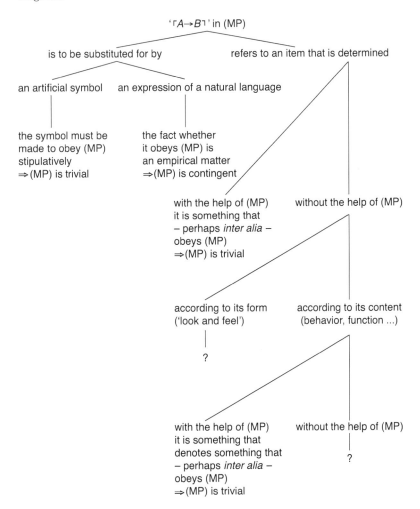

Hence it seems that to avoid the dilemma of *triviality* or *contingency* we would have to be able to fill in the place held by at least one of the two question marks in this diagram, which I do not think can be done. And as I do not think the second horn of the dilemma can be embraced (I hold the construals of logic as an empirical science, perhaps empirical psychology, were shown to be fruitless, already by Frege), I am convinced we are left with the first one.

10.5   To accept MP is to have implication

Given the difficulties with interpreting MP so that it would render Boghossian's considerations nontrivial, let us try to reassess the entire situation. Let us accept that MP is always inevitably related to a language. Languages have rules, and what is called MP is a certain rule within the context of certain other rules. In particular, MP is a rule for inferring a sentence from two other sentences:

$A, B \vdash C$

However, surely not every rule of this form deserves to be called MP: what we should require if B be the *implication* of C from A? Our answer is that it is its 'inferential behavior'; perhaps that it fulfills, aside from MP, also the following 'maximality condition' (discussed in Section 9.6):

if $A, D \vdash C$ for a D, then $B \vdash D$

Given this, *the concept of MP becomes inextricable from the concept of implication*. Hence it seems that accepting MP and acquiring implication are simply two sides of the same coin. Viewed thus, the question whether MP can be justified or whether it is a priori simply *is* the question whether we are justified in acquiring implication, and whether this acquiring is 'inevitable'. And it follows that the sense of the question is rather obscure.

Can we have a language without implication? It depends on what we call *language*. There surely is a sense in which there can be a language without anything even remotely resembling implication. However, presumably every natural language (and every formal language that can be used to *reason*) has something close to implication. Hence if we agree that thought and language are two sides of the same coin, we can say that *to be reasonable* is *to have a reasoning-apt language*, especially a language with implication, and hence a language with MP.

Do we accept MP a priori? Again, it depends on what we call a priori. I do not believe that we are born with MP in our heads: if not for other reasons, then simply because rules of the kind of MP presuppose language and we are born with no language. But presumably we are born with a disposition to acquire a certain kind of language which, besides others, contains implication (a word or a construction governed by MP). Once we acquire the language, we come to accept MP without having any external justification (for the most basic rules of our language are followed, as Wittgenstein, 1953, §219, put it, *blindly*), so *in this sense* it is a priori. But this kind of a priori is wholly, to use Horwich's (2000) term, 'semantogenic'.

The moral I suggest we draw is that *knowledge of logic* is a matter of knowledge of rules of *some* language. Therefore, if we do not believe in an inborn *language of thought* (which an inferentialist cannot, for she believes that any languages constitutively involve rules and rules are a social matter), we must conclude that the only sense in which knowledge of logic can be a priori is that we are born with predispositions to acquire languages of a certain sort, and that we cannot become what we call *reasonable* without acquiring such a language. This does not mean that there is not a sense in which logic is universal: logic spells out a structure that must be exemplified by anything that is worth being called *language* and that underlies human reason.

An objection to this conclusion might be that explicating logical validity in these 'semantogenic' terms is bound to fall prey to Quine's (1936) well-known criticism of (Carnapian) conventionalism. We cannot, Quine pointed out, assume that we know logical truths simply by knowing (and especially by having stipulated) the meanings of logical constants, for to get from the latter to the former we must apply logical rules which are one side of the coin, the other side of which are logical truths.

This, though, is an objection against the possibility of creating logical truths out of the blue, by conventionally endowing certain signs with certain meanings. And the conclusion reached above should not be read as claiming the contrary: in no way do I mean that we could 'semantogenically' create logic out of a starting point devoid of any logic. The fact is that we, rational beings, do have a logic from the beginning (that is, from the point when we are 'reasonably taken as reasonable'). But this logic is embodied within our language. We cannot turn artificial symbols into logical constants by endowing them with appropriate meanings, without already having some symbols endowed with meanings that are capable of inducing a 'logical space', a space in which we can 'move' from a claim to its negation, draw consequences, quantify, and so forth. A language of this kind is passed on to us by our elders and is a necessary precondition of any explicit conventions we may want to accept later.

As Hellman (1986) has already pointed out, the fact that we cannot *draw* the conclusions entailed by our stipulations without the help of logical rules does not contradict the fact that the stipulations do *have* these conclusions. (Or, if you prefer saying that they do not even have the conclusions before there is explicit logic around, then we would have to say that there is no emerging of the logic without the emerging of the conclusions, but to me this idiom appears to be rather mind-boggling.) Hence, we can say we do not *create* logic by the stipulations, we only give it a guise in which it can make its appearance.

This is related to the rule-following discussion we dealt with in detail in the first part of the book: we cannot follow an explicit rule without interpreting it, and to interpret it, we need further rules. As a consequence, not all the rules we follow can be explicit (and hence they require interpretation). This means that before we can have explicit rules, we must have rules that are implicit to our practices. And, similarly, before we can explicitly create logical vocabularies, we must be in an implicit possession of one.

This is, hence, the solution of the prima facie vicious circle. Though we cannot conventionally create a language without already having a language, we *can* develop (and we have done so) a language starting from a languageless state by coming to treat actions of others as right and wrong and consequently instituting (first rudimentary, and then more complex) *linguistic rules*. Parallelly, though we cannot do explicit logic without already being in possession of an implicit one, we *can* develop an implicit logic from nothing (i.e., become rational creatures) simply by developing language with a logical structure.

10.6   What is it we study when we study logical rules?

It might seem that the foregoing considerations bring us to a conception of rules of logic as utterly empirical: they appear to amount to elements of a structure that has happened to be shared by (most? all?) languages as they are currently actually used by human communities. Do we end up with the conclusion that doing logic is simply searching out linguistic universals?

Not really. Of course, logic is a matter of *rules*, and rules are, as we saw in the first part of this book, Janus-faced entities (in fact, understanding what a rule is simply *is* grasping, at least implicitly, its Janus-facedness). Rules *are* human creations and hence they are, in this sense, plainly an empirical, contingent matter; however, rules have an additional property of being able to open up the kind of 'virtual spaces' we have been discussing throughout the book. This means that we can *bind ourselves* by means of rules, and to do so means to cease taking them as merely something contingent, and to start perceiving them as something that determines how things *should* be or what we *should* do. Indeed, the very act of binding can be seen as a matter of (intentionally) giving up their contingent view, as, we may say, 'discontingenting' them.

Hence we are back with our dialectic of 'inside' and 'outside' of rules (see Section 4.7). While viewed 'from outside', any system of rules is simply a contingent human formation; viewed 'from inside' it is a necessity (in the sense of being *binding*). Stating (MP) is typically *not* stating the contingent fact that a community happened to decide to use the sign → in a certain way (namely to adopt the rule that the formula B is inferable from $⌐A{\rightarrow}B⌐$ and A); it is saying that it is *correct* to infer B from $⌐A{\rightarrow}B⌐$ and A. It is correct for me and you to the extent to which both of us consider ourselves members of the community of 'logicians' accepting its rules. (If you do not consider yourself a member of this community, you are left with the empirical reading of MP, seeing it as a report about the members of some alien community.)

Studying rules of logic *is* studying certain rules of our contingent language *which we, however, have 'dis-contingented' by our submission to them*. Logic, therefore, tells us how things *should* be. (It tells it only to those of us who are engaged with the linguistic game rendered possible by these very rules; as there is no way of being rational save playing this game, we can leave out this restriction for it is simply implicit to the meaning of the linguistic pronoun *us*.)

This notion of the rules of logic, i.e., as 'dis-contingented' regularities, stands in opposition to some other well-known construals: namely construals whereby the rules of logic constitute the ultimate boundaries of either our entire world, or at least of our thought. The former amounts to the construal of logic as an 'ultraphysics' ridiculed by Wittgenstein (1956, §I.8);[16] the latter amounts to the understanding of logic as a matter of some objectively given barriers in which our thought comes to be canalized.[17] Our view thus rehabilitates logic as the study of certain rules, a view that, during the history of the subject, has often been suppressed by the idea that logic studies some very general features of either the world or the mind. Logical rules, such as MP, are not our means of representing logic which itself resides elsewhere; our view is that they alone are themselves the very, and the only possible, residence of logic. We cannot justify unless we already are in the space of reasons; we cannot be in the space of reasons unless we have a language, and nothing is a language unless it embodies a logical structure, i.e., unless its constitutive rules comprise rules constitutive of the space of reasons.

This is not to say that we cannot tell a story explaining how it has come to the situation in which we now have our logic. The story might begin with a tale (hinted at in Chapter 6) about how our ancestors could have come to be rule followers, and might continue with another tale about how we, by developing the rules of what we now call logic, were able to outsmart our competitors, and hence have made our logic into a success. (To put it anecdotally, those who did not employ $\rightarrow$ so that $A, A \rightarrow B \vdash B$ were weeded out by natural selection.) This *is* a kind of justification, though a thoroughly pragmatic one; it is not a justification of MP, but only of the claim that it is good to obey MP (more precisely to possess a language including implication and hence MP).

10.7 Summary of Chapter 10

In this chapter we concentrated on the laws of logic, the ways they can be justified and the ways we can know them. We concluded that when considering the nature of logical laws such as modus ponens we face the dilemma of triviality or contingency: either the laws are constitutive of logical operators, and then they are trivial in that they are mere implicit definitions, or they refer to some elements of our factual language or our factual thought and then they express contingent facts. As the second horn of this dilemma is unacceptable, it is the first one we must accept. MP is trivial because it is a direct consequence of the definition of implication; what is, however, nontrivial is that implication thus defined may explicate a natural expedient of our language and our reason.

From the ensuing viewpoint, the idea of alternative laws of logic can be given only a restricted sense: we can say it is possible to have some *slight* variations on the inferential pattern constitutive of, say, implication; we also can imagine somebody utterly *lacking* anything like implication, but the possibility that implication would obey utterly different logical rules does not make sense. We concluded that the operators and the rules governing them are two sides of the same coin, and the only possible justification of the rules is the usefulness for us of the constituted operators.

This prompted us to a conclusion regarding the nature of logic: logic, we contend, is the study of the most basic rules of our language – rules that have developed contingently, but which we now, however, submit to, and which we thus study in their 'dis-contingented' form, i.e., as means of the delineation of the space of our thinking and our rationality.

11
Logic and Reasoning

11.1 Logic and 'belief management'

In the previous chapter we rejected the view that the laws of logic are a matter of the 'ontological' structure of either our world or of our thought; we concluded that the subject matter of logic is the most general rules sustaining our languages (together with the idealized versions of these rules which we develop as our logical calculi). This conclusion, together with the stress we put on the concept of inference, may suggest that we assent to the traditional construal of logic as the 'science of reasoning'. And though there is a sense in which this is true, if put this way there is a danger of serious misconstruals, so the aim of this final chapter is to clear away this last possible misunderstanding of the inferentialist approach to logic.

Perkins (2002, p. 187) gives us a nice summary of the traditional view of logic as addressing reasoning:

> For over two millennia, since the days of Aristotle and Euclid, the notion of formal logic has figured centrally in conceptions of human reasoning, rationality and adaptiveness. To be adaptive, the story goes, we must be rational about ends and means, truth and evidence. To be rational, we must reason about what means suit what ends, what evidence supports what conclusions. And to reason we must respect the canons of logic. It's common to note that transient moments of everyday cognition involve logical moves, at least implicitly. When you hear a dog bark outside, what you hear is a sound you recognize as a bark. You infer the presence of a dog, a deduction that might go:
>
> Around here, only dogs make the sound of a bark.

I hear something that makes the sound of a bark.

Therefore I hear a dog.

Examples like these intimate that formal logic is far more than a playground and workshop for philosophers, mathematicians and designers of microchips. It is, if not the warp and woof of human reasoning, at least the warp, the woof perhaps being the beliefs from which we reason. Insofar as we are successful as a species in ways beyond the reach of chimpanzees, our logical prowess may be the cause.

Similarly, Boghossian (2006, p. 76) writes:

> Many of the epistemic principles we operate with are 'transmission' principles, principles that prescribe how to move from some justified beliefs to other justified beliefs. One example of such a transmission principle has to do with moving across what we take to be deductively valid inferences, inferences which are such that, if their premises are true, their conclusions must be true as well. For example:
>
>> (Modus Ponens-rain) If S justifiably believes that it will rain tomorrow, and justifiably believes that if it rains tomorrow the streets will be wet tomorrow, S is justified in believing that the streets will be wet tomorrow.
>
> Another example is given by the principle of conjunction-elimination:
>
>> (Conjunction-elimination-rain) If S justifiably believes that it will be cold and rainy tomorrow, then S is justified in believing that it will be cold tomorrow.
>
> More generally, we endorse the principle that thinkers are justified in believing the obvious logical consequences of beliefs they are justified in having.
>
>> (Deduction) If S is justified in believing p and p fairly obviously entails q, then S is justified in believing q.

The common conviction that logic and reasoning are two sides of the same coin may result in the proof-theoretic or inferentialist attitudes to logic, as urged in this book, but it also often gives rise to the further conviction that logic spells out some directives for 'right' management of our system of beliefs, *viz.*, rules that help us to weave our web of beliefs in a 'correct' way, especially telling us when it is 'correct' to incorporate a new belief.

If the laws of logic were indeed such directives, this would deliver a straightforward answer to the question about the normativity of logic: it is normative inasmuch as it tells us what it is correct for us to do (for efficiency in coping with our environment, or expanding our collection of true beliefs, etc.). Also, it would yield a clear-cut diagnosis of the relationship between logic and rationality. If to be rational is to hold only certain patterns of beliefs, which nowadays appears to be the standard view (Way, 2010), then logic is here to tell us how to achieve this. Hence this construal of logical laws appears to put many things into place in one sweep. What more could we want?

There is, however, a major problem with this view, which, I am convinced, renders it ultimately untenable: simply put, there is no sound way of explaining the laws of logic as governing the kinematics of the web of beliefs of an individual. According to the most basic tenet of inferentialism, meanings are roles of expressions conferred by rules governing the employment of the expressions, the rules being essentially social. The same holds for propositions as a species of meanings (*viz.*, meanings of sentences). And as beliefs are propositions to which one holds a specific kind of attitude, beliefs, too, must be entities that are constituted by rules, and hence their origin is intersubjective. Thus a belief is *primarily* a *social* matter, and only secondarily a *personal* one, not in the sense that one cannot believe *privatim*, but because propositions, which constitute the vehicles of beliefs, are forged exclusively in a social mold. And the laws of logic concern more primarily this mold than any strategies of dealing with its products within an individual. (To be more precise, I think that *derivatively* these rules may *also* influence the individual belief management; however, this is only a byproduct of their primary role.) Hence, though undoubtedly *in a sense* it is true that logic is a theory of reasoning, my conviction is that the sense in which it is true is actually far more complex than generally assumed, or than the passages quoted above would suggest.

11.2   Do the rules of logic tell us how to reason?

In a book published about a quarter of a century ago, Gilbert Harman (1986) insists that logic has very little to do with reasoning, in the sense of 'reasoned change of view'. For those holding that logic is the science of reasoning, this may sound perplexing. But, on the other hand, if we consider the arguments of Harman, and indeed if we consult obvious facts at hand, we may well start to wonder why we ever thought that logic and reasoning are connected in this straightforward way. Let me quote from a more recent paper by Harman and Kulkarni (2006, p. 561):

> In the traditional view, reasoning can be modeled by a formal argument. You start by accepting certain premises, you then accept intermediate conclusions that follow from the premises or earlier intermediate conclusions in accordance with certain rules of inference. You end by accepting new conclusions that you have inferred directly or indirectly from your original premises. One problem with the traditional picture is its implication that reasoning is always a matter of inferring new things from what you start out believing. On the contrary, reasoning often involves abandoning things you start out believing. ... You regularly modify previous opinions in the light of new information.

Look, again, at modus ponens:

$$A, A \rightarrow B \vdash B$$

We can easily imagine somebody using this step in reasoning. She forms a belief, say, *that if it is raining, Tom will take his umbrella when he goes out*, and later she finds *that it is raining*. Hence, using modus ponens, she concludes *that Tom will take his umbrella when he goes out*.

But how exactly is modus ponens relevant for our reasoning? That once we have the beliefs A and $A \rightarrow B$, we should acquire the belief B? One of the problems pointed out by Harman is that we certainly do not always use modus ponens in this way. Imagine that I go home and believe *that my wife is there*. Also I believe that *if my wife is at home, the door is not locked*. I come to the door and find it locked. What I naturally do is give up my belief *that my wife is at home*.

The second, more worrisome problem tabled by Harman is that were we to work out everything that follows from our beliefs, we would never find a place to stop, whereas we obviously only work out what follows when we expect to get something useful.[1] Hence perhaps modus ponens does not tell us how we *should* amend our beliefs, but merely how we *may* do so? But if this is so, the rule would tell us how to reason merely in a very indirect, and not very helpful sense. Clearly the space of moves that are in accordance with the laws of logic is abundant, hence we would immediately need some other rules to tell us how to really steer through it. This would seem to compromise seeing the rules of logic as helpful directives for belief management.[2]

MacFarlane (unpublished) considers a third possibility of the normative reading of laws of logic, namely the reading according to which a rule tells us that believing the premises gives us reason to believe the respective conclusion. Also, he distinguishes the scope of the deontic operator: in the case of *ought*, for example, we might read a law of logic so that believing its premises we ought to believe its conclusion; or so that if we ought to believe the premises, we ought to believe the conclusion; or, finally, so that we 'ought to see it that' if we believe the premises, we also believe the conclusion. Then he makes one more distinction that cuts through the previous ones: this distinction concerns reading the conclusion of the logical law in question either as prescribing us to believe it, or not to disbelieve it. (This gives him, altogether, 18 possible normative readings of the logical laws.) MacFarlane is inclined to go for 'some combination' of (a) *you ought to see to it that if you believe the premises, you do not disbelieve the conclusion*, and (b) *you have reason to see to it that if you believe the premises, you believe the conclusion.*

Now, though I think MacFarlane may have isolated the best of the spectrum of options, whether these are acceptable remains at least dubious.[3] While (b) does not seem to quite avoid Harman's objection that it would get our mind clogged with inferences, (a) contains an unclear notion of *disbelieving*. It seems that were we to interpret *disbelief* as simply lack of belief, then *not disbelieving* would simply collapse into *believing* (thus making this first option fall prey to the same problem as the second one), whereas were we to see it more as *believing the opposite*, it would again not tell us anything helpful with respect to what to really believe.

Given all of this, it may be good to return to Harman's argument against a straightforward linking of the laws of logic to reasoning. Field (2009, pp. 252–253) summarizes the outcomes of the argument in four points:

1. Reasoning (change of view) doesn't follow the pattern of logical consequence. When one has beliefs $A_1, \ldots, A_n$, and realizes that they together entail B, sometimes the best thing to do isn't to believe B but to drop one of the beliefs $A_1, \ldots, A_n$.

2. We shouldn't clutter up our minds with irrelevancies, but we'd have to if whenever we believed A and recognized that B was a consequence of it we believed B.

3. It is sometimes rational to have beliefs even while knowing they are jointly inconsistent, if one doesn't know how the inconsistency should be avoided.

4. No one can recognize all the consequences of his or her beliefs. Because of this, it is not reasonable to demand that one's beliefs be closed under consequence. For similar reasons, one can't always recognize inconsistencies in one's beliefs, so even putting aside point 3 it is not reasonable to demand that one's beliefs be consistent.

In view of the problems with logic considered as a theory of 'reasoned change of view' we may relish a wholly different interpretation of the laws of logic. Thus Field considers the possibility of seeing the laws of logic as spelling out those forms of inference that necessarily preserve truth (Field attributes this view to Harman; Harman, however, disowns it),[4] but ultimately he dismisses this possibility as unviable. Hence, in the end, Field returns to anchoring the laws of logic in reasoning and ends up with the following probabilistic interpretation (2009, p. 262, where $P(X)$ denotes the probability of X):

Employing a logic L involves it being one's practice that when simple inferences $A_1, ..., A_n \vdash B$ licensed by the logic are brought to one's attention, one will normally impose the constraint that $P(B)$ is to be at least $P(A_1) + ... + P(A_n) - (n - 1)$.

But, again, this does not seem quite satisfactory. Unlike simply ascribing a belief *simpliciter*, ascribing its probabilistic version (i.e., a probability the ascribee associates with a belief) is a much more complicated matter with much less clear content. Moreover, it is not clear how this avoids the 'cluttering up our minds with irrelevancies', for it seems that it again concerns all the consequences of our beliefs; and adjusting all the relevant probabilities, or even checking them, would again be an infinite process.

11.3   The social and normative nature of belief

Harman's objections might be understood as protesting merely against the 'direction' in which reasoning works, and against its 'compulsiveness': the reasoning process does not (always) move from what the usual laws of logic would count as premises to what they would count as conclusions. Sometimes human reasoning appears to proceed in the opposite direction ('abandoning one of the premises rather than accepting the conclusion'), and sometimes its relationship to the laws of logic is even more disingenuous. This fact is, I think, important to note (and Harman presents very persuasive arguments against the simplistic construal of reasoning), but what is even more important, from our perspective, is to stress that the root cause for reasoning not being in perfect partnership with the rules of logic lies still somewhat deeper. In particular, I think that problems start as soon as we take for granted that the task of logic is to help us reasonably manage our beliefs (which we have and which it is not the business of logic to explain).

Once we take ready-made beliefs as an unquestioned point of departure of the application of logic, as something that must be explained by something that has nothing to do with logic (perhaps cognitive science?), we are well on the way into a blind alley. It is essentially wrong, I am convinced, to see logic as a theory of an individual's epistemic achievements. Though, of course, it is an individual who reasons, it should by now be clear that the ability to reason has an essential social dimension, and logic should be seen as related to this dimension. And it is certain rules, including the rules of logic, that license certain material vehicles, typically types of sounds or scrawls, to become 'embodiments of beliefs'.

Does this mean that there is no belief without language? Well, it does, but with two important provisos. First, what is the case is that there is no belief *in our human sense* without language; I do not mean to deny that even languageless brutes may be in states that we may tend to characterize as states of believing something. However, as we have already seen (see Section 2.4), saying about somebody that she believes something in our human sense of the word involves saying that she knows the place of the belief within the network of many other beliefs (knows, for example, what follows from it or what must be the case for this belief to become true), and language is the only substratum nourishing enough to sustain such a network.

The other proviso is that, though there is no belief without a language, this does not mean that belief would generally be something like an inner assertion. It is not possible, I am convinced, for a believer not to be a language user, but not every episode of belief must be a matter of language. I understand the constitutive connection between language and belief in the sense of Sellars's 'verbal behaviorism': 'According to VB [verbal behaviorism]', as he puts it in his characteristically cryptic way (1974, p. 419), 'thinking "that-p", where this means "having the thought occur to one that-p", has as its primary sense [an event of] saying "p"; and a secondary sense in which it stands for a short term proximate propensity [dispositional] to say "p"'.[5]

It follows from the conclusion of the previous section that the rules of logic cannot be seen as *tactical* rules dictating feasible strategies of a game; they are the rules *constitutive* of the game as such.[6] (MP does not tell us how to handle implication efficiently, but rather what implication *is*.) This is a crucial point, because it is often taken for granted that the rules of logic tell us *how to reason* precisely in the tactical sense of the word. But what I maintain is that this is wrong, the rules do not tell us *how* to reason, they provide us with things *with which*, or in *terms of which*, to reason.[7]

This brings us back to our frequently invoked analogy between language and chess. There are two kinds of rules of chess: first, there are rules of the kind that a bishop can move only diagonally and that the king and a rook can castle only when neither of the pieces have previously been moved. These are the rules constitutive of chess; were we not to follow them, we have seen (Section 5.5) we would not be playing chess. In contrast to these, there are *tactical* rules telling us what to do to increase our chance of winning, rules advising us, e.g., not to exchange a rook for a bishop or to embattle the king by castling. Were we not to follow them, we would still be playing chess, but with little likelihood of winning.

We can imagine the rules of chess as something that produces the pieces, equips them each with its peculiar modus operandi, and then see the relevant tactical rules as consisting in setting the individual modi into the most efficient teamwork. The rules of logic, viewed analogously, would then have a slightly more complex role: along with furnishing us with logical concepts (each with its peculiar modus operandi) they also provide us with a mold in which we cast all other concepts so that they acquire their characteristic shape (and thus can combine with logical ones).[8] Then we face the problem of setting the individual concepts (logical and extralogical) into effective thinking (and we might consider articulating some directives or rules that could then be seen as the tactical rules of reasoning). As we put it in the previous chapter, we become rational by mastering certain ('cognitive') tools.

Instead of assuming that argumentation is an externalization of reasoning, I am assuming that a certain, relatively recent upgrade of our reasoning faculties is effected by an internalization of argumentation. Thus I concur with Mercier's (2010) claim that 'reasoning evolved not to complement individual cognition but as an argumentative device'.

Let me summarize, in the remaining sections of this chapter, arguments that support the view of logic we have arrived at. Most of them have been implicit in what has already been presented, and now we only will make them explicit. The first point I will stress is that logical rules (and inferential rules in general), as they find their expressions within the systems of modern logic, are best seen as primarily concerned not with reasoning in the sense of belief management, but with demonstrations and proofs. Next, it is important to see that the rules that govern demonstrations and proofs can be seen as rules of certain language games, especially the games that have to do with giving and asking for reasons. The most important point is, then, that neither demonstration nor argumentation is an externalization of reasoning (but it can, to a certain extent, be internalized to constitute an extraordinary overlay of our normal reasoning proceedings). And hence logical rules are rooted in the regulation of argumentation; the rules are constitutive of the very space of argumentation and consequently of beliefs as inner correlates of assertions: they are constitutive rather than tactical rules.

Let us now consider these points in greater detail.

11.4   Logical laws as laws of demonstration

When we look at the writings of the most reflective of the founding fathers of modern logic, Frege, we can see, from the beginning, that he aims his logical system at proofs, i.e., demonstrations; he takes pains to stress that this has very little to do with actual reasoning in the sense of what happens in an individual mind (1879, p. iii):

> In apprehending a scientific truth we pass, as a rule, through various degrees of certitude. Perhaps first conjectured on the basis of an insufficient number of particular cases, a general proposition comes to be more and more securely established by being connected with other truths through chains of inferences, whether consequences are derived from it that are confirmed in some other way or whether, conversely, it is seen to be a consequence of propositions already established. Hence we can inquire, on the one hand, how we have gradually arrived at a given proposition and, on the other, how we can finally provide it with the most secure foundation. The first question may have to be answered differently for different persons; the second is more definite, and the answer to it is connected with the inner nature of the proposition considered. The most reliable way of carrying out a proof, obviously, is to follow pure logic, a way that, disregarding the particular characteristics of objects, depends solely on those laws upon which all knowledge rests. Accordingly, we divide all truths that require justification into two kinds, those for which the proof can be carried out purely by means of logic and those for which it must be supported by facts of experience. But that a proposition is of the first kind is surely compatible with the fact that it could nevertheless not have come to

consciousness in a human mind without any activity of the senses. Hence it is not the psychological genesis but the best method of proof that is at the basis of the classification.

We can see that Frege saw the laws of logic as laws of reasoning exclusively in the sense of 'way of carrying out a proof', which, unlike reasoning in the individualist sense, inevitably has to be public (the question how we can prove something is 'more definite' than to be answerable 'differently for different persons'). What the laws of logic capture is 'not the psychological genesis but the best method of proof'.

Notice that public demonstration is indeed an enterprise very different from 'psychological genesis'. To demonstrate, in a way acceptable as a proof, that something follows from something else, involves decomposing the entailment link between the premises and the conclusion into a chain of steps, each of which is (a) legitimate (in accordance with a publicly acceptable code); and (b) elementary (i.e., perspicuous for everybody relevant). The process of acquiring a belief within my mind may be very different: it may involve processes that are legitimate only in the sense that they appear to have worked before; there may be steps that cannot be clearly articulated, and there may be various kinds of serendipities and kludges.

What does the acceptability (correctness) of a step of a proof amount to? Well, any language worth the name has the property that some of its sentences follow from others. Logicians of Frege's ilk tend to make a list of elementary kinds of acceptable steps (a basic set of steps any other acceptable step can be composed of), which lead to various logical systems; the acceptability is then judged with the help of such a list. Elementary rules of this kind are seen as the basic building blocks from which we can compose chains linking the premises and the conclusion of any valid instance of inference or consequence of the language in question. (In the case of a formal language, they *define* what counts as a valid consequence, but in the case of a natural language they are supposed to *explicate* this.) On the other hand, these rules can be seen as conferring meanings on logical expressions (i.e., those expressions whose overall function in language is determined by their functioning within such demonstrations).[9]

What is crucial is that Frege's insistence on keeping with the elementary logical rules when composing proofs is *not* tactical advice designed to help us compose proofs effectively or skillfully. It is advice that should help prevent us from straying from the realm of logic, and allows us to demonstrate that we are not leaving this realm.

Now, if a demonstration faces protests or challenges (or if, vice versa, it is a reply to a challenge), the result may be an (interactive) argumentation, an instance of the game of giving and asking for reasons. This is reflected by the fact that the rules of the usual logical systems, which equip these systems with spaces of possible demonstrations and proofs, can be reframed in game-theoretical terms, as discussed in the first part of this book (see Section 5.2). We saw that by fine-tuning the rules of the Lorenzenian games, we can make the games equivalent to various logical systems in the sense that there is a winning strategy for a game associated with a formula just in the case the formula is a theorem/ tautology of the corresponding system. Such kinds of games can thus be seen as straightforward implementations of the corresponding logics, or, perhaps more appropriately, the logical systems can be seen as capturing the structure of the corresponding games.

The shift from demonstrations and logical systems to games makes it easier to explain how logic could have come into being. It is plausible that first there were rudimentary language games, which then, by growing in complexity, acquired something as a logical backbone, thereby entangling their sentences into ever more complicated logical interrelationships (such as consequence and incompatibility), and providing for the roles of logically complex sentences (negation as minimal incompatible; conjunction as inferential infimum; etc.). The explicitly logical locutions then came into being as means of explicitly expressing these implicit logical relationships (as we discussed in detail in Chapter 9).

11.5   Reasoning as inner argumentation

Independently of whether the rules of logic spell out some eternal logical truths or merely the rules of argumentation games, it would be claimed that they must be, primarily, rules of inner reasoning, of which the outer demonstration or argumentation must be expressive. Overt steps of an argument seem obliged to come into being as mirror images of some covert steps we carry out within our minds; if this were not so, the so-called arguments would be mere empty sequences of sounds or scribbles on paper. However, as I have already indicated, I am convinced that this appearance is misguided – 'putting the cart before the horse', as it were. I hold that the covert reasoning as a sequence of those steps that are articulated by the laws of logic is much more plausibly derived from overt argumentation than the other way around.

I have already mentioned Sellars's *verbal behaviorism* as a plausible theory of how such faculties of mind as this prooflike reasoning (as well as, for that matter, propositional thought in general) derived from public practices. Sellars argues that how we construe what happens in our mind in terms of a kinematics of propositions or beliefs (initially from the first-person, but subsequently also from the third-person perspective) is parasitic on how we come to perceive linguistics behavior as the kinematics of utterances.[10] Sellars (1962, p. 6) invokes 'the idea that anything which can properly be called conceptual thinking can occur only within a framework of conceptual thinking in terms of which it can be criticized, supported, refuted, in short, evaluated' which leads him to the conclusion that 'the individual as a conceptual thinker is essentially a member of a group' (p. 17).

Davidson (1991, p. 213) is even more explicit in this respect:

> Until a base line has been established by communication with someone else, there is no point in saying one's own thoughts or words have a propositional content. If this is so, then it is clear that knowledge of another mind is essential to all thought and all knowledge.

When we internalize the laws of argumentative language games we are facilitated to do covertly what was previously overt: namely, to convince an audience by citing reasons. In this way we gain a specific overlay to our prior reasoning faculties, an overlay to which we take recourse when solving certain specific tasks, or when we want to check meticulously the conclusions achieved by means of ordinary reasoning. This new skill, however, does not displace our original ways of reasoning, nor diminish their import; it is something that we do not use very frequently (if for no other reason than that it is time consuming, and most of our reasoning must be done in the 'on-line' mode).

Counterintuitive as this view might seem at first, I believe it does stand up to scrutiny. The prima facie objections are, first, that it would seem to be a plain fact that it is an *individual* who reasons (in her, as it were, *foro interno*), and, second, that it is only an individual who can forge *meaningful* sentences to do the reasoning with. The view put forward here does not reject the first point; of course it is an individual who does the reasoning (though uninternalized argumentation done by a group of people should also be called reasoning). However, it does challenge the second point: meanings are brought into the mind from a public space where they are forged within the furnace of human interaction.

11.6   Laws of logic as constitutive

The individualistic approaches to logic take for granted that logic spells out tactical, rather than constitutive, rules. Presumably, this is because prima facie there are no obvious alternatives to this construal of the rules of logic. Upgrading beliefs does not seem, on the surface, to be a game, at least not a game with any similarity to chess, *viz.*, a game *constituted* by rules.

However, let us reappraise how we look at the constitutive rules of chess. We may see them, as we have before, as constituting the *pieces* as such: kings, rooks, bishops, etc. Once we have these items, each of them coming with a specific 'behavior' (thus the bishop with the propriety of moving diagonally, etc.), we can forget about the constitutive rules and see the space of chess as delimited by whatever it is possible to achieve with them. And the achievements are nontrivial, though they are usually not particularly important for us, chess not generally playing a significant role in our lives. Now the idea is that our beliefs are analogous to the pieces; that our tactics for dealing with them are based on the natures of the beliefs, these natures being established by constitutive rules. And here the achievements we can reach when we learn to orchestrate beliefs efficiently are not only important, but also highly nontrivial: they help us steer clear of the perils of our world, and enjoy what it has to offer much more effectively than before.

But surely beliefs are 'real' entities within mind/brain, and hence must be essentially different from 'virtual' entities such as rooks or bishops? Well, rooks and bishops are also real (at least usually); they are pieces of wood or ivory or such like. What is virtual is precisely that which makes these tangible things into the individual chess pieces. Thus the fact that beliefs can perhaps qualify as 'tangible' entities does not contradict the fact that qua beliefs they might be constituted.

This explains why the rules of logic do not really tell us how to reason, at least not in a very nontrivial sense: it is for the same reason that the rules of chess do not tell us how to play chess, except in the trivial sense that they tell us what are the permitted moves. To learn how to play chess we need another kind of rules (or guidances) – the tactical ones. The former rules merely set up the stage, or produce the characters with which to play; it is only the latter ones that tell us what to do.

The fact that a proof or a demonstration consists of steps according to these very rules does not mean that this would be what we actually do when we reach new beliefs in our heads; it is a matter of the fact that a demonstration as such must be utterly transparent; in particular it must be clear that all its steps are legitimate. And the best way to make them clearly legitimate is to make them directly accord with the elementary rules. On the other hand, the fact that we have a lot of potential steps sanctioned directly by the rules does not actively help us chain such steps together appropriately to get a proof of a given claim. If this chaining were a matter of rules, then they would have to be rules very different from the constitutive rules which we borrow to assemble the proofs from.

We have already characterized human thought as differing from that of other animals (insofar as these can be ascribed something as thought at all) in that it is *conceptual*: that we humans, in contrast to our animal cousins, have *reason* (and hence are able *to* reason); that we can think and infer *logically*, etc. The picture at which we have arrived here suggests that logic is a kind of tool enhancing our thought 'from without': we have developed certain complicated and useful social practices, crucially involving language, and these practices equipped us with certain tools that we later internalized. The tools are logical concepts that help us organize and effectively maintain what we know and what we believe, and that form the furnace in which we forge, using empirical material, other concepts and propositions.

11.7   Truth once more

In the first part of the book we brought up the concept of truth and concluded that, from the inferentialist viewpoint, it is secondary to the concept of inference (Section 5.6). In Section 7.7 we concluded that analyzing inference in terms of truth-dependence would be circular and that to break the circle we need to see inference as primary. As Prawitz (2005, p. 681) puts it:

> To analyze the modal ingredient of logical consequence in terms of evidence seems a hopeful project only if truth is understood in this constructive way. From this point of view, evidence or what it is to acquire knowledge must be taken as a more fundamental concept than truth – truth may then be defined as the potential existence of evidence.

Hence, from the viewpoint presented here, truth is not a basic concept. I have indicated how I think logical laws came into being: by means of certain argumentative practices developing out of rudimentary proto-practices and out of nothing. Then, argumentation developing into an implicitly standardized enterprise, rendering possible a general consensus on what is an acceptable step in an argument and what is not, gave birth to *correct inferences*. Specific expressions that could represent steps in arguments distinguished themselves from other kinds of expressions and became what we now call *sentences*. Some of the sentences, perhaps in specific contexts, came to be used as argument starters. These sentences can be called *true*, together with all those that are inferable from them. In this way, inferences become truth-preserving, not because there is some truth independent of them which happens to be preserved by those inferences we consider correct (and not by those we consider incorrect), but because truth was simply stipulated as that which is preserved by whatever counts as correct inference.

Thus truth becomes tantamount to correct assertability. (It amounts to *one specific* kind of correctness among others also applying to assertions; an assertion can also be correct in the sense, for example, of not violating the rules of grammar or of etiquette.)[11] Hence, to say that assertion aims at truth is, from this vantage point, little more than a tautology: aiming at truth is simply being correct in the sense constitutive of the very concept of assertion. And to say that a belief aims at truth is to say that a belief inherits the liability to that assessment in terms of the rules of assertion.

Lackey (2007) reconsiders the norm claiming that one can assert only what one knows and comes to the conclusion that this norm must be replaced by the following: 'One should assert that *p* only if (i) it is reasonable for one to believe that *p*, and (ii) if one asserted that *p*, one would assert that *p* at least in part because it is reasonable for one to believe that *p*.' This, I think, is on the right track in that it replaces the subjective state of believing with the objective state of the reasonability of belief, though it still does not follow the track to its end. The reference to belief remaining in this formulation is misleading; I think that it should be replaced by the notion of *commitment* (cf. Brandom, 1994). Making an assertion we undertake a certain commitment, namely the commitment to justify the assertion if challenged. If we are unable to live up to this commitment, then we can be seen as having violated the rules of the corresponding game and are a legitimate target for criticism.

From this viewpoint, Milne (2009, p. 286) fares better:

> Logic has a normative role in determining the commitments taken on in assertion. Logic also has a normative role in determining the commitments undertaken in holding those beliefs that constitute one's evidence, those beliefs that are candidates for expression in

assertion, and may expand out to the commitments entered into in holding any beliefs. ... And some grasp of logical connexions is implicated in the very having of beliefs.

I think this *almost* agrees with what I have argued for here, though still not entirely. Yes, logic does 'determine the commitments taken on in assertion', for it spells out the rules of the game of giving and asking for reasons, which is the game that frames the practice of assertion, with commitments constituting the 'score' of the game. However, more than just implying 'some grasp of logical connexions', I would hold that the rules actually produce every one of them – all the things like conjunctions, disjunctions, or implications, which are then available for us to use as the binding of our reasonings. And, importantly, I do not think that talk about 'commitments undertaken in holding beliefs' can be taken literally (though it may be acceptable if we beware taking it thus), for if we are to understand beliefs as residing within one's private mind, then I do not think they can be subject to rules.

11.8   Summary of Chapter 11

In this chapter we have argued that logical rules are not a matter of a strategy for optimal belief management by an individual; we have urged that they have an essential social dimension. The dimension does not make the individual dependent on the society in that the conclusions she reaches are not her own, but rather in that the vehicles of her reasoning, concepts, and propositions are originally of a social making. The conjecture put forward and defended in this chapter is that the rules of logic originated as rules of demonstrations and proofs, hence as rules of certain (argumentation) language games.

Inner reasoning, then, is the internalization of public argumentation (rather than the other way around); it is not that every instance of reasoning would be a chain of covert assertions following one from another, but rather that every instance of reasoning has to take place on a conceptual and propositional level, thereby using vehicles that originated in public language games. The most important point to which this train of thought has led us is that logical rules are *constitutive* rules; they are not *tactical* rules for dealing with beliefs and other propositions, but rather rules that are responsible for there being anything such as propositions in the first place. Thus, we can say, the laws of logic are not a means of leading us in our reasoning, but rather of producing the material in terms of which we can reason.

Postscript: Inferentialism on the Go

There are many approaches to the enigma of meaning, and many of them lead us down garden paths, if not directly up blind alleys. The approach of inferentialism is quite radical; it requires us to dispense with the persistent intuition that words are *symbols*, that they *stand for* their meanings or that they become meaningful by *representing* something. Instead of this, inferentialism puts forward the picture that meaningfulness is essentially a *role*, a role that a word acquires if it is made to function within a virtual space delimited by a system of (broadly construed) inferential rules.

This picture requires us to see language as primarily a catalyst of the emergence of a new and unprecedented spectrum of actions, actions that let us manage, coordinate, and develop our social – and correlatively individual – life in brand new ways largely surpassing anything that was possible before. We come to be able, by emitting sounds, to make our peers do very complicated kinds of things, and we come to think in new and complex ways. From this perspective, what we call meanings are roles that the sounds we emit acquire when they become entangled in the web of our fantastically complex rule-governed linguistic practices, the meaningful words thus becoming ('cognitive') tools helping us to cooperate, to manage our social environment, and indeed to think in our proficient human ways.

Logic, then, amounts to the most fundamental skeleton of this web of rules constitutive of our linguistic practices, to rules without which we would not call the practices linguistic and that are, in this sense, *essential* to any language. Logic, therefore, is primarily a matter of rules, rules that form our 'space of meaningfulness'. Logical words, as a species of the 'cognitive tools' that our sounds/scrawls are transformed into when they become meaningful, constitute the fundamental pillars of the whole 'space of meaningfulness'. Unlike other meaningful words, their roles are not concerned with coping directly with the extralinguistic reality, but rather with supporting the arena in which our specific, human, 'conceptual' way of coping may take place.

We can see various detailed models of this arena in our logical calculi which are the result of the efforts of generations of logicians to create versions of our natural logical rules and logical words that would be more transparent, more manageable, and more handy than their natural prototypes. These calculi have largely acquired lives of their own and are often investigated for their own sake, but their ultimate aim is to envisage the foundations of our arena of meaningfulness.

Over the decades, modern logicians have stringently addressed the internal problems of logical calculi and developed a number of methods and attitudes that obscured the ultimate aim of logic. (This is, to be sure, not to say that their work has been in vain; many of them have produced interesting mathematics for which the ultimate aim of logic is legitimately irrelevant.) By manipulations of logical rules they reached 'formal semantics', a theory that tentatively masquerades as providing direct capture of meanings and claims to secure us a much more direct attitude to semantics than is achievable via deference to any kind of rules. But despite all positive qualities of such theories the idea that it might help us penetrate 'beyond' rules is an illusion.

In short, inferentialism offers a fresh start in looking at meaning, both in philosophy of language and logic, bypassing some of the most recalcitrant prejudices we have accumulated over the centuries of wrestling with this enigma. It suggests that what seemed to be peculiar kind of entities stubbornly resisting our anatomizations might in reality be merely projections of our specific speech acts, and hence what we must anatomize are the social, linguistic practices that bring them into 'being'. Inferentialism brings together some of the most interesting philosophical ideas of the twentieth century (the pragmatistic emphasis on the practical, use theoretic approach to meaning, the role of rules and rule following, nondogmatic naturalism) and offers a coherent and viable story about the origin, the nature, and the role of meaning.

Appendix: Proofs of Theorems

Theorem 1. Let $\mathbb{R}$ be a set of inferential rules over a language L. A sentence A of L is $\mathbb{R}$-inferable from the sequence X of sentences of L iff $X \vdash_S A$ in every standard structure $<S, \vdash_S>$ in which all elements of $\mathbb{R}$ are in force. In other words, A is $\mathbb{R}$-inferable from X iff it belongs to the smallest subset of $\mathrm{FSeq}(S) \times S$ that contains all instances of all elements of $\mathbb{R}$ and is closed under the structural rules.

Proof: Direct implication: Let A be $\mathbb{R}$-inferable from X. This means that there is a sequence $A_1, \ldots, A_n$ of sentences such that $A_n = A$ and every A_i is either an element of X or is inferable by a rule from $\mathbb{R}$ from sentences that are among $A_1, \ldots, A_{i\text{-}1}$. Let us proceed by induction. If $n = 1$, then there are two possibilities: either A is an element of X and then $X \vdash_S A$ follows from REF by EXT; or A is a conclusion of a rule from $\mathbb{R}$ with no premises, and then $\vdash_S A$ and hence $X \vdash_S A$ due to EXT. If $n > 1$ and A_n is inferable from some $A_{i_1}, \ldots, A_{i_m}$ by a rule from $\mathbb{R}$, then $A_{i_1}, \ldots, A_{i_m} \vdash_S A$, where $X \vdash_S A_{i_j}$ for $j = 1, \ldots, m$. Then $X, \ldots, X \vdash_S A$ due to CUT, and hence $X \vdash_S A$ due to PERM and CON.

Inverse implication: For every inferon $X \vdash_S A$ belonging to every standard structure $<S, \vdash_S>$ in which all elements of $\mathbb{R}$ are in force we will construct a proof of A from X by means of $\mathbb{R}$. The inferon can belong to every such structure only in force of being an instance of a rule of $\mathbb{R}$ or in force of being derivable by one of the structural rules from other such inferons. If $X \vdash_S A$ is an instance of a rule from $\mathbb{R}$, then the proof consists of all elements of X followed by A; if it is an instance of REF, then it consists of A alone. If $X \vdash_S A$ follows by EXT, CON, or PERM from an inferon to which there corresponds the proof P, then the proof corresponding to it is P. If it follows by CUT from inferons to which there correspond the proofs P_1 and P_2, then the proof corresponding to it results from substituting P_2 for A into P_1. $\square$

240

Theorem 2. A protosemiinferential structure is a structure of a semantic system iff it complies with all the structural rules.

Proof: As the proof of the direct implication is a routine matter, we will prove only the inverse one. Where $<S, \vdash_S>$ is a protoinferential structure, let us denote as $Y^{\star}$ the set of all elements of a sequence $Y \in \mathrm{Seq}(S)$. If X is a subset of S, then $\mathrm{Cn}(X)$ will be the set of all sentences A such that $Y \vdash A$ for $Y^{\star} \subseteq X$ and a subset X of S will be called *closed* iff $\mathrm{Cn}(X) = X$. Let V be the class of all closed subsets of S. We will first prove that $X \vdash_S A$ iff $X \vDash A$, where $\vDash$ is the consequence relation of the semantic system $<S, V>$. The direct implication is straightforward: if $X \vdash_S A$ and $X^{\star} \subseteq U$ for some $U \in V$, then $A \in \mathrm{Cn}(U)$ and hence, as U is closed, $A \in U$. So we only have to prove the inverse implication.

Hence let $X \vDash A$. This means that whenever $U \in V$ and $X^{\star} \subseteq U$, $A \in U$; i.e., that $A \in U$ for every U such that (i) $X^{\star} \subseteq U$ and (ii) U is closed (i.e., $\mathrm{Cn}(U) = U$). As $\vdash_S$ is reflexive, $X^{\star} \subseteq \mathrm{Cn}(X^{\star})$. As it is transitive, $\mathrm{Cn}(\mathrm{Cn}(X^{\star})) = \mathrm{Cn}(X^{\star})$. This means that $\mathrm{Cn}(X^{\star})$, in the role of U, satisfies (i) and (ii), and hence $A \in \mathrm{Cn}(X^{\star})$. Hence $Z \vdash_S A$ for some sequence Z all of whose members belong to $X^{\star}$. Due to the extendability and contractibility of $\vdash_S$, this means that $Y \vdash_S A$ for some sequence Y with the same elements as X and hence, due to the permutability of $\vdash_S$, $X \vdash_S A$. □

Definitions

Let U be a set of valuations of a set S (i.e., a subset of $\{0,1\}^S$, which can be also seen as $\mathrm{Pow}(S)$). $T(U)$ (the set of *U-tautologies*) will be the set of all those elements of S which are mapped on 1 by all elements of U; and analogously $C(U)$ (the set of *U-contradictions*) will be the set of all those elements of S that are mapped on 0 by all elements of U. (Where no confusion is likely, we will identify a singleton with its single element; so, for example, we will write $C(v)$ instead of $C(\{v\})$.) The *full* valuation is the valuation that maps every element of S on 1.

Let X and Y be subsets of a set S. The *cluster over S generated by X and Y*, $\mathrm{Cl}_S[X,Y]$ will be the set of all elements of $\{0,1\}^S$ that map all elements of X on 1 and all elements of Y on 0. (Thus U is a *cluster* iff it contains, and hence is identical with, $\mathrm{Cl}_S[T(U), C(U)]$.) A cluster U is called *finitary* iff both $T(U)$ and $C(U)$ are finite; it is called *inferential* iff $C(U)$ is a singleton.

A semantic system $<S, V>$ is called:

- *Saturated* iff V contains every $v \in \{0,1\}^S$ such that for every $A \in C(v)$ there is a $v' \in V$ such that $T(v) \subseteq T(v')$ and $A \in C(v')$.
- *Compact* iff V contains every $v \in \{0,1\}^S$ such that for every finite $X \subseteq T(v)$ and finite $Y \subseteq C(v)$ there is a $v' \in V$ such that $X \subseteq T(v')$ and $Y \subseteq C(v')$.

- *Compactly saturated* iff V contains every $v \in \{0,1\}^S$ such that for every finite $X \subseteq T(v)$ and every $A \in C(v)$ there is a $v' \in V$ such that $X \subseteq T(v)$ and $A \in C(v)$.

(Let us indicate that a set of valuations is saturated according to this definition iff it is saturated in the sense of Section 8.4. There we defined a set as saturated iff it contains the supervaluations of all its subsets, where v is the supervaluation of a set V iff $T(v)$ is the intersection of $\{T(v') \mid v' \in V\}$. In other words, v is the supervaluation of V iff for every element $v' \in V$ it is the case that $T(v) \subseteq T(v')$ and for every $A \in C(v)$ there is a $v' \in V$ such that $A \in C(v')$. It follows that a set of valuations contains the supervaluations of all its subsets – and hence is saturated – iff it contains every v such that for every $A \in C(v)$ there is a $v' \in V$ such that $T(v) \subseteq T(v')$ and $A \in C(v')$.)

Lemma 3

A semantic system $<S,V>$ is:

- A PSQI-system iff $\{0,1\}^S \setminus V$ is a union of clusters.
- A PQI-system iff $\{0,1\}^S \setminus V$ is a union of finitary clusters.
- A PSI-system iff $\{0,1\}^S \setminus V$ is a union of inferential clusters.
- A PI-system iff $\{0,1\}^S \setminus V$ is a union of finitary inferential clusters.

Proof: obvious. □

Lemma 4

A semantic system $<S,V>$ is
Always a PSQI-system;
A PQI-system iff it is compact;
A PSI-system iff it is saturated;
A PI-system iff it is compactly saturated.

Proof:
  1. It is clear that any set consisting of a single valuation is a cluster, hence any set of valuations is a union of clusters.
  2. A semantic system $< S, V >$ is a PQI-system iff $\{0,1\}^S \setminus V$ is a union of finitary clusters. This is to say that it is a PQI-system iff for every $v \in \{0,1\}^S \setminus V$ there is a finite set $X \subseteq T(v)$ and a finite set $Y \subseteq C(v)$ such that $\{0,1\}^S \setminus V$ contains the whole cluster $Cl_S[X,Y]$, i.e., iff for every $v \notin V$ there are finite sets $X \subseteq T(v)$ and $Y \subseteq C(v)$ such that V does not contain

any v' such that $X \subseteq T(v')$ and $Y \subseteq C(v')$. By contraposition, $<S,V>$ is a PQI-system iff the following holds: given a valuation v, if for all finite sets $X \subseteq T(v)$ and $Y \subseteq C(v)$ there is a valuation $v' \in V$ such that $X \subseteq T(v')$ and $Y \subseteq C(v')$, then $v \in V$. But this is clearly the definition of compactness of V.

3. A semantic system $< S, V >$ is a PSI-system iff $\{0,1\}^S \setminus V$ is a union of inferential clusters; this is to say that it is a PSI-system iff for every $v \in \{0,1\}^S \setminus V$ there is a set $X \subseteq T(v)$ and a sentence $A \in C(v)$ such that $\{0,1\}^S \setminus V$ contains the whole cluster $Cl[X,A]$, i.e., such that it contains every v' such that $X \subseteq T(v')$ and $A \in C(v')$. In other words, $< S,V >$ is a PSI-system iff for every $v \notin V$ there is a set $X \subseteq T(v)$ and a sentence $A \in C(v)$ such that V does not contain any v' such that $X \subseteq T(v')$ and $A \in C(v')$. By contraposition, $< S, V >$ is a PSI-system iff the following holds: given a valuation v, if for every set $X \subseteq T(v)$ and every sentence $A \in C(v)$ there is a valuation $v' \in V$ such that $X \subseteq T(v')$ and $A \in C(v')$, then $v \in V$. But this is clearly the definition of saturatedness of V.

4. A semantic system $< S, V >$ is a PI-system iff $\{0,1\}^S \setminus V$ is a union of finitary inferential clusters. This is to say that it is a PSI-system iff for every $v \in \{0,1\}^S \setminus V$ there is a finite set $X \subseteq T(v)$ and a sentence $A \in C(v)$ such that $\{0,1\}^S \setminus V$ contains the whole cluster $Cl[X,A]$, i.e., such that it contains every v' such that $X \subseteq T(v')$ and $A \in C(v')$. In other words, $<S,V>$ is a PI-system iff for every $v \notin V$ there is a finite set $X \subseteq T(v)$ and a sentence $A \in C(v)$ such that V does not contain any v' such that $X \subseteq T(v')$ and $A \in C(v')$. By contraposition, $<S,V>$ is a PI-system iff the following holds: given a valuation v, if for every finite set $X \subseteq T(v)$ and every sentence $A \in C(v)$ there is a valuation $v' \in V$ such that $X \subseteq T(v')$ and $A \in C(v')$, then $v \in V$. But this is clearly the definition of compact saturatedness of V. $\square$

Lemma 5

- The semantic system $\Sigma_1 = <S, \{v \in Pow(S) \mid T(v) \text{ is finite}\}>$ is a PSQI-system that is neither a PSI-system, nor a PQI-system.
- The semantic system $\Sigma_2 = <S,\{\varnothing\}>$ is a PQI-system that is not a PSI-system, and hence not a PI-system.
- If A is a fixed element of S, then the semantic system $\Sigma_3 = < S, \{v \in Pow(S) \mid A \in T(v) \text{ or } S \setminus \{A\} \not\subseteq T(v)\} >$ is a PSI-system that is not a PQI-system, and hence not a PI-system.

Proof:
Σ_1 is not saturated, for V does not contain the full valuation, which is the supervaluation of the empty set, hence it is not a PSI-system. It

is not compact, because V does not contain the full valuation, but for every finite subset X of S it contains a v' such that $X = T(v')$; hence it is not a PQI-system.

Σ_2 is a PQI-system, for it is determined by the infinite set of QI-ons $\{<\{A\},\varnothing> \mid A \in S\}$. However, it is not saturated, for V does not contain the full valuation, hence it is not a P(S)I-system.

Σ_3 is a PSI-system, for it is determined by the single SI-on $< S\backslash A, A >$. However, it is not compact, because V does not contain the valuation v such that $T(v) = S\backslash\{A\}$, while it contains, for every finite subset X of $S\backslash\{A\}$, a valuation such that $T(v') = X$ and $C(v')$ contains A; hence it is not a P(Q)I-system. $\square$

Theorem 6

(i) every semantic system is a PSQI-system;
(ii) the arrows in Diagram 1 (on page 181) capture *all* inclusions among the types of semantic systems listed on it;
(iii) all the inclusions are *proper*.

Proof: (i) and (ii) follow from Lemma 4; (iii) follows from Lemma 5. $\square$

Definitions

A *language* is an ordered pair $<S, F>$, where S is a set (the elements of which are called *sentences*) and $F \subseteq \mathrm{Pow}(S)$ (the elements of this set are called *forms* of sentences). An *instantiation* over $<S, F>$ is any function i from F to S such that for every $f \in F$, $i(f) \in f$; $i(f)$ is then called the i-instance of f. A *generalized semantic system* is an ordered pair $<<S, F>,V>$ such that $<S, F>$ is a language and $<S,V>$ is a semantic system. An ordered pair of subsets of $F \cup S$ is called a *parametric SQI-on*, or *pSQI-on* over $<S,F>$; the concepts of pQI-on, pSI-on, and pI-on are defined analogously. (It follows that every (S)(Q)I-on over S is a p(S)(Q)I-on over $<S, F>$.) The pair $<<S, F>, \vdash>$, where $<S, F>$ is a language and $\vdash$ is a finite set of p(S)(Q)I-ons over $<S, F>$, will be a *(S)(Q)I-structure*.

The i-instance of a p(S)(Q)I-on, for an instantiation i, is the (S)(Q) I-on that arises from it by the replacement of forms by their i-instances. The p(S)(Q)I-on excludes those and only those valuations of S that are excluded by some of its instances. A (S)(Q)I-structure is said to *determine* a generalized semantic system $<<S, F>, V>$ iff V is the set of all and only elements of $\{0,1\}^S$ not excluded by any element of $\vdash$. If $<<S, F>, V>$ is determined by a (S)(Q)I-structure, it is called a (S)(Q)I-system. (We drop the adjective *generalized* when the context makes it clear that we are dealing with generalized systems.)

Σ_{CPC} is the semantic system <<S, F>, V> of classical propositional logic, where S is the set of wffs of propositional logic, F is a set of sets of instances of corresponding schemata, and V is the set of all those valuations of the set that do justice to all the truth tables of the classical connectives.

Σ_{CPC^*} is the semantic system <<S, F>, V> of classical propositional logic, where S and F are as before, and V is the set of all those valuations of the set that map all axioms of a system of classical propositional logic on 1 and map a *b* on 1 whenever there is an *a* so that *a* and *a*→*b* are mapped on 1. (Note that this system, as well as the one that follows, admits the full valuation; this valuation is then usually excluded 'manually', by introducing the concept of *consistency* and banning inconsistent valuations.)

Σ_{In} is the semantic system <<S, F>,V> of intuitionist propositional logic, where S and F are as before and V is the set of all those valuations of the set that map all axioms of a system of intuitionist logic on 1 and map a *b* on 1 whenever there is an *a* so that *a* and *a*→*b* are mapped on 1.

Σ_{CPPrC} is the semantic system <<S, F>, V> of pseudopredicate logic, where S is the set of wffs of predicate logic, F is a set of sets of instances of corresponding schemata, and V is the set of all those valuations of the set that do justice to all the truth tables of the classical connectives and which map formulas of the shape $\forall x p(x)$ (or $\exists x p(x)$) on 1 iff all instances (or at least one instance) of $p(x)$ is mapped on 1.

Theorem 7

1. Σ_{CPC} is a QI-system, but not an I-system.
2. Σ_{CPC^*} is an I-system.
3. Σ_{In} is an I-system.
4. Σ_{CPPrC} is an SQI-system, but neither an SI-system, nor a QI-system.

Proof:

1. Σ_{CPC} is a QI-system, for it is determined by the set of pQI-ons (we assume that the primitive connectives are → and ¬ and we let schemata stand for the sets of their instances): {<{A, A→B}, {B}>, <{B}, {A→B}>,<∅, {A, A→B}>, <{A, ¬A}, ∅>, <∅, {A, ¬A}>}. However, it is not saturated: for any atomic *a* it admits a valuation that maps *a* on 0 and one that maps ¬*a* on 0, but no valuation that maps both *a* and ¬*a* on 0 is admissible; hence it is not a pI-system.

2. $\Sigma_{\text{CPC*}}$ is an I-system, for it is determined by the set of pI-ons: $\{<\{a, a \rightarrow b\}, \{b\}>,\ <\varnothing, \{a \rightarrow (b \rightarrow a)\}>,\ <\varnothing, \{a \rightarrow (b \rightarrow c) \rightarrow ((a \rightarrow b) \rightarrow (a \rightarrow c))\}>,\ <\varnothing, \{(a \rightarrow b) \rightarrow ((\neg a \rightarrow b) \rightarrow b)\}>\}$. (We identify an axiom of a logical system with the pI-on that has an empty antecedent and the axiom in the consequent, and we identify an inference rule, such as modus ponens, with the corresponding pI-on. In this way we can say simply that $\Sigma_{\text{CPC*}}$ is determined by the axiomatic system of classical propositional logic.)

3. Σ_{In} is an I-system, for it is determined by the axiomatic system of intuitionist propositional logic. (Note that here we have nothing corresponding to the 'non-axiomatic' version of classical logic. Intuitionist operators do not have any truth tables independent of the axiomatization of the logic.)

4. Σ_{CPPrC} is an SQI-system, for it is determined by the pQI-ons determining Σ_{CPC} plus the p(S)(Q)I-ons $<\{\forall xp(x)\}, p(t)>$, $<\{p(t)\}, \exists xp(x)>$, $<\{p(n)\}_{n \in N}, \{\forall xp(x)\}>$ and $<\exists xp(x), \{p(n)\}_{n \in N}>$ (where p and t are parameters and N is the set of all individual constants of the language). It is not an SI-system, for it is not saturated (for the same reason as Σ_{CPC}) and it is not a QI-system, for it is not compact: if p is a predicate, then for every finite set $N^* \subset N$ there is a valuation mapping $p(n)$ on 1 for every $n \in N^*$ and $\forall xp(x)$ on 0, whereas there is none mapping $p(n)$ on 1 for every $n \in N$ and $\forall xp(x)$ on 0.$\square$

Notes

1 Inferentialism: State of Play

1. Devitt's (1994) 'Semantics is a veritable Balkans of the intellectual world' thus remains an apt aphorism.
2. An influential approach to meaning has been based on the assumption that semantics is a species of semiotics, that linguistic expressions are just special kinds of symbols created in order to stand for some things external to them. I have discussed this in greater detail in the first chapter of Peregrin (2001).
3. The most usual versions of this doctrine according to which what is symbolized are some mental contents, such as beliefs (as in the picture sketched, e.g., by Searle, 1983) or sentences in the language of thought (Fodor, 1975; 2008), pose the question of how a public sign can be interlinked with an essentially private mental content in such a way that the content becomes public too; that the sign, as it were, pulls it into the public sphere.
4. Here we may think of various theories of representations as co-occurrences of a kind of thing and a mental token (Dretske, 1983; Fodor, 1998), or of theories reducing the relation of having meaning to the relation of referring to something and explaining it in a direct causal way (e.g., Kripke, 1972).
5. Quine (1960; 1992) proposes to forget about meanings altogether, and work with reference as the only link between language and the world; moreover, he goes on to argue for the *inscrutability* of reference. This leads Davidson (1979) to conclude that even this link is illusory. Sellars (1974) argued that meanings are basically tools by means of which we classify the functioning of expressions rather than things that are represented by them.
6. It follows that the quarrel between those who see meaningfulness as a matter of standing for an object and those who see meaningfulness as primarily a property should not be construed as concerning the question of whether meanings are (abstract) objects; construing them thus does no harm in any case. The crucial question is whether they are things that are objects *independent* of expressions and *represented* by them.
7. I conjecture that they are specifically human, for it is only humans who are capable of following rules in the fully fledged sense discussed in this book. However, this is not something that would be crucial for the view of rules advocated here.
8. Thus, for example, Tennant (2007) writes, 'An inferentialist theory of meaning holds that the meaning of a logical operator can be captured by suitably formulated rules of inference (in, say, a system of natural deduction).'
9. See Kreisel (1968).
10. See Negri and von Plato (2001) for an overview.
11. Hacking (1979) engaged conservativity as one of the general hallmarks of the logical, thus providing for a proof-theoretic alternative to the essentially model-theoretic attempts at the delimitation of logic due to Tarski (1986), Sher (1991) and others.

12. See Wansing (2000), Prawitz (2006), or Schroeder-Heister (2006). For the most elaborated recent versions of this enterprise see Francez, Dyckhoff, and Ben-Avi (2010) and Francez and Ben-Avi (2011).
13. See Tennant (1994).
14. The controversies over whether it is possible to base logic on (and especially to furnish logical constants with meanings by means of) proof theory, or whether it must be model theory, concern, to a great extent, the technical aspect of logic. But some logicians and philosophers have started to associate this explanatory order with certain philosophical doctrines. Thus, Dummett (1977; 1978) argued that basing logic on proof theory goes hand in hand with its intuitionist construal and, more generally, with founding epistemology on the concept of justification rather than on the concept of truth. This, according to him, further invites the 'anti-realist' rather than 'realist' attitude to ontology: the conviction that principally unknowable facts are no facts at all and hence we should not assume that every statement expressing a quantification over an infinite domain is true or false. Dummett (1991) came to the conclusion that metaphysical debates are best settled by being reduced to debates about the logical backbone of our language.
15. See, for instance, Fodor and Lepore (2007, p. 679): 'a word like "tree" could mean what it does even if there were no sentences (a fortiori, no sentence meanings)'.
16. See Greenberg and Harman (2006).
17. Block (1980).
18. The more general distinction between causal and normative functionalism is discussed by Zangwill (2005).
19. A vehement warning against falling in with such a picture is presented – and argued for in detail – by Turner (2010).
20. See Peregrin (2010a; 2014) for a more detailed discussion of this.
21. Wittgenstein (1953, § 202) argued that 'to think one is obeying a rule is not to obey a rule' and that the only context in which this essential difference may emerge and be sustained is human society with its dialectic of the individual and the social: 'Hence it is not possible to obey a rule "privately": otherwise thinking one was obeying a rule would be the same thing as obeying it.'
22. The objection of Prior mentioned above involves this kind of allegation of circularity. Prior (1964) urges that inferential role is something categorically different from meaning ('It is one thing to define "conjunction-forming sign",' he says (p. 191), 'and quite another to define "and"') and that inferences presuppose, rather than create, meaning. We will return to Prior's challenge in Chapter 8.

2   Words as Governed by Rules

1. Note especially that saying that the claim that *This is edible* 'entails' eating what is pointing at does *not* amount to saying that whoever asserts *This is edible* is committed to eating what she points at. Just as asserting *This is edible* does *not* commit one to asserting *This is not poisonous* (but rather only not to do anything incompatible with the latter assertion, at least without a further ado), it does not commit one to eating it, but rather merely not to act in a way that would be 'irreconcilable' with eating it.

2. This led many logicians in the past to conclude that the step from the premises of an inference like (2) to its conclusion involves disclosing the covert presupposition (cf. also Aristotle's concept of ἐνθύμημα; see, e.g., Green, 1995).

3. If the inference from p to q is possible only if we add $p{\rightarrow}q$ as an additional premise, then, it would seem, we must further require $(p{\land}(p{\rightarrow}q)){\rightarrow}q$, then $(p{\land}(p{\rightarrow}q){\land}((p{\land}(p{\rightarrow}q)){\rightarrow}q)){\rightarrow}q$, etc., ad infinitum.

4. The last remnants of my belief that there are some unquestionable analytic truths were shaken when I saw, in the window of a gift shop, small wooden ovals advertised as 'wooden stones'.

5. See, for example, McGee (1985).

6. 'Concepts involve laws and are inconceivable without them,' as Sellars (1948) puts it.

7. This means that it is not only rules like (2) that take part in forming (extra-logical) terms (to say that this rule takes part in forming the concept of *dog* and *animal*), but also those like (3). This might appear preposterous: is the fact that lightning is usually followed by thunder not an empirical generalization that has nothing to do with forming concepts (cf. Fodor and Lepore, 2007, p. 680)? But although the fact that a certain kind of light in the sky tends to be followed by a certain kind of sound in the air is undoubtedly not a matter of the meaning of anything, where no such interconnection obtains, the concepts of *lightning* and *thunder* would not be appropriately applicable.

8. The extension of the construal from logical to other kinds of nonempirical words, such as the vocabulary of mathematics, seems relatively unproblematic.

9. This is, of course, not to say that *any* talk about reference and representation is misguided. The point is that these two concepts, in this context, are unsuitable as 'unexplained explainers'.

10. Especially when we consider infants learning language, many sentences will be indistinguishable from words. But this certainly does not cancel the general difference between sentences and subsentential phrases.

11. To avoid possible misunderstandings, let me stress that what I mean by *football* throughout the book is football (i.e., what we Europeans call *football* and what Americans call *soccer*).

12. We have stressed (and will discuss at length later) that inferences *started* as moves among *sentences*, and that propositions emerged as a sort of values of the sentences when they became appropriately inferentially interlinked. But this does not prevent us from seeing inference, in the developed form, as moves from propositions to propositions, for the proposition is precisely that aspect of sentence that captures its inferential behavior.

13. A similar point was famously made by Davidson (1986, p. 310): 'nothing can count as a reason for holding a belief save another belief'.

14. The Myth of the Given thus amounts to the empiricist conviction that there is some fundamental layer of knowledge that is delivered to us directly by our senses and is thus definite and unquestionable. Helpful commentaries to this long and somewhat cryptic paper of Sellars were published by Brandom (see Sellars, 1997) and deVries and Triplett (2000).

15. Note, however, that in this way we subscribe to a specific sense of the word *concept*, a sense that was close, besides Sellars, also to Kant and Frege, for

both of whom a concept was constitutively a constituent of propositions or judgments. Understood thus, concepts are not prior to propositions, they are extracted out of propositions as specific 'contributions'.

16. See also Peregrin (2005a).
17. To avoid misunderstanding, let me stress that this is not to say that experience is nonexistent or that its exploration is uninteresting. But it is not substantial for the inferentialist project (therefore Brandom, 2000, p. 205, says '"Experience" is not one of my words').
18. For an interesting alternative attempt at the explication of this interface see Kukla and Lance (2009). They urge the existence of 'observatives' as specific speech acts that are conceptual, but not necessarily propositional.
19. Dummett (ibid., pp. 218–219) writes: 'A conservative extension in the logicians' sense is conservative with respect to formal provability. In adapting the concept to natural language, we must take conservatism or non-conservatism as relative to whatever means exist in the language for justifying an assertion or an action consequent upon the acceptance of an assertion. The concept thus adapted offers at least a provisional method of saying more precisely what we understand by 'harmony': namely, that there is harmony between the two aspects of the use of any given expression if the language as a whole is, in this adapted sense, a conservative extension of what remains of the language when that expression is subtracted from it.'

3 Meanings as Inferential Roles

1. Such a theory of mind has been proffered, for example, by Davidson (2001).
2. This was noted, as a general problem for the concept of dispositions, by several authors – see, e.g., Mumford (2003, §6.6). But here we do not take issue with the concept of disposition in general, but rather only with its particular deployment within the accounts for our linguistic practices.
3. As we will see later, to say that it is proper, according to the rules of language, to utter *This is a spider* when pointing at a spider, does not contradict the fact that there might be other rules and other proprieties that would trump it; it may be sometimes *proper* to do things that are *improper* from the viewpoint of the rules of language. Hence, for instance, it might be proper to say *This is a spider* when pointing at an elephant, if this leads to a pertinent joke.
4. Notice that the complexity prevents us from specifying the meaning of even relatively simple words (take, for instance, our recent examples *fun* or *spider*) *independently of the theory we want to use for it*. Hence this is *not* a problem peculiar to inferentialism.
5. See, e.g., Tennant (2003).
6. See Footnote 12 to Chapter 1.
7. There is an ongoing discussion about the compatibility of the principle of compositionality and the so-called *principle of contextuality* in the writings of Frege (Pagin, 1997; Janssen, 2001). But unless you insist that the principle of compositionality describes how meanings of complexes *result* from *pre-given* meanings of the parts, there is no incompatibility to be explained. See Peregrin (2005b).

8. In Carnap's and Quine's sense of *explication* as the replacement of a pre-formal, fuzzy, and unclear notion by a formal and precise concept.
9. Cole (2013, p. 13) speaks about 'representational function' ('RF') of certain entities 'whose inherent function is to facilitate our abilities to represent, analyze, reason about, discover truths concerning, *etc.* facets of reality that are not the entities in question'. This is precisely the function of meanings captured as set-theoretical entities, and of explications in general. Cole further claims that 'the primary reason why we introduce facets of reality to serve RFs is to allow us to represent the world using intentional states that structure it into entities with features, for, as a result of the cognitive constitution of human beings at this evolutionary stage, we find it much easier to engage in the aforementioned types of activities using such states.'
10. Hence we would hold the sentences to constitute something not very different from a Boolean algebra.
11. See Peregrin (2009) for a detailed discussion of this paper of Fodor and Lepore.
12. See Peregrin (2001, Chapter 4) and especially Peregrin (2006c).
13. Quine (1960, p. 9) writes: 'Not that all or most sentences are learned as wholes. Most sentences are built up rather from learned parts, by analogy with the way in which those parts have previously been seen to occur in other sentences which may or may not have been learned as wholes. What sentences are got by such analogical synthesis, and what ones are got directly, is a question of each individual's own forgotten history.'
14. I discussed this point in greater detail in Peregrin (2001).

4 The Rules of Language

1. As Wheeler (1986, p. 492) points out (in a different context), 'speech and thought are brain-writing, some kind of tokenings which are as much subject to interpretation as any other'.
2. At least prima facie; if we subject the very concept of regularity to critical scrutiny, things may start to look much less clear.
3. One way of expressing this is also Penrose's (1989) claim that human thought is 'non-algorithmic'.
4. As Wittgenstein (1953, §119) warned us, our understanding can 'get bumps' by being bounced off the rules delimiting language.
5. Is the constrictive power of the rules of language restricted to the level underlying that of meaningful talk? Is it so that, insofar as we have meaningful utterances, we are no longer constrained in any way? Well, if this were true, it would be true in a trivial sense only: in the sense in which we cannot make an erroneous move with a rook for if we make a candidate for such a move (e.g., move the rook diagonally), it would not count as *a move with a rook*. But actually I think it is not true: as Haugeland (1998) stresses, a game like chess must always induce an 'excluded zone' that is behind the boundaries of the game, where the pieces still manage to keep their identity as such.
6. Note also that the possibility of making the joke presupposes the existence of the rules.

7. Note that my saying *This is a dog* when pointing at a car may count as a joke only insofar I do not do this usually, hence when it is clear that I do not really think that the car is a dog.
8. Cf. the classic text of Williams (1973). A sense in which we ought to believe something (despite the fact that the *ought* does not imply *can*) was discussed by Chrisman (2008): we may be said to ought to believe something in the sense that our peers ought to criticize us for not believing it. (In this way we interpret the ought-to-believe claims, in the Sellarsian idiom discussed in Section 4.2, as *ought-to-be*'s, rather than *ought-to-do*'s.)
9. We *can* say that it is a norm that we *ought to interpret our peers as believing* the truth. This is the celebrated Davidsonian principle of charity, but this is a far cry from claiming that we *ought to believe* the truth.
10. I use the indefinite article here because truth amounts to one specific sense of correctness applicable to assertions besides other senses in which an assertion can be said to be correct. I will have more to say about truth in Sections 5.6 and 11.7.
11. From this perspective, MacFarlane's (2011) classification of the approaches to asserting is misleading: it lists Williamson-type epistemic approaches under the category *Assertion as a move defined by rules*, while putting Brandom's approach into a different category, namely *Assertion as a commitment*. But for Brandom (and certainly for the kind of inferentialism advocated here), assertion is an activity no less rule-constituted than for Williamson, for it is only the space delimited by rules that can make room for anything like *commitment*. The difference is a matter of the *nature* of the constitutive rules.
12. Cf. also Gauker (2007).
13. See Cole (2013) for a discussion of this.
14. Cf. Footnote 4 to this chapter.
15. Certain things long discussed within philosophy of law can be seen as having anticipated some of the problems now being faced by the inferentialist philosophy of language. However, from the inferentialist viewpoint, within philosophy of law they appear as if within a specific context – *viz.*, the context of all rules being explicit and codified – which makes their treatment easier than in the general case.

5   Our Language Games

1. Cf. Egginton and Sandbothe (2004). Cf. also Peregrin (1999).
2. See Hintikka and Sandu (1997) for an overview of the subsequent development of the idea.
3. And what is even more remarkable is that we can reach classical logic by canceling some of the above constraints. For example, as we saw, if we cancel (b), then there would be a winning strategy for the *Proponent* in our game.
4. See, e.g., Lorenzen (1962).
5. The notions of minimality/maximality employed here are based on considering the relation of inference as (partially) ordering the set of propositions so that B *is inferable from* A is read as $B{\leq}A$. There is also the dual possibility of reading B *is inferable from* A as $B{\geq}A$, which comes naturally if we consider propositions as something as classes of possible worlds.

6. It is remarkable how sparse empirical studies of the logical vocabularies of natural languages are; I think that they might bring a substantial corrective to the widespread conviction that the formal languages of logic straightforwardly reflect what can be found there. Cf., e.g., Bach et al. (1995) regarding quantification.
7. This appears to chime with the sense of *practice* introduced by Rawls (1955, p. 3), according to whom a practice is 'any form of activity specified by a system of rules which defines offices, roles, moves, penalties, defenses, and so on, and which gives the activity its structure'.
8. See Peregrin (1995).

6 Rules and Evolution

1. Of course that as we are talking about clashes of creatures each of which is disposed to rigidly follow a particular strategy, there is literally no deliberating and deciding in play; it is, as it were, the evolution to deliberate which of the strategies to choose, by playing them against one another.
2. Von Wright (1963) calls them *directives*, whereas Raz (1999) speaks about *technical norms*.
3. See also Noble (2000).
4. We may also think about an incompatibility that can be called mixed: an incompatibility of a situation and an action. In terms of the distinction between what *cannot* and what *should not* happen, this kind goes together with the second: it amounts to impropriety. This kind of incompatibility may be seen as underlying the extended sense of *inference* discussed in Section 2.5.

7 Inference in Logic

1. Thus, Sellars (1953), for example, points out that the concept of inference as put forward by Carnap (1934) unsuccessfully tries to ride the horses of all the three senses of *inference* distinguished above at the same time. Carnap's inference (as well as the inference of many contemporary logicians) is in fact inference$_3$, and Carnap makes a deep point of the fact that the relation is fully arbitrary. On the other hand, he refers to it as the relation of deriv*ability*, which, Sellars points out, alludes to the fact that it expresses what *is permitted to be derived* (which would be appropriate for inference$_2$). Moreover, as what is or is not permitted are human actions, viz. those of inferring, it further alludes to the classification of human inferential performances, which are a matter of inference$_1$. But Carnap pays no attention to any constraints that would be implied for his definition of inference by any normative considerations or empirical studies of human inferential activities. As a result, Sellars concludes that 'Carnap's claim that he is giving a definition of "directly derivable in S" is a snare and a delusion' (ibid., p. 329) and I think this is basically right (albeit somewhat overstated).
2. Let me, however, stress that the sense in which I use the term *formal* here differs from the one in which it is usually used in logic. I mean *form* simply in the sense of *shape*, hence *formal* properties of an expression are those that are visible. (This sense then has nothing to do with *logical* form). The requirement that a rule is formal thus excludes sets of inferons that cannot be delimited in terms of a finite number of visible features.

3. See Došen and Schroeder-Heister (1993); Restall (2000).
4. See Anderson and Belnap (1975) and Anderson, Belnap, and Dunn (1992).
5. See Girard (1987).
6. As Shapiro (2005, p. 653) puts it: 'For what it is worth, treatments of mathematical logic usually presuppose that the model-theoretic notion is the primary one. For example, one says that a deductive system is sound or complete (or not) for the semantics – not the other way around. If a deductive system is not sound for a given semantics, then that alone disqualifies the deductive system. Why? Because the deductive system allows us to deduce a falsehood from truths in some interpretation of the language.' Shapiro then continues to challenge this orthodoxy in a way that is congenial to the one put forward here: 'But one could perhaps argue instead that it is the model theory that is at fault. Any counterexample to soundness – any "interpretation" in which we can deduce a false conclusion from true premises – is perhaps not a legitimate interpretation of the language. For better or worse, however, most mathematical logicians do not think that way.'
7. I say *clearly*, but Slater (2007) claims the contrary: namely that the conclusion follows from a finite number premises; actually from a single one. He claims to prove this by means of the Hilbertian epsilon-calculus: he interprets the fact that in this calculus $\forall x P x$ is equivalent to $P(\varepsilon x \neg P x)$ as showing that the fact that every number is P is tantamount to the fact that one particular number, namely $\varepsilon x \neg P x$, is P (though we do not know – cannot know? – which one it is). But in my view, this is like saying that the fact that every man in a room is bald is not a matter of all the men in the room, but merely of one of them, namely the least bald one.
8. In fact, this is exactly what is spelled out by the structural rule (EXT).
9. It could be argued that the truth of Gödel's sentence does not follow from the axioms of arithmetic, for it is not true in all models of the axioms. However, this objection turns on the first-order regimentation of arithmetic (which admits nonstandard models), which cannot be equated with arithmetic as such. Within second-order arithmetic, there are no models of the axioms in which Gödel's sentence would be false.
10. Of course, we can try biting this bullet. There are logicians who would insist that this is how it should be. But I do not see how we could seriously claim that, say, 2+2=4 *is a consequence of* 1×1=2.
11. Or, as King (2001) suggests, perhaps much further back.
12. Languages having a logical connective of the kind of *if...then....* Obviously, this can be taken for granted for any natural language, and it is also fulfilled by common logical languages. But, of course, there may be artificial languages (or 'languages'?) lacking any such connective.
13. Namely the Aristotelian concept of ἐνθύμημα mentioned in Footnote 2 to Chapter 2.
14. The difference between the respective approaches of Tarski and Bolzano should not be overestimated. Just as Bolzano crucially needed to determine the ranges of expressions of an ideal language (which may outrun the resources of any real one), Tarski equally crucially needs to determine the ranges of entities from which expressions draw their denotations. And such a determination is no straightforward task. Tarski circumvented this by restricting his attention to languages formalized into the shape of predicate logic, fixing the denotations for their expressions stipulatively, without any

discussion of the appropriateness of such directives. (I discussed this problem in detail elsewhere; see Peregrin, 1995.)

15. As valuations can be seen as characteristic functions of sets of sentences, they can obviously be identified with the sets they characterize.
16. Van Fraassen (1971) was the first to propose this kind of explication of semantics; his proposal was further elaborated by Dunn and Hardegree (2000). I have adapted it in Peregrin (2006a).
17. Of course, it depends on the existence of the shared language and thereby on certain 'beliefs' of members of the relevant linguistic community. However, this does not rob consequence of its objectivity; at least it is surely no less objective than chess or NATO or money, which all also depend on certain 'beliefs' of people.
18. Unlike truth, consequence has no contingent or empirical component; indeed consequence is what remains of truth when it is purged of this component. While *Fido is a dog* is true both because of the meanings of the words of which the sentence consists *and* the current state of the world, for the fact that *Fido is a dog* entails *Fido is an animal* the state of the world is totally irrelevant.
19. Lorenzen (1962, p. 67) points out that although the 'semiformalism' is not 'beweisdefinit' (definite with respect to proofs), it is, however, 'dialogisch-definit' (definite in dialogue): the point is that it is easy to incorporate it into his dialogic logic (see Section 5.2).
20. As we already noted, saying this does not sound very plausible. Perhaps the concept of consequence *simpliciter* (as contrasted with logical consequence) is not really applicable to nonempirical discourse?
21. See also Koreň (t. a.).

8 Logical Constants

1. Cf. Footnote 11 to Chapter 1.
2. See, e.g., Read (2004), Tennant (2007), or Murzi and Hjortland (2009).
3. This is obviously an oversimplification in that the function of *and* in English is actually more multiverse; it is, for example, often used to express temporal succession.
4. In fact, if we agree with the inferentialist to see meaning as an inferential role, there is no deep reason not to extend the term *meaning* also to *tonk* and its kin. After all, *tonk* does have an inferential role, albeit a trivial one.
5. This makes room for various authors' attempts at filling the gap. Thus, Tennant (1997, pp. 332–333) characterized the harmony between introduction and elimination rules as follows: 'The introduction and elimination rules for any logical operator λ should be framed in such a way that (i) in the statement of the introduction rule for λ, the conclusion (with λ dominant) should be the strongest that can be inferred under the conditions specified; and (ii) in the statement of the corresponding elimination rule, the major premise (with λ dominant) should be the weakest that can be used in the way specified.' The principle, as Tennant suggests, 'serves to tailor the elimination rule to a previously chosen introduction rule, or vice versa'. Hence if we encounter λ within a proof, we know it must have been introduced in its canonical way, and can reason back to the premises of its introduction rules.

6. Obviously, in the case of some purely *extensional* languages, the constraints may exclude all valuations save a single one. However, this is clearly not the case for any natural language.
7. Of course, when dealing with the *empirical* terms of *empirical* languages, we need a way to 'connect them to the world'; we need, if not a trusted metalanguage capable of mediating the connection, then a direct connection which, however, can be established only practically.
8. See Raatikainen (2008) and Murzi and Hjortland (2009) for the most recent discussion of their significance.
9. See Shapiro (1991) for details.
10. Though sophisticated defenses of multiple-conclusion inference do exist; see, e.g., Restall (2005).

9 Logic as Making Inference Explicit

1. Hilbert and Bernays (1939, Supplement III).
2. Should it be interpreted as referring to all purely implicative theorems, then the situation would be different, for within classical logic, unlike within intuitionist logic, negation is not conservative over implication, and hence the class of implicative theorems exceeds the class of sentences provable from purely implicative axioms.
3. They are what Avron (1991) called the internal implication and conjunction, respectively.
4. I owe this observation to Greg Restall.
5. This is, in a sense, a sleight of hand; a more straightforward way would be to accept incompatibility as a new primitive concept and '$X \vdash \perp$' as a new piece of primitive notation (then perhaps better written as '$\perp X$'; cf. Peregrin, 2006a). As Tennant (1994) argues, since inference is to record truth-transmission, $X \vdash A$ makes nontrivial sense only if there is something to transmit from X to A, i.e., if X is capable of being true at all. From this vantage point, marking inconsistency is a task naturally instrumental to the task of marking truth-transmission, i.e., inference, and hence the introduction of an inconsistency marker is a natural continuation of introducing a deductor.
6. See Peregrin (2008) for details.
7. There have also been several suggestions to admit only as much of sequent calculus into natural deduction as to allow us to handle classical logic (see Read, 2000, or Milne, 2002).
8. Can we have different modal logics based on incompatibility? In principle, surely we can, provided that we add some surplus ingredient corresponding to the relation of equivalence in Kripkean models. Elsewhere (see Peregrin, 2010d) I have shown how we may reach the modal logic B in this way.
9. Došen (ibid., p. 273) writes: 'The approach starts with the assumption that logic is the science of formal deductions, and that basic formal deductions are structural deductions, i.e., deductions independent of any constant of the language to which the premises and conclusions belong. Logical constants, on which the remaining formal deductions are dependent, may be said to serve as "punctuation marks" for some structural features of deductions.'

10. The approach of Koslow (1992), mentioned in Section 8.2, is slightly different. He considers operators as mapping sentences always on minima of certain propositional functions: hence while we would propose to see disjunction as an infimum of two sentences (the maximal sentence entailed by both of them), he would want to see it as the minimum of a more complicated function. See also Footnote 5 to Chapter 5.

10 Rules of Logic

1. Usually, expressivism is taken to amount to the view that some form of discourse, most often the moral language, is not truth-apt, for it does not state facts, but rather express the utterer's attitude; see, e.g., Sinclair (2009). But see Price (2013) for some ways of intersecting this kind of expressivism with the Brandomian kind.

2. See Peregrin (2010d) for a more thorough discussion of the role of logical vocabulary of formal languages vis-à-vis that of the natural language. See also Shapiro (2011, p. 527): 'The idea is that a logical system – formal language, deductive system, model-theoretic semantics – is a mathematical model. It then becomes a matter of figuring out what, if anything, the various parts of a given logical system are models of. With mathematical models generally, it is rare for there to be a single model for a given phenomenon. There are usually trade-offs to be negotiated: one model may be better for describing some purposes, another model better for others; one model may be simpler and easier to work with, but more idealized, another model more realistic but more cumbersome.'

3. Many psychologists now speak about our cognition as consisting of two layers: while the first, and evolutionary older one, usually called System I, is devoted especially to the swift control of behavior and we share it with other animals, the evolutionary newer System II, that developed for the purposes of rehearsing and correcting the mistakes of System I, may be identified with the upgrade I am talking about (see, e.g., Evans and Frankish, 2009; or Frankish, 2010). In the following chapter we will suggest that this happened via the internalization of argumentation.

4. As Wittgenstein (1969b, §559) puts it: 'You must bear in mind that the language-game is so to say something unpredictable. I mean: it is not based on grounds. It is not reasonable (or unreasonable).'

5. While modus ponens takes us from A and $A{\to}B$ to B, *affirming the consequent* is the rule that takes us from B and $A{\to}B$ to A, a rule which is, needless to say, not valid for the usual implication.

6. Note that this certainly does not preclude a community from being mistaken in general, e.g., with respect to factual claims. See my discussion of 'Protagorean concepts' in Peregrin (2010c).

7. This standpoint is close to Quine's (1986), for whom there cannot be any really competing logics, for any change of logic is automatically a change of subject. But I would not go so far as to deny logical plurality. Logic is our way to reconstruct human argumentative practices, and this reconstruction can be carried out in various ways, reflecting various emphases and aims, which may legitimately lead us to different logical systems.

8. As Prawitz (2005, p. 682) puts it: 'what can we answer someone who questions the drawing of the conclusion $A{\to}B$, given a proof of B from A, except that this is how $A{\to}B$ is used, it is a part of what $A{\to}B$ means?'. Of course it is possible to take implication, make it not obey MP, and still call the result *implication*. (And there may be reasons for such generalizations – see, e.g., Beall, t. a.) But unless anything whatsoever is implication, there must be *something* that distinguishes it from other operators, and I think that MP is among the hottest candidates.

9. Note that this is not to say that they do not do anything that *would be describable in terms of* implication, but it is to say that such a description cannot be their own, i.e., that they do not have the concept.

10. I will talk simply about modus ponens, MP, instead of Boghossian's modus ponendo ponens, MPP.

11. This does not hold without an exception. Conjunction *does* obey MP, for B is inferable from $A{\wedge}B$ and A, though this is merely the side effect of the fact that B is inferable from $A{\wedge}B$.

12. Some more sophisticated cases against MP holding for the English *if...then...* may be found in the literature – see Footnote 5 of Chapter 2.

13. Cf. Peregrin (2000).

14. See Fodor (1975).

15. See Peregrin (2000) for a discussion of this.

16. 'Logic is a kind of ultra-physics, the description of the "logical structure" of the world, which we perceive through a kind of ultra-experience (with the understanding e.g.).' An example of a proponent of this view is Russell (1919, pp. 169–170): 'Logic is concerned with the real world just as truly as zoology, though with its more abstract and general features.'

17. See, e.g., Hanna (2006, p. 9): 'Logic is the result of the constructive operations of an innate protological cognitive capacity that is necessarily shared by all rational human animals.'

11   Logic and Reasoning

1. There is a further problem (though we will not discuss it here) with the construal of laws of logic as directives for beliefs management. What we do or do not believe is not generally a matter of our decision (cf. Footnote 8 to Chapter 4); and this would seem to compromise the possibility of seeing it as something that might be reasonably *prescribed* to us by a *rule*. The point is that a rule cannot bind us to do something that we cannot do; hence if we are not capable of changing our beliefs at will, there can hardly be rules that would bind us to do so.

2. Moreover, we can ask what kind of inappropriateness or sanction would we be liable to were we to disobey modus ponens in our mind. Surely not a social one, such as compromising our status as a rational being in the eyes of others, for nobody would know. Hence, would the sanction consist in not being successful in our reasoning? But it is clear that we can imagine circumstances when reasoning *may* be successful even if it ignores any kinds of canons.

3. It is fair to stress that as MacFarlane's paper remains unpublished (and on his home page, from where it is available, its author points out that he intends to rework it), this cannot be taken as a criticism. Perhaps it is inappropriate to refer to this kind of paper at all; however, the truth is that the systematicity with which this paper sorts out the possible deontic readings of logical laws with respect to reasoning is unmatched.

4. See Harman (2009).

5. The parenthetic comments are added by Rosenberg (2009). His exposition of Sellars's view may be consulted for a more detailed elucidation.

6. Let me stress that speaking of 'constitutive' rules I do not mean *constitutive* as opposed to *regulative* in the terminology of Rawls (1955) or Searle (1969). *Constitutive* rules in the sense entertained here are opposed to *tactical* rules: constitutive rules are those that delimit the space of the game (and it is not important whether they delimit it purely conventionally or on some natural foundations, hence even regulative rules can be seen as constitutive in this sense), whereas tactical rules are those that advise how to move within the space with success.

7. Another important point, which, however, we will not discuss here, is the dimension of the rejection of the individualist construal of belief (and for that matter, knowledge) yielding the possibility of there being two completely identical individuals such that it would be justified to say of one of them, but not of the other, that she believes something. The point is that somebody's believing something, under this construal, depends not only on his state of mind, but also, as it were, on the social context and especially on what we may call the *institutional framework*. (Compare believing thus construed with christening. It is obvious that there might be two completely identical individuals, making completely the same movements, such that it would be justified to say of one of them, but not of the other, that she is christening a newborn baby. There is nothing puzzling about the fact that christening can take place only within a clearly delimited institutional framework, and my point is that believing and knowing is, despite appearances, not entirely unlike this.) I think that this follows from the fact that our knowledge claims are underlain by what Williams (2001) calls *default and challenge structure*.

8. The other concepts are not produced by the rules of logic alone; they are co-produced by other kinds of rules. See Peregrin (2001) for details.

9. Of course, not every logical system is based *directly* on the articulation of the basic steps encountered in preformal proofs. This is mostly a matter of systems of natural deduction. Axiomatic systems often trade 'naturalness' for austerity, and provide frameworks for proving that may be – plus minus – equivalent to the pre-formal ones, but are actually rather different. Another possibility is to furnish the expressions with formal denotations, which also defines, or perhaps explicates, what follows from what. (Thus, instead of stipulating the above rules we can furnish the operator $\lor$ with the classical truth table sanctioning these rules.)

10. Sellars (1956) presents this stance in his much discussed *Myth of Jones*. See deVries and Triplett (2000) for a detailed exposition.

11. See Peregrin (2006b).

References

Anderson, A. R. and N. D. Belnap (1975): *Entailment: The Logic of Relevance and Necessity,* vol. 1, Princeton University Press, Princeton.

Anderson, A. R., N. D. Belnap and J. M. Dunn (1992): *Entailment: The Logic of Relevance and Necessity,* vol. 2, Princeton University Press, Princeton.

Avron, A. (1991): 'Simple Consequence Relations', *Information and Computation* 92, 105–139.

Axelrod, R. (1984): *The Evolution of Cooperation,* Basic Books, New York.

—— (1986): 'An Evolutionary Approach to Norms', *The American Political Science Review* 80, 1095–1111.

Bach, E., E. Jelinek, A. Kratzer, and B. Partee (1995): *Quantification in Natural Languages,* Kluwer, Dordrecht.

Beall, Jc (t.a.): 'Free of Detachment: Logic, Rationality, and Gluts', *Noûs,* forthcoming.

Belnap, N. D. (1962): 'Tonk, Plonk and Plink', *Analysis* 22, 130–134.

Belnap, N. D. and G. J. Massey (1990): 'Semantic Holism', *Studia Logica* 49, 67–82.

Bicchieri, C. (2006): *The Grammar of Society: The Nature and Dynamics of Social Norms,* Cambridge University Press, Cambridge.

Block, N. (1995): 'The Mind as the Software of the Brain', in E. Smith and D. Osherson (eds): *An Invitation to Cognitive Science,* vol. 3: *Thinking,* MIT Press, Cambridge (Mass.), 377–426.

—— (1980): 'Introduction: What Is Functionalism?', in N. Block (ed.): *Readings in Philosophy of Psychology,* vol. 1, Methuen, London, 171–184.

Boghossian, P. A. (1993): 'Does an Inferential Role Semantics Rest upon a Mistake?', in E. Villanueva (ed.): *Philosophical Issues* 3, Ridgeview Press, Atascadero, 73–88.

—— (2000): 'Knowledge of Logic', in P. Boghossian and C. Peacocke (eds): *New Essays on the A Priori,* Clarendon Press, Oxford, 229–254.

—— (2005): 'Is Meaning Normative?', in C. Nimtz and A. Beckermann (eds): *Philosophie und/als Wissenschaft,* Mentis, Paderborn, 205–218.

—— (2006): *Fear of Knowledge: Against Relativism and Constructivism,* Oxford University Press, Oxford.

—— (2012): 'Inferentialism and the Epistemology of Logic: Reflections on Casalegno and Williamson', *Dialectica* 66, 221–236.

—— (2014): 'What Is Inference?', *Philosophical Studies* 169, 1–18.

Bolzano, B. (1837): *Wissenschaftslehre,* Seidel, Sulzbach.

Brandom, R. (1983): 'Asserting', *Noûs* 17, 637–650.

—— (1994): *Making It Explicit,* Harvard University Press, Cambridge (Mass.).

—— (2000): *Articulating Reasons: An Introduction to Inferentialism,* Harvard University Press, Cambridge (Mass.).

—— (2001): 'Reason, Expression, and the Philosophical Enterprise', in C. P. Ragland and S. Heidt (eds): *What Is Philosophy?,* Yale University Press, New Haven, 74–95.

—— (2002): *Tales of the Mighty Dead: Historical Essays in the Metaphysics of Intentionality*, Harvard University Press, Cambridge (Mass.).

—— (2007): 'Inferentialism and Some of Its Challenges', *Philosophy and Phenomenological Research* 74, 651–676.

Brandom, R. and A. Aker (2008): 'Appendix to Chapter V', in R. Brandom: *Between Saying and Doing: Towards an Analytical Pragmatism*, Oxford University Press, New York, 141–175.

Carnap, R. (1934): *Logische Syntax der Sprache*, Springer, Vienna.

—— (1943): *Formalization of Logic*, Harvard University Press, Cambridge (Mass.).

—— (1947): *Meaning and Necessity*, The University of Chicago Press, Chicago.

Carroll, L. (1895): 'What the Tortoise Said to Achilles', *Mind* 4, 278–280.

Chisholm, R. M. and W. Sellars (1958): 'Intentionality and the Mental: Chisholm–Sellars Correspondence on Intentionality', in H. Feigl, M. Scriven, and G. Maxwell (eds): *Minnesota Studies in the Philosophy of Science*, vol. 2: *Concepts, Theories, and the Mind–Body Problem*, University of Minnesota Press, Minneapolis, 521–539.

Chrisman, M. (2008): 'Ought to Believe', *The Journal of Philosophy* 105, 346–370.

Cole, J. (2013): 'Towards an Institutional Account of the Objectivity, Necessity, and Atemporality of Mathematics', *Philosophia Mathematica* 21, 9–36.

Cook, R. T. (2005): 'What's Wrong with Tonk(?)', *Journal of Philosophical Logic* 34, 217–226.

Cozzo, C. (1994): *Meaning and Argument: A Theory of Meaning Centred on Immediate Argumental Role*, Almqvist and Wiksell, Stockholm.

Davidson, D. (1970): 'Mental Events', in L. Foster and J. W. Swanson (eds): *Experience and Theory*, The University of Massachusetts Press, Amherst, 79–101; reprinted in D. Davidson (1980): *Essays on Actions and Events*, Clarendon Press, Oxford, 207–224.

—— (1973): 'Radical Interpretation', *Dialectica* 27, 313–328; reprinted in Davidson (1984), 125–140.

—— (1979): 'The Inscrutability of Reference', *Southwestern Journal of Philosophy* 10, 7–19; reprinted in Davidson (1984), 227–241.

—— (1984): *Inquiries into Truth and Interpretation*, Clarendon Press, Oxford.

—— (1986): 'A Coherence Theory of Truth and Knowledge', in E. Lepore (ed.): *Truth and Interpretation: Perspectives on the Philosophy of Donald Davidson*, Blackwell, Oxford, 307–319; reprinted (with added 'Afterthoughts') in Davidson (2001), 137–153.

—— (1990): 'The Structure and Contents of Truth', *The Journal of Philosophy* 87, 279–328.

—— (1991): 'Three Varieties of Knowledge', in A. Griffiths (ed.): *A. J. Ayer: Memorial Essays (Royal Institute of Philosophy Supplement 30)*, Cambridge University Press, Cambridge, 153–166; reprinted in and quoted from Davidson (2001), 205–220.

—— (2001): *Subjective, Intersubjective, Objective*, Clarendon Press, Oxford.

Dawkins, R. (1989): *The Selfish Gene*, Oxford University Press, Oxford.

Dennett, D. (1996): *Kinds of Minds*, Basic Books, New York.

—— (2008): 'The Evolution of "Why"', in B. Weiss and J. Wanderer (eds): *Reading Brandom*, Routledge, London, 48–62.

Devitt, M. (1994): 'The Methodology of Naturalistic Semantics', *The Journal of Philosophy* 91, 545–572.

deVries, W. (2011): 'Wilfrid Sellars', in E. N. Zalta (ed): *The Stanford Encyclopedia of Philosophy* (Fall 2011 Edition), url = http://plato.stanford.edu/archives/fall2011/entries/sellars/.

deVries, W. and T. Triplett (2000): *Knowledge, Mind, and the Given: Reading Wilfrid Sellars's 'Empiricism and the Philosophy of Mind'*, Hackett, Cambridge.

Došen, K. (1994): 'Logical Constants as Punctuation Marks', in D. M. Gabbay (ed): *What Is a Logical System?*, Clarendon Press, Oxford, 273–296.

Došen, K. and P. Schroeder-Heister (eds) (1993): *Substructural Logics*, Clarendon Press, Oxford.

Dretske, F. (1983): *Knowledge and the Flow of Information*, MIT Press, Cambridge (Mass.).

Dreyfuss, H. (1999): 'The Primacy of Phenomenology over Logical Analysis: A Critique of Searle', *Philosophical Topics* 27, 3–24.

Dummett, M. (1973): *Frege, the Philosophy of Language*, Duckworth, London.

—— (1977): *Elements of Intuitionism*, Clarendon Press, Oxford.

—— (1978): *Truth and Other Enigmas*, Duckworth, London.

—— (1991): *The Logical Basis of Metaphysics*, Duckworth, London.

—— (1993): 'What Do I Know When I Know a Language?', in M. Dummett: *The Seas of Language*, Oxford University Press, Oxford, 94–106.

Dunn, J. M. and G. M. Hardegree (2000): *Algebraic Methods in Philosophical Logic*, Clarendon Press, Oxford.

Edwards, J. (2003): 'Reduction and Tarski's Definition of Logical Consequence', *Notre Dame Journal of Formal Logic* 44, 49–62.

Egginton, W. and M. Sandbothe (2004): *The Pragmatic Turn in Philosophy*, SUNY Press, New York.

Evans, J. and K. Frankish (eds) (2009): *In Two Minds: Dual Processes and Beyond*, Oxford University Press, Oxford.

Fehr, E. and S. Gächter (2002): 'Altruistic Punishment in Humans', *Nature* 415, 137–140.

Field, H. (2009): 'What Is the Normative Role of Logic?', *The Aristotelian Society Supplementary Volume* 83, 251–268.

Fodor, J. A. (1975): *The Language of Thought*, Crowell, Scranton.

—— (1998): *Concepts*, Clarendon Press, Oxford.

—— (2008): *The Language and Thought Revisited*, Clarendon Press, Oxford.

Fodor, J. A. and E. Lepore (2001): 'Brandom's Burdens: Compositionality and Inferentialism', *Philosophy and Phenomenological Research* 63, 465–481.

Fodor, J. A. and E. Lepore (2007): 'Brandom Beleaguered', *Philosophy and Phenomenological Research* 74, 677–691.

Francez, N. and G. Ben-Avi (2011): 'Proof-Theoretic Semantic Values for Logical Operators', *The Review of Symbolic Logic* 4, 466–478.

Francez, N., R. Dyckhoff, and G. Ben-Avi (2010): 'Proof-Theoretic Semantics for Subsentential Phrases', *Studia Logica* 94, 381–401.

Frankish, K. (2010): 'Dual-Process and Dual-System Theories of Reasoning', *Philosophy Compass* 5, 914–926.

Frege, G. (1879): *Begriffsschrift*, Nebert, Halle; English translation in J. van Heijenoort (ed) (1971): *From Frege to Gödel: A Source Book in Mathematical Logic*, Harvard University Press, Cambridge (Mass.), 1–82.

Gauker, Ch. (2007): 'The Circle of Deference Proves the Normativity Semantics', *Rivista di Estetica* 47, 181–198.

Gendler, T. S. (2008a): 'Alief and Belief', *The Journal of Philosophy* 105, 634–663.

—— (2008b): 'Alief in Action (and Reaction)', *Mind and Language* 23, 552–585.

Gentzen, G. (1934): 'Untersuchungen über das logische Schliessen. I', *Mathematische Zeitschrift* 39, 176–210.

—— (1936): 'Untersuchungen über das logische Schliessen. II', *Mathematische Zeitschrift* 41, 405–431.

Girard, J.-Y. (1987): 'Linear Logic', *Theoretical Computer Science* 50, 1–101.

Glüer, K. (2000): 'Bedeutung zwischen Norm und Naturgesetz', *Deutsche Zeitschrift für Philosophie* 48, 449–468.

Glüer, K. and P. Pagin (1999): 'Rules of Meaning and Practical Reasoning', *Synthèse* 117, 207–227.

Glüer, K. and Å. M. Wikforss (2009): 'Against Content Normativity', *Mind* 118, 31–70.

Green, L. (1995): 'Aristotle's Enthymeme and the Imperfect Syllogism', in W. B. Horner and M. Leff (eds): *Rhetoric and Pedagogy: Its History, Philosophy, and Practice. Essays in Honor of James J. Murphy*, Erlbaum, New York, 19–41.

Greenberg, M., and G. Harman (2006): 'Conceptual Role Semantics', in E. Lepore and B. Smith (eds): *The Oxford Handbook of Philosophy of Language*, Oxford University Press, Oxford, 295–322.

Hacking, I. (1979): 'What Is Logic?', *The Journal of Philosophy* 76, 285–319.

Hanna, R. (2006): *Rationality and Logic*, MIT Press, Cambridge (Mass.).

Hardegree, G. M. (2005): 'Completeness and Super-Valuations', *Journal of Philosophical Logic* 34, 81–95.

Harman, G. and S. R. Kulkarni (2006): 'The Problem of Induction', *Philosophy and Phenomenological Research* 72, 559–575.

—— (1986): *Change in View (Principles of Reasoning)*, MIT Press, Cambridge (Mass.).

—— (2009): 'Field on the Normative Role of Logic', *Proceedings of the Aristotelian Society* 109, 333–335.

Hart, H. L. A. (1961): *The Concept of Law*, Clarendon Press, Oxford.

Hattiangadi, A. (2006): 'Is Meaning Normative?', *Mind and Language* 21, 220–240.

—— (2009): 'Some More Thoughts on Semantic Oughts: A Reply to Daniel Whiting', *Analysis* 69, 54–63.

Haugeland, J. (1998): 'Truth and Rule-Following', *Having Thought*, Harvard University Press, Cambridge (Mass.), 305–378.

Heckathorn, D. D. (1989): 'Collective Action and the Second-Order Free-Rider Problem', *Rationality and Society* 1, 78–100.

Hellman, G. (1986): 'Logical Truth by Linguistic Convention', in L. E. Hahn and P. A. Schilpp (eds): *Philosophy of W. V. Quine*, Open Court, La Salle, 114–115.

Hilbert, D. (1931): 'Die grundlegung der elementaren Zahlenlehre', *Mathematische Annalen* 104, 485–494.

Hilbert, D. and P. Bernays (1939): *Grundlagen der Mathematik*, Springer, Berlin.

Hintikka, J. (1973): *Logic, Language-Games and Information*, Clarendon Press, Oxford.

Hintikka, J. and G. Sandu (1997): 'Game-Theoretical Semantics', in J. van Benthem and A. ter Meulen (eds): *Handbook of Logic and Language*, Elsevier/MIT Press, Amsterdam/Cambridge (Mass.), 361–410.

Horwich, P. (2000): 'Stipulation, Meaning, and Apriority', in P. Boghossian and C. Peacocke (eds): *New Essays on the A Priori*, Clarendon Press, Oxford, 150–169.

Janssen, T. M. V. (2001): 'Frege, Contextuality and Compositionality', *Journal of Logic, Language and Information* 10, 115–136.

King, P. (2001): 'Consequence as Inference (Mediæval Proof Theory 1300–1350)', in M. Yrjönsuuri (ed): *Medieval Formal Logic: Consequences, Obligations and Insolubles*, Kluwer, Dordrecht, 117–145.

Knight, C. (2008): 'Language Co-evolved with the Rule of Law', *Mind & Society* 7, 109–128.

Koreň, L. (t. a.): 'Quantificational Accounts and the Problem of Logical Consequence III: The Standard Model-Theoretic Accounts Triumphant?', *Organon F*, forthcoming.

Koslow, A. (1992): *A Structuralist Theory of Logic*, Cambridge University Press, Cambridge.

Krebs, J. R. and R. Dawkins (1984): 'Animal Signals: Mind-Reading and Manipulation', in J. R. Krebs and N. B. Davies (eds): *Behavioural Ecology: An Evolutionary Approach*, Blackwell, Oxford, 380–402.

Kreisel, G. (1968): 'A Survey of Proof Theory', *The Journal of Symbolic Logic* 33, 321–388.

Kripke, S. (1972): 'Naming and Necessity', in D. Davidson and G. Harman (eds): *Semantics of Natural Language*, Reidel, Dordrecht, 253–355; later published as a book.

—— (1982): *Wittgenstein on Rules and Private Language*, Harvard University Press, Cambridge (Mass.).

Kukla, R. and M. Lance (2009): *'Yo!' and 'Lo!': The Pragmatic Topography of the Space of Reasons*, Harvard University Press, Cambridge (Mass.).

Kusch, M. (2002): *Knowledge by Agreement: The Programme of Communitarian Epistemology*, Oxford University Press, Oxford.

Lackey, J. (2007): 'Norms of Assertion', *Noûs* 41, 594–626.

Lance, M. (1998): 'Some Reflections on the Sport of Language', *Noûs* 32, Supplement: *Philosophical Perspectives*, 12, *Language, Mind, and Ontology*, 219–240.

Lance, M. and J. O'Leary-Hawthorne (1997): *The Grammar of Meaning: Normativity and Semantic Discourse*, Cambridge University Press, Cambridge.

Lehmann, L. and L. Keller (2006): 'The Evolution of Cooperation and Altruism – A General Framework and a Classification of Models', *Journal of Evolutionary Biology* 19, 1365–1376.

Lewis, D. (1979): 'Scorekeeping in a Language-Game', *Journal of Philosophical Logic* 8, 339–359.

Lorenzen, P. (1955): *Einführung in die operative Logik und Mathematik*, Springer, Berlin.

—— (1962): *Metamathematik*, Bibliographisches Institut, Mannheim.

Lorenzen, P. and K. Lorenz (1978): *Dialogische Logik*, Wissenschaftliche Buchgesellschaft, Darmstadt.

Lyotard, J.-F. (1979): *La Condition postmoderne*, Minuit, Paris.

MacFarlane, J. (2011): 'What Is Assertion?', in J. Brown and H. Cappelen (eds): *Assertion: New Philosophical Essays*, Oxford University Press, Oxford, 79–96.

—— (unpublished): 'In What Sense (If Any) Is Logic Normative for Thought?', draft.

Maynard Smith, J. (1982): *Evolution and the Theory of Games*, Cambridge University Press, Cambridge.

McDowell, J. (1994): *Mind and World*, Harvard University Press, Cambridge (Mass.).

McGee, V. (1985): 'A Counterexample to Modus Ponens', *The Journal of Philosophy* 82, 462–471.

Mercier, H. (2010): 'The Social Origins of Folk Epistemology', *Review of Philosophy and Psychology* 1, 499–514.

Millikan, R. G. (2004): *Varieties of Meaning: The 2002 Jean Nicod Lectures*, MIT Press, Cambridge (Mass.).

—— (2005): 'The Father, the Son, and the Daughter: Sellars, Brandom, and Millikan', *Pragmatics and Cognition* 13, 59–71.

Milne, P. (2002): 'Harmony, Purity, Simplicity and a "Seemingly Magical Fact"', *Monist* 85, 498–534.

—— (2009): 'What Is the Normative Role of Logic?', *The Aristotelian Society Supplementary Volume* 83, 269–298.

Mumford, S. (2003): *Dispositions*, Oxford University Press, Oxford.

Murzi, J. and O. T. Hjortland (2009): 'Inferentialism and the Categoricity Problem: Reply to Raatikainen', *Analysis* 69, 480–488.

Negri, S. and J. von Plato (2001): *Structural Proof Theory*, Cambridge University Press, Cambridge.

Noble, J. (2000): 'Co-Operation, Competition and the Evolution of Prelinguistic Communication', in C. Knight, M. Studdert-Kennedy and J. R. Hurford (eds): *The Evolutionary Emergence of Language: Social Function and the Origins of Linguistic Form*, Cambridge University Press, Cambridge, 40–61.

Pagin, P. (1997): 'Is Compositionality Compatible with Holism?', *Mind & Language* 12, 11–33.

Peacocke, C. (1992): *A Study of Concepts*, MIT Press, Cambridge.

Penrose, R. (1989): *The Emperor's New Mind: Concerning Computers, Minds, and the Laws of Physics*, Oxford University Press, New York.

Peregrin, J. (1995): *Doing Worlds with Words*, Kluwer, Dordrecht.

—— (1999): 'The Pragmatization of Semantics', in K. Turner (ed.), *The Semantics/Pragmatics Interface from Different Points of View*, Elsevier, North-Holland, 419–442.

—— (2000): 'The "Natural" and the "Formal"', *Journal of Philosophical Logic* 29, 75–101.

—— (2001): *Meaning and Structure*, Ashgate, Aldershot.

—— (2005a): 'The "Causal Story" and the "Justificatory Story"', in J. Boros (ed): *Mind in World*, Brambauer, Pécs, 145–161.

—— (2005b): 'Is Compositionality an Empirical Matter?', in M. Werning, E. Machery, and G. Schurz (eds): *The Compositionality of Meaning and Content*, vol. 1: *Foundational Issues*, Ontos, Frankfurt, 231–246.

—— (2006a): 'Meaning as an Inferential Role', *Erkenntnis* 64, 1–35.

—— (2006b): 'Brandom and Davidson: What Do We Need to Account for Thinking and Agency', *Philosophica* 75, 43–59.

—— (2006c): 'Intersubstitutivity', in M. Bílková and O. Tomala (eds): *The Logica Yearbook 2005*, Filosofia, Praha, 149–163.

—— (2006d): 'Developing Sellars' Semantic Legacy: Meaning as a Role', in P. Wolf and M. N. Lance (eds): *The Self-Correcting Enterprise,* Rodopi, Amsterdam, 257–274.

—— (2008): 'What Is *the* Logic of Inference?', *Studia Logica* 88, 263–294.

—— (2009): 'Inferentialism and Compositionality of Meaning', *International Review of Pragmatics* 1, 154–181.

—— (2010a): 'The Enigma of Rules', *International Journal of Philosophical Studies* 18, 377–394.

—— (2010b): 'Logic and Natural Selection', *Logica Universalis* 4, 207–223.

—— (2010c): 'Language, the World and the Nature of Philosophy', in R. E. Auxier and L. E. Hahn (eds): *The Philosophy of Richard Rorty,* Open Court, La Salle, 225–245.

—— (2010d): 'Brandom's Incompatibility Semantics', *Philosophical Topics* 36, 99–122.

—— (2010e): 'Inferentializing Semantics', *Journal of Philosophical Logic* 39, 255–274.

—— (2011): 'The Use-Theory of Meaning and the Rules of Our Language Games', in K. Turner (ed.): *Making Semantics Pragmatic*, Emerald, Bingley, 183–204.

—— (2012): 'Inferentialism and the Normativity of Meaning', *Philosophia* 40, 2012, 75–97.

—— (t.a.): 'Rules as the Impetus of Cultural Evolution', *Topoi,* forthcoming.

Perkins, D. N. (2002): 'Standard Logic as a Model of Reasoning: The Empirical Critique', in D. M. Gabbay, R. H. Johnson, H. J. Ohlbach and J. Woods (eds): *Handbook of the Logic of Argument and Inference*, Elsevier, Amsterdam, 187–223.

Poundstone, W. (1992): *Prisoner's Dilemma,* Doubleday, New York.

Prawitz, D. (1965): *Natural Deduction*, Almqvist & Wiksell, Stockholm.

—— (2005): 'Logical Consequence from a Constructivist Point of View', in S. Shapiro (ed.): *The Oxford Handbook of Philosophy of Mathematics and Logic*, Oxford University Press, New York, 671–713.

—— (2006): 'Meaning Approached via Proofs', *Synthèse* 148, 507–524.

Price, H. (2013): *Expressivism, Pragmatism and Representationalism*, Cambridge University Press, Cambridge.

Prior, A. N. (1960/1961): 'Runabout Inference Ticket', *Analysis* 21, 38–39.

—— (1964): 'Conjunction and Contonktion Revisited', *Analysis* 24, 191–195.

Quine, W. V. O. (1936): 'Truth by Convention', in O. H. Lee (ed.): *Philosophical Essays for A. N. Whitehead*, Longmans, New York, 90–124.

—— (1952): 'Two Dogmas of Empiricism', *The Philosophical Review* 60, 20–43; reprinted in Quine (1953): *From the Logical Point of View*, Harvard University Press, Cambridge (Mass.), 20–46.

—— (1960): *Word and Object*, MIT Press, Cambridge (Mass.).

—— (1969): *Ontological Relativity and Other Essays*, Columbia University Press, New York.

—— (1986): *Philosophy of Logic*, Harvard University Press, Cambridge (Mass.).

—— (1992): *Pursuit of Truth*, rev. ed., Harvard University Press, Cambridge (Mass.).

Raatikainen, P. (2008): 'On Rules of Inference and the Meanings of Logical Constants', *Analysis* 68, 282–287.

Rawls, J. (1955): 'Two Concepts of Rules', *The Philosophical Review* 64, 3–32.

Raz, J. (1999): *Practical Reason and Norms*, Oxford University Press, Oxford.

Read, S. (2000): 'Harmony and Autonomy in Classical Logic', *Journal of Philosophical Logic* 29, 123–154.

—— (2004): 'Identity and Harmony', *Analysis* 64, 113–119.

Restall, G. (2000): *An Introduction to Substructural Logics*, Routledge, London.

—— (2005): 'Multiple Conclusions', in P. Hájek, L. Valdés-Villanueva and D. Westerståhl (eds): *Logic, Methodology and Philosophy of Science: Proceedings of the Twelfth International Congress*, KCL Publications, London, 189–205.

Rietveld, E. (2008): 'Situated Normativity: The Normative Aspect of Embodied Cognition in Unreflective Action', *Mind* 117, 973–1001.

Rosenberg, J. (2009): 'Wilfrid Sellars', in E. N. Zalta (ed.): *The Stanford Encyclopedia of Philosophy* (Fall 2010 edition), url = http://plato.stanford.edu/archives/fall2010/entries/sellars/.

Ross, A. (1957): 'Tû-tû', *Harvard Law Review* 70, 812–825.

Rouse, J. (2007): 'Social Practices and Normativity', *Philosophy of the Social Sciences* 37, 46–56.

Russell, B. (1914): *Our Knowledge of the External World,* Routledge, London.

—— (1919): *Introduction to Mathematical Philosophy*, Allen & Unwin, London.

Schroeder-Heister, P. (2006): 'Validity Concepts in Proof-Theoretic Semantics', *Synthèse* 148, 525–571.

Schütte, K. (1960): *Beweistheorie*, Springer, Berlin.

Searle, J. R. (1969): *Speech Acts: An Essay in the Philosophy of Language*, Cambridge University Press, Cambridge.

—— (1983): *Intentionality: An Essay in the Philosophy of Mind*, Cambridge University Press, Cambridge.

Sellars, W. (1948): 'Concepts as Involving Laws and Inconceivable without Them', *Journal of Philosophy* 15, 287–315.

—— (1949): 'Language, Rules and Behavior', in S. Hook (ed.): *John Dewey: Philosopher of Science and Freedom*, Dial Press, New York, 289–315.

—— (1953): 'Inference and Meaning', *Mind* 62, 313–338.

—— (1954): 'Some Reflections on Language Games', *Philosophy of Science* 21, 204–228.

—— (1956): 'The Myth of the Given: Three Lectures on Empiricism and the Philosophy of Mind', in H. Feigl and M. Scriven (eds): *The Foundations of Science and the Concepts of Psychology and Psychoanalysis* (*Minnesota Studies in the Philosophy of Science,* vol. 1), University of Minnesota Press, Minneapolis, 253–329; reprinted in deVries and Triplett (2000), 205–276.

—— (1962): 'Philosophy and the Scientific Image of Man', in R. Colodny (ed.): *Frontiers of Science and Philosophy*, University of Pittsburgh, Pittsburgh, 35–78; reprinted in and quoted from Sellars (1963): *Science, Perception and Reality*, Ridgeview, Atascadero (CA), 1963.

—— (1969): 'Language as Thought and as Communication', *Philosophy and Phenomenological Research* 29, 506–527.

—— (1974): 'Meaning as Functional Classification', *Synthèse* 27, 417–437.

—— (1992): *Science and Metaphysics*, Ridgeview, Atascadero.

—— (1997): *Empiricism and the Philosophy of Mind* (reprint of Sellars's paper 'The Myth of the Given' with R. Brandom's commentary), Harvard University Press, Cambridge (Mass.).

Shapiro, S. (1991): *Foundations without Foundationalism*, Clarendon Press, Oxford.

—— (2005): 'Logical Consequence, Proof Theory, and Model Theory', in S. Shapiro (ed.): *The Oxford Handbook of Philosophy of Mathematics and Logic*, Oxford University Press, New York, 651–670.

—— (2011): 'Varieties of Pluralism and Relativism for Logic', in D. S. Hales (ed.): *A Companion to Relativism*, Blackwell, Oxford, 526–555.

Sher, G. (1991): *The Bounds of Logic*, MIT Press, Cambridge (Mass.).

Sinclair, N. (2009): 'Recent Work in Expressivism', *Analysis* 69, 136–147.

Slater, H. (2007): 'Hilbert's Epsilon Calculus and Its Successors', in D. Gabbay and J. Woods (eds): *Handbook of the History of Logic*, vol. 5, Kluwer, Dordrecht, 385–449.

Tarski, A. (1930): 'Fundamentale Begriffe der Methodologie der deduktiven Wissenschaften I', *Monatshefte für Mathematik und Physik* 37, 361–404; quoted from the English translation 'Fundamental Concepts of the Methodology of the Deductive Sciences', in Tarski (1956), 60–109.

—— (1936): 'Über den Begriff der logischen Folgerung', *Actes du Congrès International de Philosophique Scientifique* 7, 1–11; English translation 'On the Concept of Logical Consequence' in Tarski (1956), 409–420.

—— (1956): *Logic, Semantics, Metamathematics*, Clarendon Press, Oxford.

—— (1986): 'What Are Logical Notions?', *History and Philosophy of Logic* 7, 143–154.

Tennant, N. (1994): 'Logic and Its Place in Nature', in P. Parrini (ed.): *Kant and Contemporary Epistemology*, Kluwer, Dordrecht, 101–113.

—— (1997): *The Taming of the True*, Oxford University Press, Oxford.

—— (2003): 'Frege's Content-Principle and Relevant Deducibility', *Journal of Philosophical Logic* 32, 245–258.

—— (2007): 'Existence and Identity in Free Logic: A Problem for Inferentialism?', *Mind* 116, 1055–1078.

Thomason, S. K. (1973): 'A New Representation of S5', *Notre Dame Journal of Formal Logic* 14, 281–284.

Trivers, R. L. (1971): 'The Evolution of Reciprocal Altruism', *Quarterly Review of Biology* 46, 35–57.

Turner, S. (2010): *Explaining the Normative*, Polity, Cambridge.

van Fraassen, B. C. (1971): *Formal Semantics and Logic*, Macmillan, New York.

von Wright, G. H. (1963): *Norm and Action: A Logical Enquiry*, Humanities Press, New York.

Waisman, F. (1984): *Wittgenstein und der Wiener Kreis: Gespräche*, Suhrkamp, Frankfurt.

Wansing, H. (2000): 'The Idea of a Proof-Theoretic Semantics and the Meaning of Logical Operations', *Studia Logica* 64, 3–20.

—— (2006): 'Connectives Stranger than Tonk', *Journal of Philosophical Logic* 35, 653–660.

Way, J. (2010): 'The Normativity of Rationality', *Philosophy Compass* 5, 1057–1068.

Wheeler, S. C. III (1986): 'Indeterminacy of French Interpretation: Derrida and Davidson', in E. Lepore (ed.): *Truth and Interpretation: Perspectives on the Philosophy of Donald Davidson,* Blackwell, Oxford, 477–494.

Wikforss, Å. M. (2001): 'Semantic Normativity', *Philosophical Studies* 102, 203–226.

Williams, B. (1973): 'Deciding to Believe', in B. Williams: *Problems of the Self*, Cambridge University Press, Cambridge, 136–151.

Williams, M. (2001): *Problems of Knowledge: A Critical Introduction to Epistemology*, Oxford University Press, New York.

Williamson, T. (1996): 'Knowing and Asserting', *The Philosophical Review* 105, 489–523.

Wittgenstein, L. (1953): *Philosophische Untersuchungen*, Blackwell, Oxford; English translation *Philosophical Investigations*, Blackwell, Oxford, 1953.

—— (1956): *Bemerkungen über die Grundlagen der Mathematik*, Blackwell, Oxford; English translation *Remarks on the Foundations of Mathematics*, Blackwell, Oxford, 1956.

—— (1958): *The Blue and Brown Books*, Blackwell, Oxford.

—— (1969a): *Philosophische Grammatik*, Suhrkamp, Frankfurt; English translation *Philosophical Grammar*, Blackwell, Oxford, 1974.

—— (1969b): *Über Gewissheit*, Blackwell, Oxford; English translation *On Certainty*, Blackwell, Oxford, 1969.

Woodcock, S. and J. Heath (2002): 'The Robustness of Altruism as an Evolutionary Strategy', *Biology and Philosophy* 17, 567–590.

Zangwill, N. (2005): 'The Normativity of the Mental', *Philosophical Explorations* 8, 1–19.

Index

Printed and bound in the United States of America